The Subject of
TORTURE

The Subject of TORTURE
PSYCHOANALYSIS AND BIOPOLITICS IN TELEVISION AND FILM

Hilary Neroni

Columbia University Press
New York

Columbia University Press
Publishers Since 1893
New York   Chichester, West Sussex

Copyright © 2015 Columbia University Press
All rights reserved

Library of Congress Cataloging-in-Publication Data

Neroni, Hilary, 1969–
The subject of torture : psychoanalysis and biopolitics in Television and Film/ Hilary Neroni.
pages cm
Includes bibliographical references and index.
ISBN 978-0-231-17070-3 (cloth: alk. paper) —
ISBN 978-0-231-17071-0 (pbk.: alk paper) —
ISBN 978-0-231-53914-2 (e-book)
1. Torture in motion pictures.   2. Torture on television.
3. Torture in mass media.   4. Psychoanalysis and motion pictures.
5. Psychoanalysis and television.   6. Motion pictures—Moral and ethical aspects.   7. Television—Moral and ethical aspects.
8. Mass media—Moral and ethical aspects.   I. Title.

PN1995.9.T67N47 2015
791.43'6352—dc23   2014034082

COVER DESIGN: *Lisa Force.*
COVER IMAGE: ©*istockphoto*

To Todd McGowan

CONTENTS

Acknowledgments   ix

Introduction: Confronting the Abu Ghraib Photographs   1

1. Torture, Biopower, and the Desiring Subject   23

2. The Nonsensical Smile of the Torturer in Post-9/11 Documentary Films   49

3. Torture Porn and the Desiring Subject in *Hostel* and *Saw*   71

4. 24, Jack Bauer, and the Torture Fantasy   95

5. The Biodetective Versus the Detective of the Real in *Zero Dark Thirty* and *Homeland*   115

6. *Alias* and the Fictional Alternative to Torture   139

Notes   161
Index   185

ACKNOWLEDGMENTS

To begin with, I would like to thank *Studies in Documentary* where a version of chapter 2 was published as "The Nonsensical Smile of the Torturer: Documentary Form and the Logic of Enjoyment." I am also indebted to Ethan Wattley and Tony Magistrale at the University of Vermont for their help in shaping the book.

Thanks to my students and colleagues in the Film and Television Studies Program at the University of Vermont, especially to my wonderful colleagues Deb Ellis, David Jenemann, Todd McGowan, Sarah Nilsen, and Hyon Joo Yoo. A special thank you to Frank and Sheila Manchel for their support and check-ins to see if I'd finished and to Rashad Shabazz for sharing his work and ideas. To our theory reading group—Joseph Acquisto, Bea Bookchin, John Waldron, and Todd McGowan, and Hyon Joo Yoo—your devotion to our discussions always buoyed me. And a special thanks to Bea for modeling just what a real intellectual looks like.

I am lucky and honored to have Emily Bernard, Jennifer Friedlander, Sarah Nilsen, and Hyon Joo Yoo as my closest friends and my excellent colleagues. Their individual strength, creativity, and passion inspire me every day. Thanks to Paul Eisenstein and Mac Davis for being friends whose intellectual integrity provides endless inspiration. Frances Restuccia invited me to talk about my ideas with her graduate class and their questions breathed new life into my own questions. I am also grateful to Frances for discussing Agamben with me and providing such careful observations about his ideas, which became important to my own. Thank you to Jean Wyatt for being such an important friend, role model, and supporter. I could not have gotten through this project without Sheila Kunkle's friendship and her astute help at all stages of the manuscript. Many thanks to Jennifer Friedlander and Henry Krips for listening to more conference papers on representations of torture than anyone else. Their patience is as boundless as their much appreciated enthusiasm, and their conference on realism at Pomona in 2013 provided yet another arena in which I encountered ideas important to this book. Thanks to Luka Arsenjuk for staging the Cinema and Violence conference at the University of Maryland in 2013 and provoking many interesting conversations around violence and torture. David Denny and Justin Clemens have each been working on torture and violence in their own insightful ways and I was lucky enough to have their questions, challenges, and encouragement over the years. Thanks to Rick Boothby for his excellent reading and comments. Thanks to Ken Reinhard both for having me present these ideas in his graduate class and for his invaluable help in bringing this book into existence. I am also grateful to Slavoj Žižek and Joan Copjec for their inspiring work and their generous support.

Thank you to my family. My parents, Jane and Del Neroni, have taught me that passions and work are not separate. I'm grateful to them for their love, support, and inspiration. To Nico Taranovsky and Sharon Preves for their kindness, wisdom, and humor. My mother-in-law, Sandi McGowan, seems to believe in me endlessly and was kind enough to provide many hours of babysitting our twin boys. Thanks as always to Diana Cataldi, Wyk McGowan, and Gina McGowan for their love and understanding. I'd also like to thank my sons, Dashiell and Theo Neroni, for their love and exuberance. I've been writing this book for half of their lives, and especially in the last couple years they have encouraged me with a compassion and understanding that always takes me aback. Finally, I'd like to thank Todd McGowan, but he thinks complements are too clichéd to be meaningful, so I'll just thank him for his always-at-hand provocations.

The Subject of
TORTURE

INTRODUCTION: CONFRONTING THE ABU GHRAIB PHOTOGRAPHS

THE HIDDEN EXPOSED

In late April 2004, the shocking photographs from Abu Ghraib depicting American military personnel and their prisoners were made public. It is not by chance that the representations in these photographs brought the question of torture to the foreground. Representations of torture have been at the heart of the torture debate in recent years, and the outcome of this debate will undoubtedly revolve around what sort of representation becomes the accepted standard. Thus, a book on the theoretical implications of torture must be, I contend, at the same time a book on the media representation of torture. This is the contemporary battlefield—and it is the terrain of this book.

The images from Abu Ghraib revealed horrible scenes of abuse perpetrated by American soldiers who seem to be thoroughly enjoying themselves rather than reluctantly performing their duty. No official doctrine could quell the questions and intense emotion that these images provoked. One photograph, for example, depicts a stacked pyramid of naked Arab male bodies with United States Army Specialist Sabrina Harmon leaning close to their bodies, smiling, and giving a thumbs-up sign, while Specialist Charles Graner stands nearby smiling with his arms crossed. The men in the pyramid have green bags tied around their heads, and they are clearly holding onto each other while struggling not to fall. Tension in their entwined outstretched bodies indicates the pain of their positions. In frightening contrast to this painful, bizarre, and sexually charged pyramid of men, Harmon and Graner's bodies, in military uniforms, seem relaxed, in control. Their smiles signify that they are enjoying themselves through the pain they are causing their prisoners. The contrast between their enjoyment and the prisoners' evident humiliation in this military environment is so charged that it bursts out of the frame of the photograph.

Another photograph depicts a prisoner naked, chained to a bed, with arms outstretched and women's underwear on his head. His bulging muscles chained to the metal frame contrasts with the underwear, a clear signifier of enjoyment that the guards are having at his expense. Yet another photograph shows a line of naked prisoners, again with bags over their heads, with Specialist Lynndie England pointing at the men, who are being forced to masturbate. In this photograph, England smiles with a cigarette hanging out of the corner of her mouth. England's enjoyment of the sexual abuse resonates at the front of the frame while the line of naked men recedes off into the dark barred hallway.[1]

As documents, these photographs revealed the widespread use of torture within the American military and created a scandal concerning this development. In recent history, the American military has abjured the use of torture, and the American commitment to the Geneva Conventions expressly prohibited it. The Bush administration, however, argued that the September 11, 2001 attacks created a situation in which torture (or enhanced interrogation) became necessary for national security. Later in his memoirs Bush revealed, "My most solemn responsibility as president was to protect the country. I approved the use of the interrogation techniques."[2] Bush's declaration of an exception to the rule of law excludes prisoners from both national and international protections. As Giorgio Agamben puts it, "What is new about President Bush's order is that it radically erases any legal status of the individual. Not only do the Taliban captured in Afghanistan [and all other prisoners in the War on Terror] not enjoy the status of POWs as defined by the Geneva Convention, they do not even have the status of persons charged with a crime according to American laws."³ Bush's declaration of a state of exception condemns prisoners to the status of ambiguous detainees and thus facilitates their torture. He also clearly links this state of exception with national security.⁴

Though the story broke on April 28, 2004, when CBS's *60 Minutes* II aired the Abu Ghraib photographs, this wasn't the first time the public was in fact made aware of torture after September 11. As early as December 26, 2002, the *Washington Post* ran a story about secret CIA detention centers, and in March 31, 2003, the *Nation* led with a cover story entitled "In Torture We Trust."⁵ In addition, other stories broke throughout 2003 that discussed allegations of abuse in POW camps.⁶ Photographs, however, accompanied none of these earlier stories. It was the Abu Ghraib photographs that finally caused the scandal, the congressional hearings, the calls for impeachment, and the widespread national debate on the ethics of torture. As powerful images, they also posed questions about violence, truth, and ideology that could not be easily answered.

Much of the discourse surrounding the photographs attempted to lessen their power by explaining the necessity for torture. Commentators suggested that torture was a useful, direct, and fast way to get information needed to win a war. Even liberals like Jonathan Alter and Alan Dershowitz began to see torture as a necessary, if unpleasant, fact of life in the new state of emergency.⁷ They viewed torture as a necessary and reasonable response to an immanent danger, and they considered it only through this prism. The photographs, however, told another story. They depicted a range of enjoyment on the part of the guards that did not fit the description of torture as a clean and effective military tactic. The justification for torture as a means for extracting necessary information in the war against terrorism runs into a contradiction with the photographic images, which shows soldiers enjoying themselves rather than seeking the truth or fighting a war. The soldiers reveal that the justification proffered by Alter and Dershowitz doesn't stand up to scrutiny. The key to the problem lies in the nature of the photographs. The sexual dimension of these photographs played an important role in the scandal that they triggered.⁸ The sexuality in the photographs reveals the shocking and counterintuitive aspect of enjoyment that resides in torture and also throws into question its legitimacy as an effective military tool with which to procure information.

In order for torture to have legitimacy in the modern world, one must obscure the various elements that constitute it—such as humiliation, degradation, and sexual elements. This is certainly what the Bush administration tried to do. In some ways, the attempt failed, as the outcry against torture in the United States and globally, Obama's executive act to stop torture, and the many media representations that revealed torture's illegitimacy all testify.[9] And yet, in other ways, their attempt succeeded: no one impeached George Bush or charged him with war crimes, and even though Obama signed the act, he failed to close the camp for detainees at Guantanamo Bay. The plethora of scenes of torture in contemporary film and television also indicate torture's continued influence. Indeed, torture scenes after the September 11, 2001, attacks began to function as naturalized plot devices at every level of media—from commercials to television shows to animated children's films. Though we can easily identify torture, understanding the proliferation of representations of torture today requires establishing a working definition.

WHAT IS TORTURE?

Through modern history, many legal documents have provided definitions of torture, and a variety of scholarly disciplines have produced books and essays that have also attempted to nail down its definition. As one might expect, these definitions vary widely, but there are a few characteristics that one can find in all the definitions. The majority of the definitions include the idea that torture is an act where severe pain or suffering, either physical or mental, is intentionally inflicted on another person in order to obtain information, punish, intimidate, coerce, or eliminate personal dignity through a significant level of humiliation or degradation.

The definition changes significantly depending on the purposes of the group or individual promulgating it. For example, since the United Nations is concerned with nation-states, its definition suggests that the definition given is torture when committed by someone acting in an official capacity for the state. The Red Cross and the World Medical Association, on the other hand, both have broader definitions that include private individuals as well as those acting on behalf of a state. Individual countries often stipulate that its citizens are protected against their own government from torture. In his *Understanding Torture*, philosopher J. Jeremy Wisnewski points out that the differences in definition make sense since these world organizations have different focuses. Of the United Nations, he says, "It would thus make little legal sense to have a definition that covered, for example, the Marquis de Sade. The treaty would have no bearing on his particular actions, regardless of whether or not these were torture."[10] It is interesting here that Wisnewski refers to Marquis de Sade as an example of one who would truly be outside most legal definitions of torture. Infamous for his use of torture for sexual pleasure, Sade seems to define the outer limits of how torture is employed. The Abu Ghraib photos suggest, however, that Sade's approach to torture may not be so far from traditional ideas about torture.[11] Or, at the very least, that Sade, as do the smiles on the faces of the guards at Abu Ghraib, has something fundamental to tell us about torture.

Originally torture was used to shore up or enact the law.[12] In Greece, for example, the courts would never torture citizens, but always tortured slaves to obtain their testimony. The theory behind this pertained to the status of truth. The courts felt that slaves would be too afraid of their owners to tell the truth; thus torture had to be employed in order to validate what they had to say. Even at this time, the belief that torture produced truth was not unanimous. But Greek society as such accepted that torture was needed to mark a difference between the truth of the citizen and the truth of the slave.

The Greek system's approach to torture can stand as a larger metaphor for torture in the way that it looked to torture to inaugurate truth.[13] Important to note here is that the violence of torture marks the very impossibility of ever being totally sure of the validity of truth. One tortures in order to ensure that one obtains the truth, but the very necessity driving the torture reveals that truth will always remain suspect. Once court systems developed other ways of validating the truth—certain types of evidence, ways of corroborating witness reports, technological aid in determining aspects of truth claims—torture became obsolete in the court system. Wisnewski argues that most likely it was a combination of the belief that torture was degrading to humanity and a change in the epistemology of the juridical proof that made torture obsolete. When looking at these different forms of torture, what is essential is the shifting relations between violence, truth, and language.

Torture remains a more public and accepted phenomenon in societies up to the 1700s. Even when it serves no legal purpose, torture proliferates in the premodern world. Michel Foucault captures its public visibility in his famous account of the torture of Damiens the Regicide. In the opening pages of *Discipline and Punish*, Foucault provides an unforgettable description of the horrors of premodern torture. He cites the punishment planned for Damiens: "the flesh will be torn from his breasts, arms, thighs and calves with red-hot pincers, his right hand, holding the knife with which he committed the said parricide, burnt with sulphur, and, on those places where the flesh will be torn away, poured molten lead, boiling oil, burning resin, wax and sulfur melted together and then his body drawn and quartered by four horses and his limbs and body consumed by fire, reduced to ashes and his ashes thrown to the winds."[14] It is clear that the point of this torture is to teach a lesson to the onlookers and to use Damiens as a negative example. The law displays its authority and encourages obedience through the public act of torture. This can no longer be the justification for torture in the modern world.

The modern public would never accept this kind of spectacle of state-sponsored cruelty. Even as we see the photographs from Abu Ghraib, it remains impossible to imagine a return to the world in which torture served as a source of spectacular punishment. Today, torture can only exist under the veil of secrecy. *Discipline and Punish* itself follows the historical trajectory of state-sponsored punishment as it moves from a public spectacle to a necessarily hidden endeavor. The standard of state-sponsored punishment also changes from brutal violence, such as torture, to institutionalized incarceration. With the development of modern democratic society, there was no legal room for torture. Laws against torture appear alongside this society. In the United States, the stance against torture occurred in the Eighth Amendment to the Constitution, which is part of the Bill of Rights (ratified in 1791) that directly stipulates against the government inflicting "cruel and unusual punishment" on its citizens.[15] The wording for this amendment was very closely based on the English Bill of Rights of 1689. Torture fell under these laws against cruel and unusual punishment, and the ban on torture was an essential part of the idea of political rights and a foundational part of the institution of modern law.[16] Since the founding of the United States, torture has been alternately a private crime, the dirty secret of law enforcement that was a punishable offense, or a public spectacle that was completely unsanctioned by the federal government (as in the case of lynching). That is, torture occurred in the United States, but it was always an illegal activity, which meant that the perpetrators could theoretically be punished.[17]

Of course, the laws against torture are all geared toward protecting citizens of the United States and do not apply to how our military treats citizens from other countries. Nonetheless, the United States is a member of the United Nations, whose charter, signed in 1945, insisted on human rights and thus implicitly rejected torture. The United States also ratified the Geneva Conventions, originally formed in 1929 and revised in 1949. These conventions specifically protect prisoners of war against acts of violence or intimidation as well as from prolonged confinement. They also prohibit the use of violence to procure information.[18] Even more recently, the United States ratified the Convention Against Torture and Other Cruel Inhuman or Degrading Treatment or Punishment in 1988.[19] Of course, the conventions all rely on both parties in a war agreeing to these rules that they have accepted by their previous signing and ratifying of the conventions. There is no fully empowered authority to ensure that nations are following the rules. But in the case of the Geneva Conventions, a country that violates them can be brought in front of the international court and tried for war crimes or other nations can place sanctions on them as a punishment.

American law and involvement in United Nations and Geneva Conventions positions it as a democracy that does not support torture. The underlying theory here is that inflicting cruel and unusual punishment erodes the basic system of law (in which individual rights and the social good are balanced). Even when the United States military has tortured in the past, civilian and military authorities have seen it as a misstep and not taken it up as a new military practice or law of the land. But this is no longer the case. What ideological shifts occurred to change our fundamental beliefs against torture? Clearly, the shift begins with the September 11, 2001 attacks and the trauma of that event. The reaction is a seismic shift. All of a sudden torture becomes a method of interrogation that promises to reveal valuable information, which the state can employ with impunity. Barack Obama's attempt to curtail this impunity in 2009 stands as an important indication that this shift is not yet a complete transformation. But his attempt was not a reversal either in the realm of law or culture. Something changed with George Bush that Barack Obama could not rectify.

In order to inaugurate the state use of torture, the Bush administration first classified those involved as non-POWs, simply as detainees. By classifying all prisoners as enemy combatants or detainees, the Bush administration felt confident that it was not violating the Geneva Conventions or Convention Against Torture. These classifications, however, reveal themselves to be justifications for stepping out of the bounds of the belief system in basic political rights that the United States has been invested in since its birth as a nation. Inflicting cruel and unusual punishment on thousands of people, confining these people to unsanitary prisonlike environments, refusing to charge detainees with a crime, using violence to try to procure information, and systematically attempting to degrade their human dignity as an official United States military policy reveals a radical shift in our approach to the idea of law and in the ideological structure that surrounds official doctrine. The basic ideological structure of our times has undergone a revolution when it comes to torture. Regardless of its lack of practical success, the idea of torture has now entered the public imaginary in an unprecedented manner, and, if we use media representations as a gauge, it doesn't seem to be evanescing.

During this recent decade in which torture occurred at Abu Ghraib, Guantanamo Bay, Bagram, and other places, the Bush administration continued to release statements that the United States was against torture. Bush was clearly aware of the U.S.'s longstanding commitment to the worldwide stance against torture. Ironically, not long before the Abu Ghraib photos were leaked to the press, Bush released a statement on the United Nations International Day in Support of Victims of Torture. It read, "The United States is committed to the world-wide elimination of torture and we are leading this fight by example."[20] In part, Bush was able to publish such official statements because he had retooled the definition of torture.

He had asked the Office of Legal Counsel to respond to the Convention Against Torture and investigate whether the United States military could employ torture on its detainees in the Middle East. In 2002, John Yoo submitted the infamous torture memos. He had narrowed the definition of torture down to only interrogation that causes organ failure or death, making all other types of interrogation, including waterboarding, acceptable. The torture that inflicts pain but doesn't cause organ failure or death would later come to be known as "enhanced interrogation." Yoo's memo explains, "Physical pain amounting to torture must be equivalent in intensity to the pain accompanying serious physical injury, such as organ failure, impairment of bodily function, or even death."[21] The memo also suggests that having to abide by the conventional definition of torture erodes the president's right to conduct war and that it impinges on the United States' right to self-defense. The United Nations reviewed the United States in 2006 and accused it of both torturing and of outsourcing torture. The United States denied all these accusations.[22] Meanwhile, news organizations reported widely on the fact of the United States military using torture.

Even after the end of the Bush presidency and with increasing temporal distance from September 11, the American government's position on torture has not unequivocally changed. Wrapped into the discussions of torture are fears about national security and another attack against the United States, which further muddies the call to protect the rights of all people from being tortured established with the Geneva Conventions. By examining contemporary representations of torture, I intend to bring to light the underpinnings of these discussions and fears. Representations of torture provide a unique insight into the ideological structure encasing our ideas about torture. These representations reveal a fundamental presupposition that informs the policies and approaches to torture, one which sees the individual as reducible to its body. Understanding the individual as a desiring subject irreducible to its body, however, would instead prompt us to view torture not only as unthinkable but also as completely ineffectual. Representations of torture reveal that ideology today doesn't interpellate individuals as subjects; it interpellates them as bodies.[23] Today's representations of torture are the terrain in which this reduction to the body receives its clearest elaboration. By examining these representations, I hope to understand why the contemporary fantasy of torture can function today and how one might potentially disrupt it.

We can define torture as physical or mental harm done to humiliate, punish, seek revenge, degrade, or force a confession (usually a faked one). But one must add to this an element of the torturer's pleasure in the victim's pain. This pleasure may arise out of the satisfaction of revenge or simply out of the act of humiliating another human being. Often torturers believe the victim deserves to be tortured for one reason or another, and they feel emboldened by this belief. Significantly, defenders of torture disregard all other considerations (such as its illegitimacy or its ineffectualness) and insist on a single justification: torture helps authorities procure information and thus shores up national security. In order to torture in the contemporary world, one must then believe that the body is a repository for truth and that performing violence on the body will cause the truth that the body hides to emerge. Without this foundational belief, no one would conceive of torture as an effective strategy for fighting terrorism or for any police action. Recourse to torture thus has an ideological foundation in the idea of biopower, a political idea that focuses on the body itself rather than on its representation or signification. Those who sanction torture as an information procurement tool believe that the body holds the key to a person, and they have recourse to torture in order to turn this key. There have been to date no revelations that the Bush administration or the military personnel involved articulated a desire to seek revenge and purposely degrade the humanity of those in captivity on an official level. Instead, they believed torture was effective and that it was their only recourse.

A DIFFERENT STORY ABOUT TORTURE

But the Abu Ghraib photographs tell a different story about torture. They document a level of eerie enjoyment, and it is in this enjoyment that we find the actual purpose of the torture. Torture exists for the sake of the sadistic enjoyment that it produces, not for its effectiveness as an information procurement device. In order to recognize this fact about torture, we can't simply pay attention to the tortured body. This body is an ideological entity that blinds us to the dynamics at work in the torture chamber. In the Abu Ghraib photos, we see a series of desiring subjects, subjects who are irreducible to their bodies. The radical difference between the biopolitical body and the desiring subject lies at the heart of the debates about torture, and chapter 1 of this book confronts this opposition as it lays out what defines this contemporary fantasy about torture versus what occurs in actual torture. It shows that the only way to combat torture is to insist that there is no such thing as a pure body, that the idea of a body that just wants to survive is simply an ideological figure. The fight against torture, I argue, must begin with the psychoanalytic conception of the subject. The first chapter of the book explains this idea of subjectivity and contrasts it with the prevailing biopolitical idea that the body is the only basis of politics.

For many contemporary theorists, focus on the body provides respite from centuries of philosophical idealism that neglected embodiment through a privileging of the mind. For the opponents of philosophical idealism, the problem begins with the onset of modern philosophy and Descartes' separation of thought and the body.[24] This separation marks the beginning of the denial of embodiment that continues through twentieth-century thinkers such as Jean-Paul Sartre and Ludwig Wittgenstein. Biopolitical theory focuses on the mind's fundamental dependence on the body, a dependence that renders any philosophical slander of the body, such as we find with Descartes, untenable. The problem is that emphasizing the body at the expense of the mind, as I argue in chapter 1, plays into the hands of the torturers and provides them an inherent justification for their activity. If we are just bodies, then torture is the best way to obtain information and fight against terrorism. Privileging the body leaves one with no recourse. Theorists like Michel Foucault are not guilty themselves of creating a climate where torture would be acceptable, but they do strip us of the means to struggle against this climate. Theorizing the subject as a subject of desire, however, reveals that torture is destined to fail every time as an information procurement device, even when it doesn't degenerate into the extreme perversities revealed in the Abu Ghraib photographs. Revealing the desiring subject's role in the practice of torture begins to dismantle contemporary torture's edifice and in the process brings back discussions of political rights.

The desiring subject, as theorized by psychoanalysis, involves the body, but is not identical to it. This subject is wholly opposed to the bare body presupposed by both biopower and biopolitical theorists. Colette Soler states this directly: "psychoanalysis . . . is in direct confrontation with the operation of capitalist bio-power."[25] This confrontation stems from the emphasis that psychoanalysis places on the act of signification. The signifier divides the body from itself, and in this way creates a desiring subject irreducible to its body. But this subject is equally irreducible to its mind.

Psychoanalysis, I argue, doesn't involve a return to the dichotomy between mind and body.[26] Instead, it focuses on the desire that emerges when the body collides with the mind or when instinct encounters signification.[27] When one tortures this alienated desiring being, one evinces a fundamental misunderstanding of the nature of subjectivity. In contrast to the body, the subject does not privilege its survival above all else, and this skewed relation to survival renders the torture of the subject problematic. Even more than its survival, the subject treasures its mode of enjoying itself, its specific way of desiring. Contemporary justifications for torture do not acknowledge the subjectivity of the torturer nor the tortured that ultimately renders the contemporary torture fantasy impossible. Chapter 1 offers an account of the subject that is irreducible to the body, and it claims that this represents the only conceptual path out of the torture chamber.

In chapter 2, I consider a group of documentaries—*Standard Operating Procedure* (Errol Morris, 2008), *Taxi to the Dark Side* (Alex Gibney, 2007), and *The Ghosts of Abu Ghraib* (Rory Kennedy, 2007)—that try directly to address the Abu Ghraib photographs. Most specifically, they aim to delegitimize torture as a practice. The subject of these documentaries is not the desiring subject or the bizarre nature of what the photographs from Abu Ghraib reveal about human subjectivity. Instead, the documentaries work to expose the inhumanity of torture. The films also tear down the Bush administration's claim that the United States military did not directly order those specific acts of torture at Abu Ghraib. To do this, the documentaries follow the commands to torture all the way to the highest level. The tortured body at the heart of these documentaries remains an ambiguous body trapped in the frames of the photographic stills. Working hard to prove that torture is ineffective, these films keep torture on a specific ideological terrain. They do prove both the ineffectual nature of torture and Bush's involvement in the decrees to torture. This ends up avoiding, however, the question of the enjoying subject who smiles at us in the Abu Ghraib photographs, and this avoidance ultimately leads these otherwise excellent documentaries to miss the real issue at stake in torture.

In many ways, the documentaries share a similar problem with Amnesty International. Along with other organizations, Amnesty International publicized their research showing that torture was inhumane and did not work. Their arguments are indisputable. Their explanations, however, never had the intended effect of convincing the American public and the American president to ban torture. To convince people, William F. Schulz, former executive director of Amnesty International USA, tried to debunk the usual justifications for torture. He argued, "the number of true, confirmed ticking bomb cases is infinitesimal, certainly in comparison to the number of innocent people who have been tortured around the world." [28] The "ticking bomb" scenario is a favorite of torture advocates. In this scenario, a bomb (or some type of weapon of mass destruction) is about to explode and kill large numbers of people. The authorities have a suspect in custody that they believe knows where the bomb is located. Under these circumstances, proponents argue that potential mass murder justifies the use of torture. Schulz countered that a history of human experience shows us that these situations aren't the norm and that in this way they misrepresent how torture actually functions. The reason Schulz could not make his case was neither because he argued it poorly nor because he had the facts wrong. Instead, Schultz could not easily convince people because torture had ceased to be a simple practice and had become enmeshed in a torture fantasy.[29] Chapter 2 lays out the misconception that haunts so many outspoken opponents of torture, including Amnesty International and the documentary filmmakers.

In chapter 3, I consider a filmic genre that seems to be responding to these documentaries by essentially staging fictional versions of what happened in the torture chamber at Abu Ghraib. This chapter investigates the tortured body in the new filmic genre dubbed "torture porn," where the possible role of desire in the torture chamber is actually explored. Excessive spectacle and performance provide the stage for torture in the *Hostel* and *Saw* films. In this visual environment, the tortured body becomes an enjoyed body, a body coveted by the torturers who pay for or seek out torture for the enjoyment of humiliating and degrading rather than for procuring information. In this sense, they refer to more traditional ideas of the role of torture.

Chapter 3 explores these ideas as they become evident in the film form and narrative structure. In *Hostel* (Eli Roth, 2005), for example, one of the three main male characters, Josh (Derek Richardson), has been caught and brought to the torture factory. The scene opens by putting us in his perspective, since we only see out a small hole in the hood that is over Josh's head. We hear that Josh is breathing heavily and is scared. The camera pans over instruments of torture and the dank cellar where he is trapped. The torturer comes in and takes off his hood, and the film cuts to a shot of Josh, which reveals that he is naked except for his underwear. The shot also reveals Josh's shackles. The torturer comes over, and despite Josh's pleading, drills a hole in Josh's shoulder. The torturer then sits down to talk with Josh and explains that he always wanted to be a surgeon, but he never passed the requisite tests. He says, "A surgeon, he holds the very essence of life in his hands. Your life, he touches it. He has a relationship with it. He's part of it." During this explanation, the man touches Josh's leg. He then reveals that no amount of money would stop him from doing what he wants to do to Josh. In fact, he is paying the torture factory for the experience of torturing Josh.

The scene proceeds as he horribly mutilates and eventually kills Josh. In this exemplary scene, the torturer pays for the enjoyment of torturing his victim, and he explains that he does this because the human body holds something in it and yet more than it that defines the essence of life, which he wants to hold in his hands. Another way to explain this is that he wants to touch the elusiveness of the subject itself. He believes this can only be achieved through the pain, fear, and anxiety of the torture victim. He knows this is elusive, and yet he seeks it out nonetheless. The viewer witnesses Josh's experience of the horror of anxiety in the face of the enjoying torturer. These films thus suggest that the torturer's enjoyment is a defining element of torture itself.

The mise-en-scène of the torture scenes in *Hostel* combine a postindustrial decayed building with instruments of medieval torture scenes and dark ominous lighting. This further emphasizes the gruesome enjoyment encountered here. It has not gone unnoticed that it is in fact the imagery in these torture porn films that best evokes the images from Abu Ghraib. In her essay on documentaries about these photographs, Julia Lesage notes, "the Abu Ghraib photographs are echoed in mass culture in torture porn, which began with Eli Roth's *Hostel* in 2005."[30] The Abu Ghraib photographs depict an obscene underside of the contemporary torture fantasy, which is a highly sexualized torture that most representations on film and television since the September 11 attacks do not depict. It is torture porn that represents a genre engaging the depiction of torture as useless and, at the same time, replete with enjoyment.

In this way, torture porn struggles with the smiles in the Abu Ghraib photographs by pushing our idea of what motivates the guards into fantastical realms. In the fourth chapter of the book, I turn to television and the series *24* and investigate the contours of the torture fantasy itself as well as its ideological ramifications. Biopower's emphasis on the body helps to define the contours of this contemporary torture fantasy. The imperative for survival of the body animates both sides of this fantasy. It refers to the survival of those in danger and suggests that the quantity of the lives in danger invalidates any rights of the suspect in custody. It also informs the idea that the person being tortured values their survival above all else and thus will divulge any needed information when their body is threatened or in pain. This then leads to an association of truth with the body.

A POLITICAL FORM OF VIOLENCE

The ideas about the body, which are at the heart of the contemporary torture fantasy, are especially animated by a sense of urgency, a belief that time is running out. This belief manifests itself most clearly in the ticking bomb scenario. The ticking bomb scenario—most succinctly articulated in the Jean Lartéguy's 1960 novel *Les Centurions*—articulates the belief that torturing the body will result in the information that will lead us immediately to the bomb.[31] What *Les Centurions* introduces is not torture itself but rather the contemporary justification of torture. It suggests that truth can be retrieved like a material object out of the body. The ticking bomb scenario reinforces two biopolitical presuppositions: that truth can be accessed as if it is a material object and that a person who feels her or his life is in danger will reveal anything to stay alive.

The importance of the ticking bomb scenario was reenergized following the terrorist attacks of September 11. Whenever proponents of torture justified torture with the ticking bomb scenario they were also referring back to the September 11 terrorist attacks.[32] The subtext that clings to these arguments takes the form of a question: "Wouldn't you have approved of torture if it could have stopped the September 11 attacks?" This justification at the heart of the contemporary torture fantasy is indeed a very narrow fictional fantasy that plays on the trauma of those attacks. What should be surprising here is that the ticking bomb scenario itself came together most clearly in a work of fiction. The justification much touted by torture proponents did not emerge out of a famous historical example or set of examples. Instead, it sprang from fiction itself, a hypothesis of what might happen rather than a recounting of what actually happened.

Jean Lartéguy wrote *Les Centurions* during the time France was violently occupying Algeria. The book was award winning and extremely popular.[33] The story chronicles a paratrooper who beats a female Arab dissident as well as a dentist. In the process, he uncovers and stops two separate plots to explode bombs all over Algeria. While the use of torture for various reasons has long been a part of human history, thinking of torture as an effective military tool to uncover hidden clues that will immediately lead to victory is a recent phenomenon. Political scientist Darius Rejali explains that Lartéguy was himself a former paratrooper and a war journalist whose novel fictionalized the battle of Algiers. Through extensive research Rejali details that the military won the battle of Algiers not through information gotten during torture, but rather through informants within the Algerian population and other police work. Torture during this military operation served the purpose of intimidation, not information gathering as the military constantly claimed. Rejali argues, "Torture served 'to make them understand— who wielded power.' It was 'above all a *political* form of violence.'"[34] But then Rejali details that the cases in which the military received the most useful information were ones in which torture was not used. Even the most famous torture cases during the battle of Algiers did not actually lead to useful information.[35] But French authorities constructed a fiction about the torture being productive, which they then used to justify the torture of nearly one hundred thousand people.

Les Centurions, as well as the film *The Battle of Algiers*, contributed to shoring up this torture fantasy. These two fictions are obviously quite different. Film scholars, filmmakers, and even actual revolutionaries have historically embraced Gillo Pontecorno's *The Battle of Algiers* (1967) as a radical film. Despite its depiction of revolutionary attacks on civilians, it clearly privileges the Algerian side over the colonial French military. But, as Rejali astutely points out, the film does include a torture scene that yields information and helps the French military stop a bomb. Therefore, it too rearticulates a falsity about the Battle of Algiers and reinforces the contemporary torture fantasy. Critics often tout the film for its unflinching realism, and this only solidifies this fantasy. That the popularity of the ticking bomb scenario—and the subsequent belief in the efficacy of torture—has its origins in fictional portrayals (whether spun by the French military, *Les Centurions*, or *The Battle of Algiers*) is certainly essential to consider. But no work of fiction is sui generis. It responds to and comes out of a cultural moment. In chapter 4, I will discuss the direct impact the television show *24* had on the military's idea of the productive nature of torture. Even with the military quoting *24* to each other, it's clear that *24* is not to blame but rather it comes out of, as much as it may inform, a larger ideological moment. Nonetheless, it was fiction rather than a historical event that dominated the torture debate. All sides used *24* as a point of reference, and this reveals the truly fantastical nature of our contemporary justification for torture.[36]

Not only does the justification for torture emerge out of a fiction, but the continued support for it has its roots in fictional representations. An unprecedented quantity of torture scenes from 2001 to the present reveals that torture has become embedded within our cultural imaginary. According to the Parents Television Council, which keeps a programming database, from 1995–2001 there were 110 scenes of torture on prime-time television, but from 2002–2007 there were 836 scenes of torture. This sevenfold increase testifies to the profound ideological shift that occurred after 2001.[37] Representations of torture, however, run the gamut. Some representations depict torture as effective and fully embody the tenets of biopower and the ticking bomb scenario, while others completely eschew this and depict the desiring subject's relationship to torture, thereby exposing torture's ineffectiveness. Still other representations of torture offer an essential way to address the ideological ramifications of torture as well as understand the origin of this new trend in cinematic violence.

The paradigm of the torture fantasy, which is the main focus of chapter 4, is the television series 24 (2001–2010). This series adheres to the notion that the body is wholly biopolitical, and it is a media representation that sees torture as a useful tool of war. This is largely contextualized through the plot but has visual ramifications as well, and analyzing representative scenes from the series reveals a great deal about the larger ideological structure surrounding torture as well as about its media representation.

Though not discussing the series in the context of biopolitics, Stephen Prince gives a precise description of this biopolitical body when he describes torture victims on 24. He says, "In the series' political vision, people are vessels containing information, which is a kind of material substance that can be physically extracted from them; when the vessel breaks, the information pours forth."[38] Prince's imagery of the body as vessel containing information is apt. On 24, bodies are objects on which violence has the particular effect of unlocking the necessary information. This is especially the case with violence performed by the hero Jack Bauer (Keifer Sutherland).

A scene from season 5, episode 6 ("Day 6: 12pm-1pm"), is exemplary. Jack has information that Walt Cummings (John Allen Nelson)—the president's chief of staff—is orchestrating an attack on America. He gains access to the president and says, "Mr. President, my name is Jack Bauer and I'm sorry to have to confront you like this but your chief of staff is withholding information that is vital to this nation's security." Jack signals that his project is firmly rooted in the ticking bomb scenario by invoking national security. After preventing Cummings from calling security by brutally punching him, Jack explains, "Mr. Cummings is guilty of conspiring with terrorists. He facilitated the theft of a military grade nerve gas." After punching him again, Jack screams at Cummings and demands that he reveal the location of the nerve gas. But Cummings claims not to know. Jack points a knife at Cummings eye and says, "I'm done talking to you. You hear me. You've read my file. First thing, I'm going to do . . . I'm going to take out your right eye then I'm going to move over and take out your left. Then I'm going to cut you and keep cutting you (he waves his knife around his face) until I get the information I need." This speech by Jack that announces the torture also reminds the viewers, as much as Cummings himself, of Jack's history and track record.

At this point in the series, Jack's own reputation as a brutal torturing Counter Terrorist Unit (CTU) agent serves as part of the torture itself, or at least it authenticates Jack's intentions. But Cummings still won't confess, so Jack grabs Cummings and moves behind him and then places his knife directly on his face under his eye causing him pain, threatening mutilation while slightly choking him with the other arm. A close-up of the befuddled president signals his desire to hear the confession, but also aligns him with the audience in wondering how far he should let Jack go. Just as the show cuts to a close-up of Jack's hand on the knife pressing into Cummings right eye so that his eye is actually bulging out, Cummings says through grunts of pain, "Stop, Stop, I'll tell you. It's on the freighter leaving Long Beach at 2:30." In the end, through several direct punches and the threat of Cummings losing his eye within the space of a few short moments, Jack has procured the information. By applying a kind of science of violence to Cummings' body, Jack seems to easily crack the code or break the vessel, as Prince describes it, and the information spills out. This is not a complicated process on *24*. All it takes is someone willing to be violent enough (like Jack Bauer) to find the answers lodged in the body.

Other representations, however, consider the role of the desiring subject as it relates to torture in a completely different way. The television series *Alias* received criticism for having torture scenes and was often grouped with *24* by watch-groups tallying these depictions. But the portrayal of torture in *Alias*, which I investigate in chapter 5, is entirely different than *24* because torture in *Alias* rarely works. In *Alias*, it is exactly the desiring subject, the subject of fiction, who reveals the needed information, not during torture sessions but instead in the web of a CIA agent's fictional aliases that Sydney Bristow (Jennifer Garner) takes on. As a result, bodies on the series are not the bodies as defined by biopower but instead desiring subjects. The effect this has on the actual representation of torture, when contrasted to 24, reveals vastly different concerns. Through its recourse to fiction, *Alias* reveals that the torturer is always face to face with a desiring subject, and this desire renders torture ineffective.

Though *Alias* shares the investment of 24 in the project of national security, its political valence is the opposite. The emphasis that *Alias* places on fiction rather than torture as the privileged vehicle for truth bespeaks a political challenge to the contemporary ideology of biopower. Once one recognizes the necessity of the fiction in order to arrive at truth, one enters the terrain of dialectics, even if one is not a Hegelian or a Marxist.[39] The fundamental contention of dialectics is that we cannot separate truth from its dependence on the fiction that allows it to emerge as such. This is precisely the position that *Alias* adopts. In addition to showing the effectiveness of the fiction in revealing truth, the series refuses to create stable oppositions between friend and enemy.[40] Friends are constantly becoming enemies, and enemies often show themselves to be friends. Even late in the series, regular viewers must confront the possibility that the heroine's father Jack Bristow (Victor Garber) is a traitor or that her chief antagonist, Arvin Sloane (Ron Rifkin), has changed allegiances.

With its commitment to locating truth within the fiction, *Alias* necessarily adopts a political position that 24 cannot. Its rejection of torture follows from its implicit acknowledgment that the subject is not reducible to a body. But *Alias* and its political position have not become dominant. Though the series has concluded, 24 continues to prevail ideologically. Most of the films and television series that have followed in its wake have accepted its biopolitical premises, even if they have rejected its full-throated embrace of torture. This is the case even with Hollywood's most celebrated interventions on the subject. The public debate over torture found a second wind recently with the release of Katherine Bigelow's *Zero Dark Thirty* (2012). Though many celebrated *Zero Dark Thirty* for its authenticity, its elision of the enjoyment in torture and its wholly ideological implication that torture leads to truth reveal that we remain fully ensconced in the torture fantasy despite the apparent transformations that have taken place within the debate surrounding torture and its representations in fiction and nonfiction media.

Fictionalized images of scenes of torture rose dramatically while America struggled with the images from Abu Ghraib. These scenes of torture that began to rise on prime-time television and in film shortly after the September 11 attacks eventually exploded across genres and media outlets after the Abu Ghaib scandal in 2004. Torture has replaced some of the traditional plot devices and has become a violent staple in many genres that one would expect (such as spy thrillers, horror films, or action movies) but has also become common in dramas where one would not expect it. Even comedies and commercials increasingly rely on depictions of torture. This book investigates what these representations reveal about torture and the ideological formation that crystalizes after September 11, 2001. Representations of torture today reveal new formal patterns of violence and their engagement with and often challenge to contemporary ideologies of biopower. What comes out of this encounter is simple: when we understand that torture concerns how we enjoy and not how we know, we will find ourselves incapable of continuing to practice enhanced interrogation.

1
TORTURE, BIOPOWER, AND THE DESIRING SUBJECT

COMPETING REPRESENTATIONS

Recent years have seen a remarkable rise in scenes of torture on television and in film. How the scenes are depicted and situated in narratives reveals not only America's various cultural reactions to the attacks of September 11, 2001, but also the latest development in a far-reaching ideological shift that impacts every facet of contemporary existence. The various deployments are far from simple or one-sided; instead, these violent scenes are often used in opposing ways in different films or television series. Since September 11, 2001, however, some clear patterns across these various representations have begun to establish themselves. By examining these patterns, we can understand the significance of torture and the reasons for its growing popularity. It is impossible to grasp contemporary torture without a thorough investigation of the different ways that contemporary film and television represents it. Representations of torture hold the key to the practice of torture and the belief system that underlies it because they interact with the fantasy that supports contemporary torture. It is not by accident that authorities seeking to justify torture turn to media representations in their defense of what seems like an indefensible practice. On the other hand, it is also through media representations that we can find a way out of the practice of torture. Representations both provide the justification for torture and reveal that torture is not our destiny today.

Some representations depict the body as an information depository that torture can mine, while others present the body as enigmatic and thus resistant to torture. Some representations concern torture as a policing technique, while others investigate torture as a site of sexual perversity. But the decisive question is simply whether a film or television series generally perpetuates the belief that torture is effectual or ineffectual as a fact-finding procedure. This assumption is tied, I argue, to other more fundamental assumptions about the body and about subjectivity. Throughout this book, I will be investigating these contemporary patterns of torture, what stance the narrative takes toward the violence, and how it is represented visually. I will begin, however, with a theoretical investigation into the ideological and philosophical assumptions underlying the repeated tropes within representations of torture. Such an investigation into the assumptions that inform depictions of torture will thus shed light on the role of the exponential rise in depictions of torture in the contemporary world . These assumptions provide the ideological background for every depiction of torture, and they inhere in these depictions through the possibilities and impossibilities that govern them.

Representations of torture suggest two general ways to approach and define the body. One type of body manifests itself in the official or accepted justification for torture. The other body emerges in the failure of the practice of torture to align itself completely with the official justification. The first body is a biopolitical body, a vital body oriented around its own flourishing and survival. The second body is one that doesn't coincide with itself. This body that doesn't coincide with itself has a precise name in psychoanalytic theory—the subject. Contrasting the official justification for torture with the practice of torture permits us to see the difference between the biopolitical body and the psychoanalytic subject. These two competing theories of the body function as the basis for the understanding of torture in the chapters that follow.

The biopolitical body and the psychoanalytic subject are not two new approaches to the body that emerge with the renewed popularity of torture. But they are organized in a very specific way in relation to our new fixation on torture. One approach sees the body as a simple biological vessel whose worth is dependent solely on its survival, and because of this the body can be controlled, contained, or eliminated, depending on what is best for the survival of the greatest number of people. Utilitarian in nature, this approach takes a quantitative approach to the good. It adheres either to the ideas of evolutionary theorists and those who champion biology above all else or to vitalist thinkers who locate an inherent value in life itself. The perpetuation of life becomes, according to this way of thinking, the driving force behind political and social decisions.

Beginning from this position, one believes that the body exists as a fact repository whose information was stored in an archive that just needs to be accessed by medical procedures, health initiatives, or even torture.[1] This biological approach to the body predominates today and provides the theoretical foundation for torture. If the body is nothing but a biological entity that wants to survive and flourish, torturing the body is the best way to retrieve the secrets that it harbors. Under the threat of pain and death, the body reveals the truths that it contains.

The other conception of the body, which is not nearly so widespread, rejects the idea that the body has an inherent vitality and that it aims at survival. The origin of psychoanalysis lies in the fact that subjects do not seek their own good but instead endeavor constantly to undermine their own self-interest. The problem for psychoanalysis is not aiding subjects in overcoming their egoism—which separates it from the confessional and from moral philosophy—but in helping them to avoid completely destroying themselves through their various modes of enjoyment. The body, as understood by psychoanalysis, is then entrenched within a subjectivity that enjoys itself through painful repetition and thus does not aim at its own good. It is a body we don't have access to, a body that traumatizes and delights us, a body that plays a significant role in our desires and yet that we cannot totally control when it comes to satisfying those desires. This body is a body that can only exist in its connection to our psyche, and it must be understood through the complex relationship between mind and body, which is precisely where psychoanalysis places its emphasis. Because of this mind/body connection and its unpredictable results, this body is difficult to know or to control, and it is difficult to elicit any information from this body that really makes sense or is useful in a direct way. Dealing with this body, then, requires other ways of thinking about the greater good and politics.[2]

When Descartes first conceives the modern subject, he posits a strict division between the mind and the body. This dualistic approach both shaped subsequent centuries of philosophizing and earned him the opprobrium of many thinkers in the late twentieth century. According to Descartes, "there is a great difference between the mind and the body, inasmuch as the body is by its very nature always divisible, while the mind is utterly indivisible."[3] Though Descartes theorizes a divide, he places much more emphasis on one side of the divide than the other. If subjectivity for him does include the body, it is nonetheless the mind that predominates. As he makes clear in the *Meditations*, the mind, not the body, is the essence of the self. The body serves as a source of doubt—we can't trust our bodily sensations—while the mind provides epistemological certainty through the act of thinking. Contemporary emphasis on the body has emerged to counter this one-sidedness of the modern conception of subjectivity, but the result has been an inverse one-sidedness. Today's common sense views the body as determinative in relation to the mind. This is evident in the privileged position that neuroscience holds as a popular explanatory device. Neuroscience can demonstrate the lack of any autonomy on the part of the mind in relation to the physiology of the brain. Psychoanalysis does not at all reject the insights of contemporary neuroscience, but it does insist on sustaining the idea of a split between the mind and body.

Taking the Cartesian conception as its starting point, psychoanalysis rejects both the apotheosis of the mind and the reduction of the mind to the body. According to the psychoanalytic approach, subjectivity emerges through the collision of mind and body, a collision that produces desire. Desire is born out of the intersection between the mind and the body. Desire is not reducible to biological impulses, and, in fact, it often compels subjects to act against these impulses. Unlike the knowable body, the subject of desire bespeaks the ineffectiveness of torture because the body does not hold the key to the subject. The body is instead marked by its enigmatic status. The subject's relationship to bodily pleasure or violence is unpredictable, and the subject doesn't always do what is best for the body. For example, in terms of bodily health, subjects notoriously undermine it through excessive eating or ingesting substances that harm the body immediately or in the long term. Though it is counterintuitive, the subject has the capacity to enjoy its suffering and thereby work to sustain it rather than put an end to it.

Both the biopolitical and the psychoanalytic body are showcased in recent cinematic and televisual depictions of torture, and they signify very different projects. When investigating the embodied nature of the representations of torture, these two theoretical positions, biopolitics and psychoanalysis, are essential to consider. They provide the foundation for the contemporary torture fantasy and for the possibility of articulating an alternative that might disrupt this fantasy. These theories have long been influential on film and television studies and have long been at odds when confronting the question of the body itself.

My basic claim is that these two theoretical approaches to the body are thoroughly opposed to each other. One cannot reconcile biopolitics with psychoanalysis or the machinelike body with the desiring subject. There is, I contend, no possible compromise position.[4] Our contemporary political predicament depends on which approach we decide on, and this decision will also determine the role that torture will play in our political future. Today, biopower represents the ruling ideological structure and remaining within the paradigm of biopower guarantees that society will continue to live under a regime of torture.

THE BIOPOLITICAL BODY

Though I often use the terms interchangeably, there is an explicit distinction between *biopower* and *biopolitics*.[5] Theorists who analyze biopower see it as a new form of power that focuses on the living body rather than on the threat of death, which is the way that traditional forms of power operated.[6] These theorists are uniformly critical of biopower. Theorizing biopower as the most recent form of power does not entail endorsing it but rather critiquing it and trying to discover a mode of resistance appropriate to this new form of power. This mode of resistance, according to many of the theorists of biopower, is biopolitics, a politics that takes the body and its pleasure rather than the desire of the subject as its starting point. The apotheosis of the body as resistance to biopower finds its most straightforward expression in the thought of Gilles Deleuze and Félix Guattari, who conceive of the body without organs as the opposite of the psychoanalytic desiring subject. For them, psychoanalysis is part of the problem rather than the solution.

Deleuze and Guattari argue that the body exists independently of its subjection to the signifier, a subjection that turns our attention to specific organs rather than to the body as an assemblage. The body becomes reified by the despotism of the signifier. According to Deleuze and Guattari, "There is a primacy of the machinic assemblage of bodies over tools and goods, a primacy of the collective assemblage of enunciation over language and words."[7] In other words, the body is more fundamental than the way it is used or the way it is taken up in language. It is the way the body speaks the words rather than the words themselves. The emphasis here on the body, combined with the critique of language, reveals the distance that separates biopolitical theorists from psychoanalysis. But, at the same time, their unapologetic investment in the body bespeaks a failure to break fully from the regime of biopower that they criticize.[8]

Though the regime of biopower and the articulation of biopolitics are distinct and in some basic sense opposed, there is a common ground that the two share, and it is this common ground that psychoanalysis contests. Both biopower and biopolitics view the body as the sole political battleground, and both see subjectivity as inessential or epiphenomenal in relation to the body. According to the premises of both biopower and biopolitics, the body has no necessary relation to signification but can be approached in its immediacy. This is why I will theorize biopower and biopolitics as similar projects, despite the explicit opposition that the proponents of the latter advance against the former. The great theoretical divide today is not between biopower and the biopolitical opposition to it. It is between biopower and biopolitics, on the one side, and psychoanalysis, on the other. For psychoanalysis, one cannot theorize the social order or politics without an idea of subjectivity as expressed in desire, enjoyment, fear, anxiety, and so on. But for biopower, and even for the biopolitics criticizing it, this aspect of subjectivity is unimportant if not deceptive. These aspects of subjectivity are considered utterly ideological and therefore misleading. This is why biopolitics speaks of bodies rather than subjects. Psychoanalysis certainly theorizes the unconscious (and its expression in desire and so on) as embroiled in ideology, but not as wholly within ideology. The potential for subjects to react against their own interest or against what ideology is asking of them is an essential part of subjectivity and is not quantifiable. While biopolitics and psychoanalysis are truly in opposition around the idea of the subject, they are united in their recent attacks on the impact of biopower. To understand biopower, it is essential to begin with its analysis by biopolitics since biopolitical thinkers, much more than psychoanalytic theorists, have made it their business to grasp how biopower functions and why it dominates today.

Theorizing the effects of biopower largely takes on momentum with Michel Foucault's work on the body and its relation to politics. Foucault sees politics as revolving around the body itself and the use that power makes of bodies. For him, modern politics posits the body as the only essential aspect of a person, and this is the way the modern state has power over the individual. In contrast to thinkers like Kant and Hegel, who emphasize freedom, equality, and other political values, Foucault believes that the survival of the body becomes the focal point of every social institution. The politics of the body becomes a powerful way to control people, and Foucault refers to it as biopower. Biopower has not always been the predominant form that power takes, but it has taken on increasing importance since the nineteenth century.

Foucault sees biopower as the politicization of biology. Within the regime of biopower, biology becomes not just one science among others but the privileged site for the deployment of power. This begins with the consideration of humanity as a species. In his lecture course at the Collège de France entitled "Security, Territory, Population," Foucault describes the emergence of biopower in the following terms: "the set of mechanisms through which the basic biological features of the human species became the object of a political strategy, of a general strategy of power, or, in other words, how, starting from the eighteenth century, modern Western societies took on board the fundamental biological fact that human beings are a species. This is roughly what I have called bio-power."[9] Biopower concerns itself with the betterment and the survival of the species, and this justifies the measures of security that leave bodies under an everincreasing control. Power must constantly care for the bodies that constitute the species.

Biopower, according to Foucault, emerges out of the logic of the Christian pastoral. Pastoral power takes care of those who belong to its flock and occupies itself with every aspect of the lives of those it oversees. Though regimes of biopower are secular rather than religious, they have imported, he argues, the Christian pastoral into their deployment of power. This is why Foucault uses interchangeably the terms *biopower* and *pastoral power*. The Christian pastoral doesn't retain the devotion of its members through the threat of death but through the act of giving life. This is exactly how Foucault sees biopower functioning.

The emergence of biopower changes the way that power operates. As Foucault sees it, sovereign power—the traditional form of power—creates a sense of fear in those it governs. It punishes those who disobey and it avails itself of death to punish the most egregious offenders of its law. In the lecture course entitled "Society Must Be Defended," Foucault proposes that biopower reigns in a quite different manner. He says, "Sovereignty took life and let live. And now we have the emergence of a power that I would call the power of regularization, and it, in contrast, consists in making live and letting die."[10] The turn from sovereignty to biopower entails a shift in our way of thinking about power. It is not vertical but horizontal. Power is productive, not repressive.

Power exists within intersubjective relations, and thus power operates at every social level. It is not simply imposed from above but manifests itself even at the bottom of the social hierarchy. That is to say, even those who are the victims of social power can act to perpetuate this power. Foucault abandons the idea that oppression involves external oppressive force acting on a group of people and contends instead that oppression inheres internally within every group.

Foucault also sees contemporary power relations developing out of a certain historical progression. He argues that this history develops from sovereign power to disciplinary power to pastoral power, though he readily grants that much historical overlap exists between these three forms. Foucault claims that the onset of biopower occurs within pastoral power when the state begins to see its job as controlling and organizing individual behavior and routines. This grows into the extensive carceral, medical, and educational institutions of contemporary society, whose purpose is to regulate all aspects of individual behavior. About this final stage of power, Foucault explains, "Power would no longer be dealing simply with legal subjects over whom the ultimate dominion was death, but with living beings, and the mastery applied at the level of life itself; it was the taking charge of life, more than the threat of death that gave power its access even to the body."[11] Foucault suggests that this happens through the concept of population and the issues attached to it, such as hygiene, health, incarceration, and reproduction.[12]

Foucault's theorization of the shift in power is well illustrated in his writings on disciplinary power and the shift in types of punishment. As I mentioned in the introduction, he begins his study of this shift with a description of torture used as a public display that acted as a punishment, but also as a warning to the population watching the spectacle. He describes power at this time as sovereign power. The sovereign utilized torture as punishment and a way to control the populous through fear. Sovereigns relied on their own personal leadership style and ethical codes rather than a ubiquitous national or global standard. During disciplinary power, torture retreats behind closed doors as discipline becomes more and more internalized and embedded in the structure of society. In the eyes of the state, however, torture became something that was a barbarous practice of the past. During this shift the importance of political rights rises and becomes the cornerstone for democracy. Built into the idea of political rights and of freedom is the right not to be tortured by one's own government. In the United States, this manifests itself in the Eighth Amendment of the Bill of Rights, and other modern nations have similar foundational codes that proscribe the practice of torture.

But under biopower torture has begun to return. Sovereign power thought it could force people to do what it wanted by threatening their deaths. Biopower, on the other hand, thinks it can make people do what it wants by manipulating what people think they have to do to stay alive. It works in a productive manner rather than a repressive manner. While the logic of torture doesn't seem to fit into the tenets of democracy, it does fit into biopower's regard of the body as productive. Political rights find themselves more and more in contradiction with the demands of biopower. To change this mode of power would obviously not be to return to an earlier mode but rather to shift the emphasis to political rights and subjects and away from productive power and bodies.

The body under biopower is a body made visible; it is a body that is known, characterized, catalogued, and completely controlled. Power, according to Foucault, arises out of control of the body and by making the individual believe that the life of the body is more important than anything else—more important, for example, than political rights. Foucault doesn't often suggest an antidote to what he sees as our contemporary quagmire, but, famously, at the end of *The History of Sexuality*, volume 1, he intimates that it is through bodies and pleasure that we might be able to fight biopower.[13] This seems like a strange suggestion in reaction to his critique of the way our bodies have been defined by contemporary power, and many critics have commented on the inappropriateness of this solution. His point, however, is that it is through these very controlled bodies that we can break the hold of power.[14] This has nothing to do with subjectivity for Foucault. He is adamantly against any recourse to the subject, which he sees as a concept used by biopower to control us and make us believe that we have agency when in fact we do not. Biopower is in charge.

Without a conception of the subject, however, there is no avenue for contesting biopower. Without the subject, one ipso facto accepts the premises of biopower and accedes to the efficacy of torture. Though a biopolitical thinker like Foucault can argue against the practice of torture, he has implicitly given it his theoretical endorsement by insisting on the ontological privilege of the body. Foucault sees the problem that leads to the contemporary outbreak of torture, but he refuses the tools that would enable him to respond to this problem.

At the close of *The Order of Things*, and throughout his work, Foucault's refusal to see subjectivity as a possible mode of contesting biopower stems from his rejection of humanism. The subject is always an illusion, and it is an illusion that Foucault associates with the concept of the human. But psychoanalysis makes clear that the subject is distinct from the human, that the subject is the inhuman—what exceeds and cannot be assimilated to humanity. The biopolitical human controls itself and has agency in the world, while the psychoanalytic subject continually stumbles over its unconscious. The unconscious marks the point at which the subject's agency exceeds the subject. That is to say, the subject has agency, but this agency has nothing to do with the conscious will of a self-identical being that knows what it wants. Foucault's inability to see subjectivity in this light, his reduction of subjectivity to an effect of power, leads him to cling to the body as the sole mode of resistance to biopower, and it is a theoretical decision that reverberates among later biopolitical theorists.

It is this suggestion of a possibility of the body as an antidote to biopower that biopolitical theorists such as Michael Hardt and Antonio Negri take as a jumping-off point. For Hardt and Negri, biopower is, as for Foucault, the controlling political power that figures the survival of the body as the sole goal. Biopower for them is also at the heart of our contemporary political and social problems. Biopolitics, as a political strategy, is a way of responding to the ubiquity of biopower. Their biopolitics entails refiguring the body as the unique site for the resistance of this biopower.

Like Foucault, Hardt and Negri reject the idea of the subject and argue that the subject is a construction of power that limits hybridity. Instead, they proffer the idea that we can see bodies as linked in a community that has the potential to dismantle biopower, a community they call the multitude. Defining the multitude, they explain, "The figures that coalesce in the multitude—industrial workers, immaterial workers, agricultural workers, the unemployed, migrants, and so forth—are biopltical figures that represent distinct forms of life in concrete places, and we have to grasp the material specificity and spatial distribution of each."[15] Hardt and Negri emphasize the singularity of each person in the multitude and strive to hold onto differences while advancing the concept of the multitude that they believe has revolutionary potential. The singularity and differences, however, are biopolitical in and of themselves, as they have to do with differences of place and identity. In this way, Hardt and Negri are trying to theorize how bodies and identities can resist and potentially dismantle biopower while never quitting the terrain of biopower.[16] Thus they repeat the error of Foucault's critical response to biopower, and his attempt to construct a biopolitics, because they do not leave room for the subject's desire to either undermine or propel it toward a revolutionary change.

THE SUBJECT THROUGH THE BODY

In a related vein to Hardt and Negri, Georgio Agamben analyzes biopower and theorizes a way to dismantle it. He argues that we live in a time when bare life has become more important than political values, when politics has dissolved into an obsession with bare life.[17] He explains bare life by suggesting that previous forms of life had combined animal life with political life. Agamben's own name for this previous political being is a *form-of-life*, a form he feels has been bifurcated by biopower. Biopower foregrounds bare life to the detriment of a form-of-life. In other words, the political life becomes lost to the privileging of animal life, what he calls, in its modern form, bare life. As he explains, "The same bare life that in the ancien régime was politically neutral and belonged to God as creaturely life and in the classical world was (at least apparently) clearly distinguished as *zoē* from political life (*bios*) now fully enters into the structure of the state and even becomes the earthly foundation of the states legitimacy and sovereignty."[18] Biopower creates a zone of indistinction where politics and political struggle disappears under the dominance of bare life, which vitiates the possible development of any form-of-life.

At the heart of biopower, for Agamben, is the structuring and formative nature of the sovereign's invocation of a state of emergency. Agamben turns to such different thinkers as Hannah Arendt, Walter Benjamin, and Carl Schmidt because they all emphasize the risk to politics occasioned by the turn to bare life and the corresponding invocation of the state of emergency.[19] The sovereign invokes the state of emergency and creates zones of exception; these zones are at first spatially confined but then spread through the society. Agamben cites the Nazi concentration camps as well as the prison at Guantanamo Bay. He also points to the Patriot Act, an act declaring a state of exception and thus lifting various rights that all Americans previously had. In these zones of exception, *zoē* and *bios* are decoupled, and the people are reduced to just bare life. Agamben emphasizes that as a result today we are in a constant state of exception and bare life has become the controlling mechanism of power.

Agamben agrees with Foucault on some important levels. He explains, "Foucault's thesis—according to which 'what is at stake today is life' and hence politics has become biopolitcs—is, in this sense, substantially correct."[20] Agamben's term *bare life* comes directly out of Foucault's ideas and yet seems to more specifically define what Foucault meant by life itself. Despite his clear debt to Foucault, Agamben's explanation as to how we arrive at this point is somewhat different. Foucault theorizes the receding of the sovereign and the rise of a more regulatory power that inaugurates life as the sole concern of politics. Agamben, on the other hand, sees the sovereign as still the nexus of political power, a power located in the proclamation of the state of emergency. Agamben also emphasizes that this stripping down to bare life is a constant process, one that therefore can be resisted. By bringing back the importance of the sovereign, while at the same time acknowledging the power of disciplinary and regulatory practices, he opens up the possibility for creating a contemporary political being that is not reducible to its bare life and that his term *form-of-life* embodies.

In this way, Agamben goes further than Foucault in theorizing various places where we can disrupt this contemporary political environment in which people are controlled by the idea that their body is more important than their political being. Agamben, after Foucault, asks: how do you reignite the political and thus resist biopower? He suggests, for example, that we can work to decouple concepts such as violence and right, which would unravel a nexus, he argues, that greatly defines our society controlled by biopower. He also wants to repoliticize other categories, such as the term *refugee,* that force politics to reexamine its terrain. Like Foucault, he also turns to the body itself by theorizing the potential for gesture to show us something far different about the body than bare life suggests. But it is precisely where he returns to the body that the distinction between Foucault's politics and Agamben's becomes clearest.

Gesture, for Agamben, shows us something beyond the body, something about the person that goes beyond just the person's physicality. This places him more proximate to the psychoanalytic conception of subjectivity than the biopolitical body. He explains, "The gesture is, in this sense, communication of a communicability."[21] In other words, for Agamben gesture suggests a communicability that is form beyond content. While we may be controlled by biopower today, communicability and the power of language itself suggests something beyond biopower, beyond the mere body. Even when Agamben sees resistance in terms of the body, his distance from Foucault is evident. Resistance doesn't involve simple "bodies and pleasures" but the implication of the body in language, precisely what other biopolitical theorists like Foucault want to avoid.

Agamben argues that the way to prevent the stripping down to bare life is to enact a politics of thought and communication in which form and content are so clearly linked that bare life can no longer be isolated. In his discussion of gesture, Agamben mentions cinema, and he suggests, "Cinema leads images back to the homeland of gesture."[22] Here I would insert that the way "back to the homeland of gesture" is through the desiring subject, and it is cinema, and its related forms of television and other media, that constantly brings the desiring subject to the fore. Cinema (to one degree or another) almost always reveals—through its unique form—the psychoanalytic subject rather than just the bare life body, and it does this through its presentation of the body.

Though it is impossible to marry the basic tenets of biopolitics and psychoanalysis, Agamben actually forms a bridge between the two modes of responding to biopower. He takes Foucault's critique of biopower as his starting point, but he formulates resistance in a way that approximates psychoanalysis. Agamben is not a psychoanalytic theorist, but concepts like that of gesture reveal a thinker sympathetic, even if unconsciously, to the psychoanalytic subject and suspicious of Foucault's body in pleasure.

The important contribution of biopolitics is its analysis of biopower and the changed relationship between power and the body. Clearly, many representations of the body in scenes of torture depict this bare life body produced and controlled by biopower and thus illustrate, if not participate in, biopower. Understanding biopower is essential to theorizing how the body is coded and depicted, and biopolitics has had the great virtue of bringing the critique of biopower to the fore. There are many ways, however, either through the torture scene itself, its placement in the plot, and its thwarting or satisfying genre expectations that these scenes at times also reveal the way in which biopower can fail and not fully control or define the body. This is why cinema does not fit smoothly into the regime of biopower and why Agamben turns to it when he theorizes the politics of gesture. In analyzing scenes of torture in film and on television as well as the Abu Ghraib photographs, it becomes apparent that the bare life body is at the heart of biopower's contemporary fantasy but completely disintegrates in the face of the actual practice of torture whose violation of political rights is so glaring.

BIOPOWER AS IDEOLOGY

Rather than dismissing biopower or biopolitics, my claim is that it functions as the prevailing ideology of our epoch. Biopower, in other words, does not describe the totality of the structure within which we live, as Foucault would argue. Instead, it operates on the level of ideology. Its emphasis on the body works to confuse and deny the individual's subjectivity, which is always in play. But biopower is nonetheless omnipresent in the way that power manifests itself today. The discourses of biopower, which privilege survival and the health of the body above all else, exist as an ideology. Of course, ideology has real-world and often material ramifications, but it also requires the work of fantasy to fill in the gaps and evident impossibilities of the structure of belief itself. Thinking of biopower as an ideology is certainly not what biopolitical theorists have in mind, but this way of conceptualizing it doesn't minimize the impact that biopower has on society. It is rather a more precise way of understanding how we as desiring subjects interact with biopower.

The traditional understanding of ideology sees it as multiple: there are various ideologies, and one can accept or reject them as one pleases. This conceptualization leaves ideology on the level of consciousness and thus misses its significance for those who exist within it. Ideology is not a set of ideas that individuals either accept or reject. It was Louis Althusser who first recognized this, and he made a fundamental advance in the theory of ideology when he positioned the process of interpellation as the foundation of ideology. According to Althusser, "*all ideology has the function (which defines it) of 'constituting' concrete individuals as subjects.*"[23] In this vision, ideology permits individuals to see themselves as subjects—that is, as agents who have control over the direction of their own existence.

This theory of ideology remained the predominant one for twenty years, and many contemporary theorists still accept it. But, despite Althusser's debt to psychoanalysis, his theory represents a betrayal of the psychoanalytic conception of the subject. Althusser conceives of subjectivity as always ideological, but this conception makes it impossible to imagine the emergence of resistance. In order to make sense of how resistance is possible, a different theory of ideology is requisite, one that retains Althusser's notion of interpellation but transforms the position of the subject in this interpellation. The subject is not the result of interpellation, but what interpellation attempts to escape.

Ideology is an effort to avoid the trauma of subjectivity, and this is why individuals too often accept their ideological interpellation rather than rejecting it out of hand. Ideology is a reaction to a fundamental lack in the subject, a lack that is constitutive of the subject. This conception of ideology appeared for the first time in Slavoj Žižek's *Sublime Object of Ideology* in 1989. As Žižek explains, "The function of ideology is not to offer us a point of escape from our reality but to offer us the social reality itself as an escape from some traumatic real kernel."[24] Theorizing ideology as covering over some lack or unsymbolizable divide prompts an investigation into the relationship between the subject and the ideology they are ensconced in rather than assuming they are wholly defined by this ideology. It also explains both why ideology usually works and why it sometimes fails.

A powerful ideology, biopower defines various aspects of our contemporary social and political landscape. The biological explanation for the phenomena of social life almost always prevails, and this explanation has the virtue of avoiding the gaps that problematize other explanations. The power of biopower as an ideology stems directly from the thoroughness of its approach. It leaves no area of social existence beyond its purview. But, like every ideology, the ideology of biopower nonetheless has points where its symbolization of phenomena breaks down.

We can see the manifestation of the ideology of biopower in various contemporary social practices, such as biometric identification and genetic investigation. Biometrics is a technological science that relies on bodily characteristics to identify individuals. Often it is used to identify and characterize groups under surveillance. Some of the most common modes of identifiers used are fingerprints, facial recognition, DNA, palm prints, iris recognition, and retina recognition. Used by New York City Police in a systematic way to identify criminals in the early 1900s, fingerprinting as a mode of identification was one of the first modern biometric identifiers. Like all the techniques that followed in its wake, fingerprinting seemed to be an infallible way to identify an individual. Because no two fingerprints are exactly the same, fingerprinting carries with it the idea that it can identify an individual with complete certainty. All biometric forms of identification follow from this same precept.

Biometrics relies on the idea that each individual is a distinct biological entity so as to be identifiable, marked by unique physical patterns. Under biopower, this uniqueness makes the individual knowable. According to this ideology, as a subject of the signifier the individual can lie, but as a body with biometric markers of identification no deception is possible. The uniqueness of the body is the truth of the individual, and no individual can obscure this truth entirely. This is why courts trust DNA evidence much more than they do eyewitness testimony. DNA cannot lie, and it can exonerate convicted felons with perfect certainty.

Biometric identifiers are most often used to track citizens and to catch criminals. In both of these uses, the ideological idea of biometrics—that the bodily identifier equals the individual—becomes inscribed as a foundational way that the state relates to the individual. The most powerful biometric identifier is one that the individual literally cannot fake and thus escape. With each advance in science, a new biometric identifier is created, and the old ones appear as outmoded and ineffectual relics. Of course, the waning of the power of a biometric identifier should itself give the lie to the idea that the individual can be fully identified by their bodily characteristics. And yet, these very advancements in biometrics work to solidify the ideological resonance of biopower. The very developments that should shake our faith in biometric identification have the perverse effect of augmenting this faith.

Nowhere is this perverse paradox more evident than in the phenomenon of cloning. The existence of cloning should function as an argument against biopower insofar as it reveals that DNA cannot define an individual. But cloning advances rather than halts the march of biopower. This is a point that W. J. T. Mitchell makes, as he argues that one of the most important expressions of the dominance of biopower today can be found in cloning and its media representations. Mitchell says, "But the most dramatic and symbolic innovation of this sort has been, as I have argued, the invention of cloning, which combines the revolution in information science with the one in biotechnology to inaugurate an age of 'biocybernetic reproduction,' one that promises to literalize and technologically realize many of the premonotional fantasies of biopower and biopolitics."[25] Mitchell investigates how the science of cloning, an expression of biopolitical ideology itself, is then also employed as a fantasy in media representations specifically to cover over the gaps in the conception of cloning.

It is easy to look at biometric identification and believe that biopower is simply how power functions today. It doesn't require an act of interpretation on the part of the theorist to arrive at this conclusion. One simply needs to cross an international border, board an airplane, or watch an episode of *C.S.I.* The manifestations of biopower are ubiquitous. But it is precisely this self-evident ubiquity that reveals biopower to be an ideology and not the totality of the structure of all aspects of society or potential expressions of the subject. If biopower really structured our contemporary social order, we would not be able to recognize it so clearly.

Biopower enables those invested in it to believe that they are self-identical, to avoid encountering their self-division as subjects, and this is the fundamental task of ideology as such. Biopower is especially effective in this task because it has the backing of biology. The subject's belief in science (which is not necessarily wholly ideological) functions as a support for the subject's investment in the ideology of biopower. But the accuracy of biological claims tells us about the body and not about the subject. Unlike the subject, the body doesn't lack, and this absence of absence provides a sense of security. The individual interpellated into the ideology of biopower can know who it is and can experience the sense of self-identity that stems from considering oneself a pure body, even if the authorities can use this knowledge to track the subject's every move. Biopower imprisons the subject not through its technological apparatuses but through the psychic investment that it demands. For example, people's psychological investment in tracking their calories, heart rate, and cholesterol levels outweighs their understanding of the lack of privacy that goes along with this.

But despite its seeming infallibility, biopower suffers from incompleteness just like every ideology, and the necessary incompleteness of every ideology demands a collective fantasy to fill the gaps within an ideological structure. The existence of fantasies is one proof that an ideological structure is not whole because they testify to amendments that subjects must make to ideology in order to continue to function within it. In the case of biopower, the gaps exist not in the realm of knowledge—the knowledge always appears complete—but in the emergence of the knowledge, the act by which we acquire knowledge that provides a complete explanation. As a result, it is difficult to discern these gaps, but they manifest themselves when we examine the fantasy that operates within the ideology of biopower. A key fantasy of this ideological structure is the torture fantasy.

The torture fantasy imagines the body as the source of the information that explains its own actions. According to this fantasy, the body holds within it the secrets to how it will act in the future, and torturing the body—threatening its welfare and even its survival—will inevitably cause it to disclose these secrets. The tortured body gives itself away because it simply wants to live and flourish. We believe that torture produces information and that this information provides the answer to how bodies behave and how they will act. This fantasy that torture is the key to truth underlies every contemporary practice of torture and most popular representations that justify the practice. This is one of the fundamental fantasies of the ideology of biopower, which is why it proliferates so widely today. The ideology of biopower cannot explain why bodies blow themselves up or act more generally against their own good. This is a gap within the ideology, and the torture fantasy comes along to fill this gap with the body's self-confession.

It is not at all surprising that it was a suicide attack perpetuated by middle-class terrorists that led to the outbreak of torture and its representation. The impoverished suicide bomber who has nothing to lose presents a challenge but remains comprehensible to a biopower. The suicide bomber who has a decent existence, however, completely upends the capacity of biopower to explain this figure's actions. The recourse to torture is an attempt to bring the suicidal terrorist back into the explanatory ground of biopower. Even if torture can't reveal the terrorists' real motives, it can lay bare all other aspects of their lives.

When we confront the ideology of biopower and the torture fantasy that supports it, the limitations of the biopolitical response to biopower become evident. Any insistence on the body as the site of resistance sees a power structure where an ideological structure is actually at work. As a result, biopolitics can perpetuate the system that it is trying to contest. It falls victim to the ideology of biopower because it fails to recognize it as an ideology. What is needed is a conception of the body that sees the body's subjection to the signifier as a transformative event that renders the body alien to itself. This is the point at which one must turn to psychoanalytic theory as a way to respond to the ideology of biopower and the torture fantasy that accompanies it.

THE PSYCHOANALYTIC SUBJECT

The basis of psychoanalytic theory is the subject of the signifier. This subject has a body, but it bears little resemblance to the body conceived by biopolitics. The advent of psychoanalysis begins, of course, with Sigmund Freud and his discovery of the unconscious. For Freud, and later for Jacques Lacan (the most important psychoanalytic theorist after Freud), the body is *an* essential part of the subject, but it is not *the* essential part. Clearly, without a body there is no subject; nonetheless, psychoanalysis theorizes that we do not experience our bodies in any direct way. We experience the body through the mediation of the psyche. Our experiences of touch, sight, hearing, and all bodily functions are always already mediated and interpreted. There is no immediate bodily experience that later suffers mediation. Instead, mediation is present from the beginning. And since for psychoanalysis the subject is not the ego but the unconscious, the body is also not totally under conscious control. Unbeknownst to the conscious mind and the ego, the body can speak the unconscious through gesture, expression, physical position, and so forth. Like all elements of the psyche, the unconscious is formed through the interaction between the body and the social order. This doesn't leave the body out, but it suggests that for the subject the body is not the whole story. Therefore, it would be impossible, as biopolitics does, to view the subject as just a guise for the body. This impossibility stems from the role of signification in the constitution of the subject.

Beginning with Freud's theory of the subject as subject of the unconscious, Lacan emphasizes that the unconscious forms through the individual's encounter with language.[26] He theorizes that when the animal body is subjected to the signifier the result is the formation of the unconscious and thus of the desiring subject. Here desire is a very different idea than an animal instinct that derives from the pure body. The subject relates to its body through the mediation of the signifier, and even bodily instincts are experienced through this mediation. For psychoanalysis, the body is not just the animal body, nor is it just a construction of signification. Psychoanalysis is neither naturalist nor is it constructivist.[27] According to psychoanalytic thought, a constant interaction between the body and the signifier occurs, and any attempt to separate them or minimize the violence of their collision necessarily misses subjectivity itself. Thus there cannot ever be, contra Agamben (and also Foucault), a time in which the body (animal instinct) is separate from the mind (political being). Certainly due to ideological shifts and new political regimes, this ideological assertion of the bare life body can dominate, but the subject and its relation to signification are still present.

It is important to note that this desiring subject does not follow the Cartesian model, with the mind on the one side and the body on the other. Instead, the mind and the body are each divided from themselves: there is no pure access to one or the other, either to the signifier or to the body, which is why both naturalism and constructivism are untenable alternatives for psychoanalysis. The mind doesn't totally understand its own motivations, and, additionally, the mind doesn't have direct access to the body. By the same token, the body can't express itself or know itself outside the mind. This lack of access, as counterintuitive as it sounds, is in fact at the heart of the subject's potential radicality, of its ability to act, of its ability to create. All this can't be completely controlled for either good or not good ends.

The fact that the mind doesn't have complete control over the body is a key aspect to the experience of the subject. In this way, the body isn't completely subsumed by signification and fully mastered. Psychoanalysis developed as a theory in reaction to the way that the body refuses to be fully signified. The birth of psychoanalysis occurred with Freud's study of physical symptoms—points on the body that resist the signifier. In other words, patients had bodily functions that marked a refusal to accept the social demand articulated through the signifier. These symptoms could not be explained through medicine. And yet they also could not be explained away as nonexistent.

Freud followed the path of these symptoms through the patients' analysis to repressed trauma and unconscious desire that motivated these symptoms and had complex relationships to the social and its ideologies. For example, Freud's patient Dora initially presented a persistent cough, which had no medical explanation and would last for many months. Frequently the cough would also be accompanied with a complete loss of voice. Freud assessed that in her case the cough and aphasia were symptoms, bodily markers that pointed to a web of repressed trauma and desire, which he details throughout his case study. In Freud's analysis these bodily symptoms indicated past trauma and sexual desire that was continually inflamed by one particular family friend. After analyzing the details of this case, Freud argues, "sexuality does not simply intervene, like a *deus ex machina*, on one single occasion, at some point in the working of the processes which characterize hysteria, but that it provides the motive power for every single symptom, and for every single manifestation of a symptom."[28] In this case and others like it, the body is telling the truth, but not a factual or evident truth. Instead, it points to an unknown truth, unknown especially to the person who has the symptoms. Following the path of these symptoms led Freud to the unconscious again and again, a path he had begun to forge in his study of dreams. Thus began the path of psychoanalysis as a theory that addressed this incongruent mind/body relationship.

When Jacques Lacan takes up the project of theorizing psychoanalysis, he adds to it a structural dimension, one in which he brings together the insights of linguistics, structural anthropology, and philosophy. Lacan broadens Freud's thought to focus on the question of subjectivity. Lacan argues that in the case of Dora, Freud shows that the unconscious can deceive, but that even in its deception it reveals its own truth. After explaining this nuance in Freud, Lacan then claims, "In this way, I have distinguished the function of the subject of certainty from the search for the truth."[29] What psychoanalysis reveals, Lacan posits, is that the Cartesian subject's certainty of its identity is utterly distinct from the subject's search for truth, an impossible and not wholly articulated truth that arises in the relationship between the psyche and the body. This search for truth is better represented by the structure of one's desire.

Psychoanalysis theorizes our psyche as motivated by different repeated structures: the structure of desire and the structure of the drive. Ultimately the structure of desire is nestled in the repetitive structure of the drive, but it is the more consciously present structure.

Desire has a structure in which we desire an object and go after that object. The pleasure is in the pursuit and the idea of satisfaction that we will have once we acquire the object. Once we do reach the object, however, it doesn't end desire all together. Instead, our desire turns to a new object. Both Freud and Lacan, point out that this is because what we are really searching for is a lost object; the actual objects just stand in for this original loss. Of course, there is no object that was once lost. In the end, it is loss itself that haunts us and motivates our desire toward an endless string of objects that may cause some pleasure but never end desire all together. Freud's important discovery here is that we are not only motivated by pleasure or by seeking pleasure.

There is a type of enjoyment that comes out of pain or self-sabotage and that often surprises us. This enjoyment is linked more to the drive and its compulsion to repeat, and it arises when language fails. In fact, it is often an enjoyment of that failure, a kind of pleasure in pain. Jacques Lacan calls this enjoyment or jouissance. Theorists often use the French when referring to Lacan's concept of jouissance because the distinction between that and pleasure is more precise in French whereas in English pleasure and enjoyment are, in casual speech, quite similar. Psychoanalysis sees the phenomenon of jouissance as a key part of the psyche. Or, rather, it is an expression of our deep investment in our own form of repetition. In this way, it is a type of symptom: a marker of our own unique pathology. In *Seminar XVI*, Lacans claims, "everything that is repressed in the symbolic reappears in the real, and it is for this reason that enjoyment is absolutely real, because, in the system of the subject, it is nowhere symbolized, nor symbolizable."[30] It is precisely because enjoyment exceeds every signification that it consumes the attention of subjects of the signifier. They derive enjoyment from what the symbolic structure does not provide for them, and it is through sex and violence that this excess becomes visible.

Considering this complexity of the subject, the psychoanalytic point regarding violence begins at the intersection between psyche and body that defines the drive, an intersection that one cannot fully pin down or make understood. It is not scandalous, for example, to point out that there is a kind of pleasure in destruction and in violence. This is evident throughout the history of humanity. The pleasure is a pleasure of self-destruction as well. It is the inexplicable proclivity of subjects to self-sabotage and undermine their own interests, to hurt the ones they love, and to offend those they desire.

Psychoanlaysis can reveal that what torture ultimately signifies is a failure of our ability to find the truth or know what to do. It is employed when we can't find the truth, whether that means we can't solve a crime or stop an attack. Torture doesn't help the problem; it doesn't lead to the truth. Instead, it redirects libidinal energy and anxiety toward this violent activity. It allows us to avoid the trauma of an attack or potential attack. This ritualized practice entails myriad violent tactics, many of which are laced with a libidinal charge. Freud first theorizes the link between torture and enjoyment in his analysis of the Rat Man (Ernst Lanzer) in 1909. The Rat Man gains his moniker from his obsession with a form of torture described to his superior, an army captain. The Rat Man haltingly describes this torture to Freud. Freud recounts, "'the criminal was tied up . . . a pot was turned upside down on his buttocks . . . some *rats* were put into it ... and they . . . '—he had again got up, and was showing every sign of horror and resistance—' . . . *bored their way in . . .* '—Into his anus, I helped him out."[31] Though this method of torture horrifies the Rat Man, it also provides enjoyment for him, and the struggle with this enjoyment is the source of his neurosis. Freud adds that he displays "*horror at the pleasure of his own of which he himself was unaware.*"[32] Though Freud doesn't take up the occasion to theorize torture as a practice, his analysis of the Rat Man nonetheless provides the key to understanding this phenomenon. Even as it horrifies both the torturer and the victim, torture is a libidinal irrational practice that can never be a fact-finding tool. It can even provide a shameful enjoyment, which is why many torturers and victims suffer the fate of the Rat Man or even worse. Rather than confront this destructiveness, society employs the torture fantasy as a screen that allows it to continue unabated though disavowed. The fantasy that truth can somehow be accessed through violence gives this violence a false structure or container within which it can be employed. The torture fantasy underwrites acts of torture today and justifies the expression of an otherwise unacceptable violence.

Torture and its representation provide a vehicle for contemporary violence.[33] People feel a range of emotions when committing violence, from disgust to anger to equanimity to enjoyment. But torture channels violence into a specific avenue. Torture is an extreme and specialized violence that involves an element of ritual and performance in the way it is structured. But, for all this structure, it doesn't take away the element of irrationality that is at the heart of violence. Torture aims to harness violence, to force it to be productive. The contemporary torture fantasy offers potential respite from the irrationality of violence, but this irrationality always trumps the fantasmatic structure.

The torture fantasy emerges out of a failure to discover the truth. It promises access to the ultimate truth—the truth of the body. And yet, the practice of torture acts as a fundamental barrier to the truth of the subject. Torture prevents us from finding the truth that it promises because truth is not bodily but inheres in the act of the subject. Slavoj Žižek describes torture as "the extreme expression of treating individuals as *Hominini sacer*," a term he borrows from Agamben's *Homo Sacer*. This is a biopolitcal way of understanding torture. But then Žižek turns to the psychoanalytic point when he argues, "The tortured subject is no longer a Neighbour, but an object whose pain is neutralised, reduced to a property that has to be dealt with in a rational utilitarian calculus (so much pain is tolerable if it prevents a much greater amount of pain). What disappears here is the abyss of the infinity that pertains to a subject."[34] In other words, the contemporary fantasy about torture tries to cover over the desiring subject. The infinite abyss of the subject that Žižek refers to here is the infinite nature of the desire and the drive and the lack that marks its pursuits. We might look at torture, then, also as an attempt to destroy the subject. Or to destroy what we can never understand about the subject, its desire. The effects of torture are quite often devastating. The trauma of prolonged and frightening violence and degradation often creates lifelong psychic problems for both the torturer and the victim. But the torture fantasy continues to hold sway in the public imagination today because of the rampart against the trauma of the subject that it provides. We would rather confront the trauma of torture than that of the desiring subject.

The opposition between a biopolitical conception of the body and a psychoanalytic one has not often been straightforwardly posed. And no one has raised the question of representations of torture in these terms. But representations of torture themselves highlight the opposition between the biopolitical body and the psychoanalytic subject. Though representations of torture most often try to convince spectators that the body is nothing other than a body, there are representations today that point spectators in the opposite direction—toward the desiring subject. The representation of torture thus marks a nodal point in the contemporary ideological landscape. Where the tortured body appears on the screen, we must be able to decipher the contours of a subject that the body in pain tries to obscure.

2

THE NONSENSICAL SMILE OF THE TORTURER IN POST-9/11 DOCUMENTARY FILMS

The contemporary torture fantasy relied upon by the Bush administration and reinforced by television shows like 24 became the object of an attack by a spate of documentary films appearing after the Abu Ghraib photographs revealed torture and abuse in U.S. military prisons in Iraq. In the aftermath of the September 11, 2001 attacks, documentary films played an important role in providing the facts behind the War on Terror that emerged in response to these attacks. The deployment of American power by the Bush administration occurred through unprecedented opaqueness and concealment, and the documentary form acted as a counterweight to the ruling nontransparency. In the midst of an unrelenting commitment to waging war in the shadows, just bringing the facts of the war on terror out in the open became an exigent political project. When it comes to the question of shedding light on the hidden facts of the American use of torture at Abu Ghraib or elsewhere, Errol Morris's *Standard Operating Procedure* (2008), Rory Kennedy's *Ghosts of Abu Ghraib* (2007), and Alex Gibney's *Taxi to the Dark Side* (2007) represent major interventions in the contemporary political landscape, and their success on the level of facts is unqualified.

These documentaries also came out at an important moment in this decade. Appearing a few years after the Abu Ghraib scandal, the films participate in a cultural moment no longer about revelation or surprise but rather about an attempt to influence the national discourse that has arisen in response to the initial revelations about the use of torture. These films then are working to challenge the set of beliefs that took hold in favor of torture. They are successful at attacking the torture fantasy because they address it on the level of its logical structure.[1] Point for point, they refute the claims of this fantasy by revealing that torture doesn't provide information, that the ticking bomb scenario is completely unlikely, and that those performing torture do not do it on their own outside of the system of law but instead are told to do it through a chain of command that reaches the president of the United States. In other words, these documentaries attack the public pronouncements of the defenders of contemporary torture and prove that these pronouncements are disingenuous. In this way, they discredit torture as a practice.

What the documentaries have a harder time addressing, however, is the enjoyment expressed by the torturers in the Abu Ghraib photographs. Oddly enough, it becomes the one thing that very few of the interviewees or experts will mention, and yet it overwhelms the screen every time the photographs or videos taken at Abu Ghraib are shown. Pursuing the facts, then, leaves these documentaries just short of the most horrifying aspect of the Abu Ghraib photographs: the smiles on the faces of the torturers. And it is the enjoyment evident on their faces that gives us the most important clue to what underlies the torture fantasy: a certain kernel of nonsense is revealed that is at the heart of this fantasy.

This kernel of nonsense—the uncanny enjoyment at the center of torture in these photographs—acts as a distortion or stain in the image. At once familiar and completely out of place, the smiles become the focal point that alternately holds the meaning in the image together and tears it apart. Turning to theories of vision can begin the process of unpacking the Abu Ghraib images and their role in these documentary films. Seeing itself is mediated, but we often only become aware of this when we encounter a stain or absence or marker that makes us reevaluate our own complicity in the image. The stain is the index of our inability to look in a neutral fashion. Seeing, like all senses, occurs at the intersection between mind and body. Encountering markers in the visual field or within representation makes us aware of the interpretive aspect of sight and thus makes us aware of our own desire and its relation to the cultural context.

Jacques Lacan suggests that our visual field is not an objective or undisturbed arena but, like language, incorporates and relies on gaps. Our vision sees some things because it doesn't see everything, and the image necessarily indicates this failure. For Lacan, then, there can—and must—be a point in one's visual field that seems to stain the image and reflects back the subject's own unconscious structure or its lack. Lacan calls this point the gaze and explains, "the relation between the gaze and what one wishes to see involves a lure. The subject is presented as other than he is, and what one shows him is not what he wishes to see."[2] What Lacan points out here is that the gaze fascinates but can also horrify because it reveals something about ourselves that we may not want to see.[3] Recent psychoanalytic film theory has begun to work out the potential that Lacan's concept of the gaze has for the analysis of cinema.

The gaze in Lacan's sense of the term is different from Laura Mulvey's concept of the male gaze, which is a look of mastery rather than a stain in the visual field. Lacan suggests that what we don't want to see is precisely our own libidinal investment in looking. Mulvey's assumption—and that of other theorists associated with the journal *Screen*—was that the image was wholly defined by ideology and that the subject has no recourse but to be completely interpellated into this ideology.[4] Lacan's point, however, is that where there is mastery there are also always points of failure wherein we realize our complicity. This is a horrifying experience, but one that also offers the possibility of reflection and potential challenge to ideology. The gaze in this sense allows us to understand ideology as a constant push and pull between mastery and failure. This movement has the inherent potential to enhance and shore up power but always already the potential to dismantle it.

The gaze is the site of enjoyment within ideology. It indicates the incompletion of the ideological structure as it indicates the incompletion of the field of vision. Ideology includes this point of absence—this point that sticks out—within itself, and it marks a disturbance in the functioning of ideology. But this disturbance is not wholly subversive relative to the ideology. Ideology uses the enjoyment that threatens to undermine it in order to cement its hold over subjects.

The reliance of ideology not just on mystification and obfuscation but on obscene enjoyment is a constant motif in the work of Slavoj Žižek. His enduring contribution to political thought and the critique of ideology lies in his discovery that ideology is primarily a libidinal category. In *Living in the End Times*, he states, "subjects obey not only because of physical coercion (or the threat of it) and ideological mystification, but because they have a libidinal investment in power. The ultimate 'cause' of power is the *objet a*, the object-cause of desire, the surplus-enjoyment by means of which power 'bribes' those it holds in its sway."[5] Understanding power in this way focuses on the subject's libidinal investment rather than an idea of the subject as completely and successfully interpellated. Žižek's approach allows for insight into why the subject can be so invested in the power that oppresses it and why, at the same time, there's room for failure, disinvestment, and rebellion.[6]

The Abu Ghraib photos themselves act as an interesting metaphor for this structure. When faced with these photos, the viewer must figure out what is going on. The initial logical answer that the military turned to torture as a tool in the war against terrorism isn't satisfactory in light of the smiles on the guards faces. In the case of the Abu Ghraib photos, this libidinal enjoyment manifests itself in the smiles of the torturers, which in turn reveals an enjoyment that associates us as viewers with the torturers in the image. In other words, it is a stain of enjoyment that makes us feel complicit in the scene. The viewer is unable to turn away from questions that threaten to tear apart the prevailing ideology: are we responsible for this torture? Is there something about the structure of our society, our relationship to global politics, our value system that could have produced this? Or, possibly more threatening, is there something about our individual psychic makeup that might lead to this behavior? Where does torture fit in our understanding of humanity and our everyday lived experience? Analyzing the stain of enjoyment in the Abu Ghraib photographs and the documentary films that investigate them sheds light on the potential for the kernel of nonsense or the inexplicable (as embodied in this stain) to tell the truth about ideology.

Slavoj Žižek notes that analyzing this stain is essential to fully comprehending ideologies and the social order as such. Rather than being extraneous, it is often the key to understanding the structure and its libidinal charge. The stain exposes the point of excess that ideology requires and that simultaneously renders it vulnerable. When we recognize the stain, we grasp the structural imbalance that the image itself obscures. Žižek explains this by recounting Claude Lévi-Strauss's example of an anthropologist asking members of a village to draw the configuration of the houses that make up the village. One group of the inhabitants drew it as a divided community, and the other group of inhabitants drew it as a whole circle. This opposition suggests that either one side is right or that both sides misidentify the true structure.

Žižek points out that the logical solution would be to fly above the village and take a photograph to prove once and for all the spatial layout. The aerial view promises to provide the objective nonstained view of the village. He argues, "what we obtain this way is the undistorted view of reality, yet we miss completely the real of social antagonism, the unsymbolizable traumatic kernel that found expression in the same distortions of reality, the fantasized displacements of the 'actual' disposition of houses."[7] In a certain sense, these documentaries in their admirable quest to affect the political landscape have taken a snapshot of the reality of torture, akin to the helicopter shot of the divided village that Žižek describes. But in doing this they missed the real of torture, that traumatic, impossible to define kernel at the center. In other words, it is the torturers' enjoyment itself that reveals the real antagonism that underlies the ideology of torture or, as Žižek puts it, "the trauma around which social reality is structured."[8] This trauma is what we see in the enjoyment of the Abu Ghraib torturers.

Psychoanalysis sees ideology as composed of the symbolic fiction and the fantasy that arises to fill in the gaps when that symbolic fiction fails. Yannis Stavrakakis offers an exact formulation of the role that fantasy plays in relation to ideology. He notes, "the symbolic aspect of motivation, identification and desire cannot function without a fantasy support and this in its turn—the imaginary promise entailed in fantasy—cannot sustain itself without a real support in the (partial) *jouissance* of the body."[9] The gaze, as I've described it, is the point of symbolic failure that fantasy obscures. Typically, fantasy helps to repress the traumatic kernel that would undermine ideology. But when the gaze becomes overwhelming, fantasy ceases to function in this ameliorative fashion. The presence of the gaze makes the gap within the symbolic order evident. In this way, the gaze is a return of the repressed or the real within the image.

All the photographs from Abu Ghraib are traumatic because of the torture that they reveal, but the most scandalous ones are those in which the torturers are smiling. In the photograph mentioned in the introduction, for example, Sabrina Harmon leans over a group of naked detainees who are piled into a pyramid while both she and Charles Graner are smiling and giving a thumbs-up sign. In a photograph like this one, replete with trauma and abuse, it is the smile of enjoyment that stains the image. It seems out of place and yet it also tells the truth of the entire image and of torture as such. It is not so much that the enjoying torturer seems completely impossible as it is that the stain of enjoyment reveals the American soldiers' relationship to the Arab prisoners. It is the nature of this relationship that uncovers what is at stake in the activity of torture.

The question is: what are they enjoying? To begin to unravel this, it's essential to note that interweaved with the abuse photographs were pornographic photographs of the members of the military police (MPs) having sex with each other. Commentators have discussed these photographs but have not linked them with the photographs of abuse. And yet, as Susan Sontag points out, they are a very important element to understanding both the abuse and the expressed enjoyment. Sontag argues, "It is surely revealing, as more Abu Ghraib photographs enter public view, that torture photographs are interleaved with pornographic images of American soldiers having sex with one another. In fact most of the torture photographs have a sexual theme, as in those showing the coercing of prisoners to perform, or simulate, sexual acts among themselves."[10] We can add to Sontag's example the video that is shown in each documentary of the male detainees being forced to masturbate. And *Salon.com* has posted photographs in what they are calling "The Abu Ghraib Files" in which a female detainee bares her breasts for the camera.[11] This is not totally separate from the sexual nature of the torture. The MPs forced the prisoners to be naked for days and weeks on end and to be interrogated while naked. At Abu Ghraib, they shackled the detainees into sexual positions in order to "soften" them and prepare them for torture. The three documentaries do describe these acts, but they do not delve into any of the questions about the sexual nature of the torture. In other words, the films point to where the symbolic fiction of torture breaks down, but they do not investigate the enjoyment that erupts at the point of this rupture.

RACISM AND THE FAILURE OF TORTURE

As the documentaries prove, the symbolic fiction of torture breaks down when torture doesn't produce the information that the contemporary torture fantasy promises it will produce. At this point, the ideology behind torture—much touted by the Bush administration, CIA leaders, as well as shows like 24—begins to break down and the fantasy that fills in the void of this failure is multilayered. On the one hand, it is a fantasy about torture working regardless of reality, combined with a racist fantasy built around the American soldiers' ideas of their Arab prisoners. This latter fantasy is replete with sexuality. That is, the guards sexualize the Arab men by torturing them through practices directed at the prisoner's sexuality (panties over their heads, being handcuffed into sexual positions, being forced to drag their genitals along the ground, and so on), which is seen as a point of vulnerability. The American military had the actual Arab men in front of them, but their idea of torture didn't work unless they disavowed the existence of these actual men and substituted their own fantasy of Arab men. This was done in various ways.

The guards' superiors told them that the prisoners were dogs and that they should be treated like dogs. In other words, they thought of them as inhuman in order to torture them. But they also thought of them as highly sexualized and aberrant. One of the myths that the MPs relied on was that Arab culture hides sexuality and that performing sexuality would break their resistance because it would be humiliating. The MPs were ensconced in the competing fantasies of the prisoner as an animal who is less than human and the prisoner as a sexualized enjoying subject who is excessively human. They were caught between these fantasies as well as the fantasy that torture works and will save American lives. Whether their smiles indicate an enjoyment of the violence, of the sexual abuse, or of something else, they reveal the irrationality at the heart of torture. This revelation points to torture as a gesture of failure and of self-sabotage on the part of the government and the military. It is a failure of good detective work, and it is a failure of an egalitarian worldview, one that becomes most evident in the ways in which racism enacts the choices within the torture chamber.

The textbook for the guards' understanding of Arab culture was Raphael Patai's 1973 work *The Arab Mind*. American authorities believed that Patai's work would help the guards unlock secrets harbored by the prisoners because of its grasp of the Arab psyche. This book positions itself as an anthropology of the Arab culture, and it is a portrait of a world replete with sexual naïveté. Even though it was highly criticized and discredited, the military still assigned it as reading.[12] Journalist Brian Whitaker reports, "According to one professor at a US military college, *The Arab Mind* is 'probably the single most popular and widely read book on the Arabs in the US military.' It is even used as a textbook for officers at the JFK special warfare school in Fort Bragg."[13] Whitaker mentions that the chapter on sexuality is the one often privileged. Patai's view of Arab sexuality is then used as the basis for different techniques of torture. According to Patai, "the average Arab, unless he happens to live in a larger town where prostitutes are available, or where, as in Beirut, Western sexual mores have begun to penetrate, has no sexual experience with women until he marries. If we add the fact that the average Arab does not marry until his middle or even late twenties (what with the necessity of paying a bride price to the father of his chosen), we find that usually years pass between sexual maturation and the beginning of licit heterosexual activity."[14] Patai combines this observation with a reading of the Islamic religion and concludes that any expression of sexuality would be a truly disorienting affront to an Arab man.

This image of Arab masculinity is a caricature. In summing up the scholarship that has disproved the book, Whitaker points out, "The result is a collection of outrageously broad—and often suspect—generalizations. . . . All this adds up to an overwhelmingly negative picture of the Arabs. Positive characteristics are mentioned, but are given relatively short shrift."[15] Armed with this (mis)information, the guards would approach the torture of Arab prisoners by emphasizing sexuality. Doing so would, according to this position, completely destabilize the psyche of the prisoners. The book thus gave an anthropological explanation for a reductive fantasy about Arab sexuality. It also presented this fantasy as the main focus of how to understand Arab culture. The torture of Arab prisoners focused on sexuality because the torturers, informed by *The Arab Mind*, believed that confronting Arab men with sexuality would destabilize them.

Oddly enough, the three documentaries discussed here never question the MPs about or investigate the pornographic photographs, their relationship to what was happening in the torture chamber, nor their own fantasies of Arab sexuality. The enjoyment as the stain in the photographs, however, unlocks these highly sexualized and racialized fantasies that were working in concert with the symbolic fiction in order to create the fabric of the contemporary torture fantasy. But the stain is not something we are supposed to see; fantasy sustains the symbolic fiction by obscuring the stain. The photographs themselves captured these fantastical qualities and became a screen of sorts depicting the excess of this military operation. This is why the release of the Abu Ghraib photographs so completely threatened the ideological edifice behind torture and provoked such frantic discourse on the part of the Bush administration and other supporters of torture. The inability of the form of the documentaries to address successfully this stain of enjoyment sheds light on the political inefficacy of revealing truth while ignoring enjoyment.

There are certainly many ways in which documentary form itself has addressed the role that enjoyment plays in the stories that documentaries recount. This occurs in the recent popular documentaries, with Michael Moore's juxtaposition of President Bush golfing and making pronouncements on terrorism in *Fahrenheit 9/11* (2004) and Morgan Spurlock's depiction of the excessive enjoyment associated with McDonald's in *Super Size Me* (2004). It also takes place in lesser-known features, when Agnès Varda reveals her own complicity with the gleaners in *The Gleaners and I* (2000) or Ross McElwee depicts himself sidetracked from making his film *Sherman's March* (1986) because of his involvement with various women. And indeed whole movements within the documentary tradition, such as feminist autobiographical video artists and filmmakers from the 1970s and 1980s, have founded their stylistic practices on incorporating their own enjoyment into the picture.

The enjoyment present in torture, however, is not investigated in the documentaries that focus on torture and the war on terror. The drive to reveal the unknown information seems to override any sustained exploration of the role that enjoyment plays in making torture possible in the first place. Rather than confessing or avowing their enjoyment from the process, the interviewed torturers downplay it at every turn, even when the photographs seem to belie these denials. The enjoying face of the torturer in Abu Ghraib stains American history, and it similarly haunts these documentary filmmakers as they pursue the truth of the facts of this story, all the while continually bumping up against the difficulty of representing the fantasies of sexual excess at the heart of the story and at the heart of torture. The way each documentary deals with the issue (or avoids it), however, expresses the way that enjoyment acts as a stain that points to the symbolic failure of the violence of torture.[16]

The form of the documentaries is geared toward proving that the "a few bad apples" argument is completely disingenuous.[17] The Bush administration claimed that the MPs involved in the scandal were perverted individuals and that their actions did not represent the American military. The distinction between official military policy and the perverse actions of individuals was essential to the defense of American policy in the face of the Abu Ghraib photograph revelations. All three films successfully reveal that the military chain of command knew what was going on and either authorized it through their silence (as in Abu Ghraib and Bagram) or officially authorized it (as in Guantanamo Bay). As detailed in *Taxi to the Dark Side* and *Ghosts of Abu Ghraib*, Rumsfeld personally approved many of the techniques used at Guantanamo Bay. Army Major General Geoffry Miller, who was in charge of Guantanamo Bay, was then sent to Iraq to advise the interrogators there. In *Standard Operating Procedure*, Janis Karpinski (brigadier general, Military Police) details Miller's arrival in Iraq and his orders to redefine the command structure so that the military interrogators would be in charge instead of her. She also explains that he was told to "GITMOize" the Iraq prisons. In addition, *Ghosts of Abu Ghraib* notes that Rumsfeld was openly angry about the lack of intelligence information and proclaimed, "Why is it that Guantanamo gets me good intel, just what I want, and I don't get this out of Iraq? I've had it with this. I want you to get Miller out to Iraq and GITMOize the situation and do it fast." The documentaries also prove at length that Guantanamo produced very little intelligence information. Instead, the torture produced what the interrogators wanted to hear, what Rumsfeld wanted to hear. The films show that the extreme techniques shown in the photographs were employed at Guantanamo Bay and Bagram on thousands of prisoners by countless other guards and interrogators who were being supervised and witnessed by military officers.

These documentaries track how the techniques used at Abu Ghraib—shackling prisoners into stress positions, having them stand on a box or hold a box with a hood over their head for long periods of time, leaving detainees naked for hours and days, sleep deprivation, sexual humiliation, and so on—were not unique ideas thought up by the Abu Ghraib MPs. This was not, as President Bush claimed, just some perverted "Animal House." Instead, these were techniques being used throughout the American military prisons that the MPs were ordered to perform. They were also techniques that have long histories both within the United States and elsewhere. Shockingly, they were not the most violent techniques employed at the Abu Ghraib prison. The most violent techniques did not appear in photographs and took place in the interrogation rooms, although these interrogations were not devoid of tactics with a sexual nature. Military interrogators or contracted interrogators were responsible for these extreme abuses. Rory Kennedy's *Ghosts of Abu Ghraib* is one of the only documentaries that points out that the detainees were far more frightened of the interrogation room than anywhere else.

In the face of these facts, the documentaries argue for a top-down policy prohibiting torture that is strictly adhered to in order to ensure that this never happens again. The films suggest that when experiencing the dangers of warfare, in combination with the extreme pressure to extract intelligence information from prisoners and with the orders to "take the gloves off" (and move away from the Geneva conventions), the young MPs would torture prisoners in ways that even they themselves would never have expected. Each director also makes clear, however, that oftentimes military officials did not give the MPs precise directions but simply told them to do what was necessary to make a detainee miserable, and along with some vague guidelines the rest was left to the soldiers' imagination. It is their imagination that the documentaries do not investigate, and it is the MPs' imagination that holds the key to the perpetuation of torture. Rather than being a separate unknowable component of torture, the soldier's imagination is in fact the quilting point around which torture revolves. It is their imagination or fantasy that covers over the ultimate symbolic failures of torture, which in turn allows the practice of torture to continue to function.

BATTLING TORTURE THROUGH DOCUMENTARY FORM

The information in the three documentaries is largely presented to us through interviews, the photographs, and the footage of war that supports the interviews. All the interviews in these three documentaries are seated and done in a studio, home, or office. The films make the surroundings inconsequential by blurring out the backgrounds, and the directors carefully light each interview. This choice in many ways indicates to the viewer that it is what these interviewees have to say, rather than how they live, that is important to the larger story. Formally, this focuses the attention on the events they are investigating, but it potentially misses any extraneous clues to the MPs' personalities. It leaves the image of the interviewee in the interview and the interviewee's words as our only sources of information to answer the powerful questions posed by the photographs. This formal decision also minimizes any experience of the gaze: the interviews appear to present objective information rather than depicting an image replete with the stain of enjoyment.

All three films center on interviews with the MPs who tortured detainees and others involved (such as ranking military and government officials, detainees themselves, and political experts). In spite of their different structures, the interviews with the MPs provide the foundation for the inquiry that each film articulates. By itself, this does not preclude approaching the issue of enjoyment, but none of the interviewees directly addresses this issue (which is often literally staring them in the face when the filmmaker has handed them one of the famous photographs). In these moments, the filmmaker and the interviewee are both staring at the enjoyment—whether in the form of the smiles, the sexual nature of the torture, or the very attempt to pose the detainees for the photograph—as the stain in the image, but the interviewee simply disavows the stain by speaking to the symbolic fiction—the facts about their missions and what they were told to do.

Standard Operating Procedure has the most highly stylized interviews and the least amount of footage or other interviewees to intervene in the MPs' story.[18] Errol Morris concentrates on interviewing the MPs involved in the Abu Ghraib prison scandal. Morris shoots his interviewees against a dark gray and black marbled background that fades completely to black at the side of the frame. The interviewee is lit well with no shadows on her or his face so that each seems to be in a literal spotlight. She or he is often decentered which adds some tension to the frame and allows Morris to jump cut between sides of the frame. The shot is a medium close-up that shows us only their heads and shoulders, which means we don't see their hands during the interview. It also does not allow us to contextualize them in their homes or other nonmilitary environments. In this sense the film keeps us relentlessly focusing on the faces of the same MPs.[19] Morris's clean presentation of the interviewees contradicts their actions. As Julia Lesage notes about this interview style in many of the documentary films on Abu Ghraib, "As they speak, I search their faces for signs of remorse and any indication that they are lying or telling the truth. My emotional response, especially to the Abu Ghraib photographs, conflicts with these people's expressed attitudes about past events and about themselves."[20] This seems especially true in *Standard Operating Procedure* where Morris does not prompt the interviewees to answer questions about their own feelings and actions, and their stark polished presentation gives us no further information. Any clues about what it was like to torture or why they seemed to be enjoying themselves or about their fantasy structure that upheld the practice of torture can be gleaned only through their words—the stories they tell. The films address torture on a symbolic level but do not touch on it as a real phenomenon, on an irrational or emotional level.[21]

The starkness of the interviews is matched only by the crispness of the photograph presentation.[22] Each photograph we see is placed center screen on a black background with a crisp white border. Obviously, the clean and orderly presentation of the photograph in no way matches the content, which depicts almost unimaginable brutality. The presentation of the photographs mimics the look of the interviews, neither of which evinces directly the impact of the enjoyment obvious in the photographs.[23] At times, the photographs show desolate prison hallways, but most often the photographs depict horrific scenes of violence, humiliation, and degradation, where the interviewees play the part of the oddly joyful aggressors. While the photographs often serve to illustrate an interviewee's story (for example, about the circumstances behind the detainee being pulled on a leash), no interviewee ever provides a satisfying explanation for her or his behavior in the photo. Thus there is no direct investigation into enjoyment as the stain in the image. There are a few attempts to explain specific actions in the photographs but not in a way that touches on the emotional state of the guards or begins to explain the enjoyment displayed in the photographs. Obviously the interviewees might not be able to explain their actions, but the documentary filmmaker could find other ways to consider this question.

Since Morris doesn't push the interviewees to any such revelation or investigate the enjoyment exhibited, we are left with the answers floating somewhere in the void between the cuts.[24] Morris addresses the symbolic fiction of torture by investigating the facts through the interviews and in this way does point out the failure of that symbolic through the facts, but his only investigation of the enjoyment that is displayed in the photographs is through his presentation of the photographs themselves. It's the odd contrast between the stoic interviewee and the Abu Ghraib photograph that keeps the question of enjoyment circulating but never explicitly addressed. Enjoyment and the irrationality at the heart of torture are present as a conspicuous absence in the interviewee's stories while being at the same time overtly present in the photographs displayed in *Standard Operating Procedure*.[25] This contradiction between the verbal symbolic fiction and the stain of the enjoyment in the photographs prompts the viewer to consider the role of the irrationality in torture, but it doesn't make possible an exploration of its structural necessity.

Taxi to the Dark Side certainly is a more comprehensive documentary than *Standard Operating Procedure*. It provides much more background footage (both shot by the filmmaker and found footage from the news or elsewhere) and many more interviewees whose opinions buttress and contextualize the MPs interviews. In contrast to Morris, Gibney interviews MPs from both Bagram and Abu Ghraib. Interestingly enough, however, Alex Gibney's *Taxi to the Dark Side*, which won the 2007 Academy Award for best documentary feature film, has a somewhat similar visual style to its interviews with most of the MPs and military intelligence (MIs). They are placed in a tighter medium close-up in front of a very dark background (usually a dark red curtain that is almost too dark to see) that fades to black at the edges of the frame. Though the interviewees are seemingly in a spotlight in *Taxi to the Dark Side*, the difference between this film and *Standard Operating Procedure* is that Gibney's film keeps half the interviewee's face in the shadow.[26]

This evokes a more criminal or underworld feel—or at least suggests a Dr. Jekyll and Mr. Hyde syndrome, which compares the unemotional telling of their stories with the unchecked emotion displayed in the photographs of the actions. In other words, the half-shadow suggests that the interviewees are hiding something, but the film leaves unexamined what this something is. It is as if the lighting here is meant to literalize the gaps in the verbal symbolic fiction. Clearly, Gibney's impetus to shoot his subjects in this way came from an idea of them as characters in this dramatic scandal, but the film never thematizes this formal development.[27]

In opposition to *Standard Operating Procedure* and *Taxi to the Dark Side*, Rory Kennedy's *Ghosts of Abu Ghraib* shoots the interviewees in a far more naturalistic way. None of them appear to be emerging from the shadows. Instead, they appear in their homes with the background blurred out and their faces evenly lit. This certainly creates a less dramatic style and gives it more the feel that these are average Americans who have lives outside the theater of the scandal they were involved in. It also allows us a very small glimpse of other enjoyment in their lives: the jersey from a favorite team, the carefully designed home with artwork on the walls, and so on. These small details hint at the fact that these MPs are enjoying subjects. But this only exists around the edges of the frame and isn't brought to the fore. Even when we are allowed more visual information about the interviewee (which might reveal more of their own personal fantasy structures) Kennedy does not work to explore these areas, instead they remain enigmatic hints. This forces us again to rely primarily on their verbal information in which they largely address the symbolic fiction rather than the fantasy upholding the practice of torture.

Like Morris, Kennedy concentrates on the Abu Ghraib scandal and interviews many of those involved. In fact, Kennedy interviews some of the same people as are interviewed in *Standard Operating Procedure* and *Taxi to the Dark Side*. Kennedy interviews Javal Davis, Sabrina Harmon, Megan Ambuhl, and Janis Karpinski (who are also interviewed in *Standard Operating Procedure*), and she interviews Ken Davis, Tony Lagouranis, Rear Admiral John Hutson, and Alberto Mora (who are also interviewed in *Taxi to the Dark Side*). The sometimes precise repetition of the stories to two different filmmakers provides an added layer of meaning for those watching more than one of these films. On the one hand, it reveals a desire to tell the truth about what happened. On the other hand, it detracts somewhat from the authenticity of the telling when it is told in exactly the same way. That is to say, the viewer becomes more aware of what might be at stake for the MP herself or himself to explain away the charges. In addition, the inability to talk more specifically about why they did what they did becomes more apparent with their own repetition of generalities to explain their actions.

Kennedy's documentary is an interesting combination of the focus of *Standard Operating Procedure* with the breadth of investigative reporting that marks *Taxi to the Dark Side*. Of the three films, *Ghosts of Abu Ghraib* is also the only one to give significant voice to the detainees. Kennedy interviews many former detainees. This not only allows for corroborations of certain claims (such as the interrogators being aware of the MPs torturing the detainees) but also puts a face and a name to the many people in the photographs. Giving weight to the voice of the men imprisoned in Abu Ghraib brings out an essential part of the story largely left underdeveloped by the other two films. Kennedy includes and personalizes the voice of the detainee because she is interested in the psychological effects of the events on all involved as well as an explanation of how these events came about. Interestingly, this rounding out of the total picture, by including the detainee's stories, makes the torturers' libidinal investment far more apparent. It is the detainees who describe further and thus verbally address the smiles on the faces of the MPs.

Kennedy frames *Ghosts of Abu Ghraib* with a reference to Dr. Stanley Milgram's 1961 experiment at Yale University about obedience. In this famous study, experimenters asked participants to shock someone in the next room with increasing voltage. The subjects hear screams from the next room (which, unbeknownst to the subject, come from actors), but most end up eventually administering the highest voltage. Kennedy includes footage taken of the actual experiment at the beginning of the film in order to set the stage for her exploration of contemporary torturers. At one point one of the participants of the study asks, "Who is going to take responsibility if anything happens to that man in there?"

The doctor says, "I'm responsible," and the participant turns back and continues with the torture process.

At the very end of her film, Kennedy returns to this footage and to a voice-over of Dr. Milgram saying that, considering his findings of what these average men would do in this scenario, one could only imagine what the government could make soldiers do. Through this example, Kennedy points to what is psychologically likely in terms of conditioning and obedience, and then she illustrates that this is exactly what happened at Abu Ghraib. In proving that the military conditioned the MPs to do what they were told, she is also proving (like the other documentaries) that the orders to abuse and torture detainees had to come from higher up. Like *Taxi to the Dark Side*, she works on two fronts: she investigates the psychological environment and experience of the MPs and she investigates the chain of command that ordered the torture.

Kennedy pushes the interviewees the furthest to reveal the psychology behind the torture, but even *Ghosts of Abu Ghraib* does not ever directly address the enjoyment that is flaunted in the photographs. The film does, however, circle the issue through the attempt to make psychology a pillar of the film's investigation. By addressing the psychological, she does address the level of fantasy and its role in upholding the symbolic fiction and hiding the failures of that symbolic. But, for Kennedy, this occurs at the level of obedience and shame rather than enjoyment. The film moves back and forth between the psychological and the political, which creates a juxtaposition that forces the viewer both to accept the findings (about the culpability of the top military and government officials) as well as remain confounded as to the mystery of the emotions that the MPs exhibited in the photographs.

There are moments when the MPs and MIs do try to directly explain the photographs. For example, in *Ghosts of Abu Ghraib*, Kennedy does push Sabrina Harmon to justify her actions by handing her a large print of the photograph depicting Harmon smiling broadly and flashing a thumbs-up behind a naked pyramid of detainees. Harmon looks at the photograph and then gives an explanation: "If I saw something I took a photograph of it. The first thing I think of is to take photographs; that probably sounds really sick, but I'm always taking photographs, that's just me. I've always taken photographs. I was taking a photograph from behind and Sergeant Frederick said, 'hey get in the photo.' And Graner's behind me and I just gave a thumbs-up and smiled. I realized it was a pretty stupid thing to do right away ... but it happened." After Harmon says this, Kennedy cuts to a full-screen version of the photograph so that the viewer may contemplate it again before she cuts to another topic. Interestingly, Harmon responds to questions about this photograph first with an explanation of why the photograph (or at least the ones she took) exists at all. In doing this, she attempts to reduce the horror of the stain of enjoyment in the photograph to an explanation of the chronology of events.

THE PERSISTENT TROUBLE OF THE PHOTOGRAPH

Harmon makes clear that the photographs themselves are the source of the trouble surrounding the torture. If there hadn't been any photographs, no one would have gotten in trouble. Some of Harmon's fellow MPs were convicted for their part in these actions because of her photographs. This is also heavily emphasized in *Standard Operating Procedure*, when Errol Morris has Harmon read the letters out loud that she sent home to her wife Kelly, and in which she states: "The only reason I took the pictures is to prove that the US is not what they think." In this age of photojournalism and the importance of the amateur photographer in capturing historic events (such as in the Rodney King video, the Zapruder film, and the many photographs and videos used on the nightly news sent by the hobbyist or bystander), the impulse to document traumatic events is one we sympathize with and even applaud. And yet Harmon, in *Ghosts of Abu Ghraib*, classifies her own desire to document the torture as "sick." At this point in the interview, the film moves to the edge of the enjoyment present in torture.

The word *sick* itself sticks out and further emphasizes the smile as stain since it indicates Harmon's inability to explain her own desire to photograph what was happening. This point of inexplicability continues to stand out as a stain in the ideology of torture (both in relation to the symbolic fiction and the fantasies upholding it) throughout her explanation. When confronted with the question of her smile in the photograph of torture, she says that she "realized it was a pretty stupid thing to do right away," and then she pauses and says in a straightforward way, "but it happened." She admits that it was "stupid" but has no explanation except "it happened." She doesn't, for example, admit that she was in fact enjoying and that now she is shocked and ashamed that she felt this enjoyment. Here the word *stupid* is the key. By saying that her actions were "stupid," she is saying that they were not done within the realm of duty but rather solely for some sort of nonsensical enjoyment that is indissociable from photography itself. By filming Harmon provide this explanation, Kennedy's film allows the question of the relationship between enjoyment and violence and thus the instability of torture to arise without fully broaching it.

Later in *Ghosts of Abu Ghraib*, Kennedy questions Harmon again about a different photograph, which Kennedy also hands her and puts on-screen for the viewer, that depicts Harmon with the same broad Doris Day smile and thumbs-up over a dead detainee whom they later discovered was murdered by the military interrogators. Harmon here tries to address the smile and thumbs-up. She says, "Well, the thumbs-up, I got that from the little kids, the smile I always smile for a camera, it's just the natural thing you do when you are in front of a camera. It really wasn't anything negative towards this guy. I didn't know he was just murdered. I just thought it's war, it's another dead guy, no big deal." Kennedy lets this answer linger as we review the photograph and consider that her answer only brings up more questions.

Her answer suggests that the camera has culturally conditioned her to perform enjoyment. While this may certainly be part of the truth, it also becomes the avenue for the libidinal expressions that these MPs might not consciously be willing to claim. In other words, the presence of the camera allows for expressions of the enjoyment of the sadism through this cultural codification of the snapshot. Certainly owning the enjoyment in any conscious way would also demand a feeling of shame. Once the enjoyment would be identified, then it could no longer continue—at least not in the same way.

By presenting Harmon with the photographs themselves to comment on, Kennedy pushes the interview format to address the photograph directly. She demands that Harmon see her enjoyment as the stain in the image of the torture. But the subject—Harmon—is ultimately unwilling to address her own enjoyment. The question here might be, what other mode of documentary presentation might have probed more deeply? If the interviewees themselves are unable to verbally address their irrational response and/or its role in torture, how else might these documentaries unearth the link between their smiles and the torture that is so clear in the photographs themselves?

Taxi to the Dark Side has several moments in the film in which the MPs look at a photograph of themselves performing abuse and/or smiling over that abuse as well. When asked what was happening in the photo, the MPs simply respond with a description and state that they were told to do those things. Certainly, the absence of any emotional revelation may reflect Gibney's different focus. He is not investigating the psychological dimension of torture as doggedly as Kennedy, so he may not have pushed the question. But it is also a common response across all three documentaries: that the photographs reveal what they were told to do. This contextualizes the MPs' actions to some extent, but it does not explain their facial expressions. Were they told to enjoy themselves? Certainly, they couldn't have been told what to feel. Feeling, as even Immanuel Kant points out, represents the ontological limit of duty. One can't command a feeling because no one can feel on demand: we could never fulfill a duty to be happy or sad.[28] And yet, in some more metaphorical way, the enjoyment of the MPs is inextricable from the orders they received.

The logic of the justification that the MPs present avoids and yet points to the problem of their enjoyment. All the documentaries chronicle the different responses of the MPs, and these different responses give them all a structuring order. One common explanation that the MPs provide for their actions—and thus possibly for their displays of enjoyment—is the life-threatening environment in which they had to live and work. Kennedy makes much of this by highlighting the MPs' description of Abu Ghraib as having the feel of a haunted prison. Pfc. Damien Corsetti in *Taxi to the Dark Side* references the life-threatening environment and pressure from the higher-ups to find intelligence information and then concludes with, "You put people in a crazy situation, people do crazy things." Here we have to assume that one of those crazy things is that the soldiers began to enjoy what they were doing. Or rather that the enjoyment described and photographed is at the heart of the definition of the "crazy things" they did.

From a psychoanalytic perspective, those "crazy things" constitute the MPs' enjoyment and act as a precise marker of the failure of the symbolic fiction.[29] These "crazy things" reveal the MPs response was irrational and yet also inevitable once the torture began. When publicly aired, the photographs reveal this enjoyment as an obscene by-product of the symbolic fiction that then points to the places it fails, which belies the reasons for torture much touted by the Bush administration. In other words, the enjoyment acts as a symptom of the symbolic failure.

When the MPs muse on their actions reported on and captured in the photographs, there seems to be three kinds of responses: 1. they explain in a matter-of-fact way what events led to the photographs, 2. they just state they were told what to do, 3. they cite the conditions and suggest that they just lost control in such a bleak and violent environment. Even within the structure of each documentary, this creates what Freud describes as kettle logic, in which too many reasons begin to cancel each other out.[30] It is at the center of this logic that the paradox of their enjoyment lies. Kettle logic appears when we are trying to hide or explain our inherently inexplicable enjoyment. We provide too many reasons for an action precisely because we are acting without reason.

The problem with enjoyment is that it is unquantifiable. That is, enjoyment cannot be reduced to the signifier. Enjoyment resists all attempts to define it because it exists in the gaps of signification, at the points where signification fails. Or, as Joan Copjec puts it in *Imagine There's No Woman*, "jouissance flourishes only there where it is *not* validated by the Other."[31] We enjoy only when we surpass the terrain of significance, and this enjoyment necessarily disrupts any attempt to account for it from within that terrain. This is why the soldiers stumble when they try to explain their own enjoyment in reaction to the violence of torture.

Abu Ghraib was not just a case of soldiers reluctantly doing their duty and trying to procure needed information from recalcitrant prisoners. It was, instead, a fully sexualized drama, as much as a lynching or a sadomasochist ritual. At Abu Ghraib, enjoyment is at the heart of the drama, but it remains elusive for both the interviewees and the form of the documentary films. To address the peculiarity of this enjoyment, many bloggers, journalists, and academics have already pointed out the similarities between the Abu Ghraib photographs and American lynching photographs. For example, Susan Sontag argued in 2004, "If there is something comparable to what these pictures show it would be some of the photographs of black victims of lynching taken between the 1880s and 1930s, which show Americans grinning beneath the naked mutilated body of a black man or woman hanging behind them from a tree."[32] Horribly, the enjoyment here seems tied to a pride in the torture itself. As art historian Dora Apel notes when comparing lynching photographs to the Abu Ghraib photographs, "The viewer is meant to identify with the proud torturers in the context of the defense of a political and cultural hierarchy."[33] The nonwhite body being proudly tortured in sexually explicit ways for a cause that is supposed to be rooted in patriotism has a long and painful history in the United States. As Apel notes further, "For white supremacists, souvenir lynching photos became ways of reliving the erotic thrills of torture and mutilation produced under the guise of righteous civic actions, as well as a way of reaffirming a racial and gendered hierarchy that kept white men on top and blacks at the bottom."[34] The link between the Abu Ghraib photographs and lynching photographs reveals the status of the torture that occurs during the war on terror. The MPs who took these photos circulated them among themselves and to other guards. Distributing and viewing the photos becomes part of the fantasy structure that supported the torture itself.

As this parallel with lynching photographs makes evident, one cannot subtract the enjoying subject from the act of torture. Though exposing the facts of torture might shock and horrify the American populace, it will not uncover the entirety of the stakes involved because this fact-finding process—at work in the three documentaries that I have discussed—remains within the logic that the torturers themselves employ. The proponents of torture justify it as a technique designed to uncover a hidden truth. But acts of torture are in fact a turning away from truth. One cannot unlock the nature of this failure by just exposing the facts; one must instead force the enjoyment into the light of day, where it can reveal how it shapes subjectivity.

3
TORTURE PORN AND THE DESIRING SUBJECT IN *HOSTEL* AND *SAW*

A NEW TREND IN HORROR

The term *torture porn* has a recent vintage. David Edelstein coined the term in an essay that appeared in the January 28, 2006, issue of *New York Magazine*. The essay, entitled "Now Playing at Your Local Multiplex: Torture Porn," identifies a group of films that seems to belong to the horror genre and yet has characteristics of pornography (which is why this moniker has stuck). Scholars, film critics, and filmmakers alike now refer to this group of films that revel in depictions of torture as "torture porn."[1] The odd yet popular term describes the recent spate of films that reveal essential aspects about torture in America after September 11, 2001, that are not overtly represented in any other genre. What stands out about the films is the extremes to which they go in order to shock and titillate spectators. In discussing this trend, Edelstein explains, "As a horror maven who long ago made peace, for better and worse, with the genre's inherent sadism, I'm baffled by how far this new stuff goes—and by why America seems so nuts these days about torture."[2] The extreme depictions in these films justify the act of identifying a new genre.

The popularity of representations of torture in the world of contemporary media spans genres and mediums (from television series such as 24, *Alias*, and *Rubicon* to blockbuster films such as Marc Forster's *Quantum of Solace* [2008] to more independent films such as Jeffrey Nachmanoff's *Traitor* [2008]).[3] But none of these recent representations approaches the gore and sadism shown in torture porn. The films commonly included in this category include *Saw* (1–6),[4] Eli Roth's *Hostel: Part I* (2005) and *Hostel: Part II* (2007), and Greg McClean's *Wolf Creek* (2005), but sometimes films as wide-ranging as Mel Gibson's *The Passion of the Christ* (2004) to Rob Zombie's *The Devil's Rejects* (2005) receive this categorization.[5] Torture porn films don't simply represent the act of torture but thematize the enjoyment that derives from it. These films are not radical in that they do not confront the viewer with this enjoyment. They do not make the viewer aware of her or his own complicity or investment in the enjoyment that they depict deriving from torture. Instead, these films allow the viewer to enjoy torture without seeing the source of that enjoyment. Torture porn does not radically undermine the contemporary legitimization of torture, but it does help to give the lie to the fantasy that subtends this legitimization. The narrative structure of torture porn remains steeped in horror genre expectations and does not push the films in such a way as to make larger social critiques by upending genre traditions. And yet their depictions of torture are unusual because of their emphasis on the torturers enjoyment of torture.

What is unique about these films is their direct investigation of the violence of the torture chamber and its relation both to the psyche of the torturer and that of the victim. The insights these films reach arise not through careful study of the psyche—they are not meditative dramas of introspection—but rather through an excessive style and gruesome spectacle that root them firmly within the traditions of the horror film. This excessive spectacle that is the mainstay of the horror genre allows torture porn to investigate contemporary torture, especially as it is manifested in the Abu Ghraib photographs, that other genres avoid. This avoidance becomes most evident, as I have pointed out, in the documentaries that attack state policies on torture without ever attempting to understand why the modern state resorts to torture in the first place. There is no straightforward logical explanation that sufficiently addresses the smile on the guards face as they stand in front of a tower of naked and shackled bodies. Similarly, there is no satisfying rational explanation for the elaborate Kafkaesque tortures that the detainees in the war on terror endured (such as months of loud music, weeks without darkness, forced masturbation, and days of forced standing).

Torture porn, in a sense, takes this as its starting point and expands into the realm of fantasy to push these limits even further.[6] What these films discover in extreme representations of torture is the truth that the contemporary torture fantasy obscures—that, contrary to what the legal memos declare, torture is never about attaining information but instead aims at the domination and humiliation of the psyche. This is done for the sake of the torturer's own fears, anxieties, and desires. Beliefs about the effectiveness of torture today derive from a biopolitical idea about the body, an idea that sees only a body and refuses to see the desiring subject and the subject's relationship to the truth. Though it presents different conceptualizations of torture at its most excessive, ultimately the torture porn genre highlights the persistence of the subject beneath the appearance of the biopolitical body. There are times that torture porn does stress the body, but throughout the genre the presence of the subject still resonates.

Sometimes on the level of plot, but always on the level of form, torture porn makes the connection between the violence of torture and enjoyment, a connection that is difficult to talk about but hard to ignore. Torture porn films suggest that there is a relationship between torture and enjoyment by presenting torture as a spectacle to be experienced in the way we experience other cinematic spectacles such as depictions of sex or musical numbers.[7] Torture porn films are quite varied in their approaches, but a structural similarity marks them all. In these films, the torture is a spectacle that we see sporadically throughout the film, and finally the spectacle culminates at the climax of the film. These films present torture in the way that pornography presents sex.

In her pathbreaking work *Hard Core*, Linda Williams links the structure of pornography to that of the musical. Her idea—that in both cases the spectacle arrests the flow of the narrative—helps to make sense of how torture functions in torture porn. If we consider these films formally, the acts of torture occupy the space that the musical number occupies in the musical, and this is the site of enjoyment. These films present torture as a performance that has its own anticipated ritual and spectacle. Both performances, the musical number and the scene in the torture chamber, highlight the capacity of spectacle to disrupt the narrative flow of daily life.[8]

Representations of torture have their own repeated formal codes that work to create a spectacle of this violence. It breaks the flow of the narrative, occurs in confinement, mimics a performance with an emphasis on props and ritual, and generally transpires between two individuals. Throughout the performance, horrific and gruesome violence is on display. But, at the same time, the violence is private rather than public and takes place behind locked doors. The privacy of torture then allows for an added element to the spectacle in the form of surveillance. Some of the films depict guards or others watching the torture through surveillance cameras. Evangelos Tziallas explains, "A consistent cinematographic motif in torture porn is the constant alignment between the filmic camera and story camera's surveillance lens. Even when the surveillance apparatus is missing from the storyline, the films, at times, position the camera at a 'surveillance angle.'"[9] The surveillance acts as another layer to the spectacle of the torture chamber. One that defines the space, links technology to the torture chamber, and emphasizes the spectacle by redoubling the act of viewing within the film itself. In these cases, surveillance adds to the fantasy space of the torturer. The violence depicted in torture porn always occurs in a fantasy space that highlights the enjoyment that this violence provides for the torturer. One of the key aspects of the way these films represent torture is that, both visually and narratively, they present the torture chamber as a space purposely set up to enact fantasies of enjoying torture.

The fantasy in torture porn is, of course, a sadistic one. The act of torture attempts to produce enjoyment through the logic of sadism. But the logic of sadism is not as straightforward as it appears. The sadist does not just assert power over the victim and enjoy this demonstration of control. Instead, the sadist wants something more than just control. Sadists depicted in these films want to inflict pain, instill fear, and kill or nearly kill their victim. They want to interact intensely with their victim, even emotionally, in a way they would never normally act in their daily lives. In other words, they want to violate or decimate the structure of intersubjectvity and intimacy through emotional excess (in the form of fear, anxiety, and causing pain). These torturers are not looking for information, but they are looking for something; they are looking to provoke extreme emotion and the libidinal charges that go along with these emotions of fear and anxiety. As Jacques Lacan notes in his famous discussion of sadism in "Kant with Sade," "the sadist discharges the pain of existence into the Other."[10] The victim suffers, but this suffering is not just suffering but also the core of the victim's subjectivity. Through extreme acts of violence, the sadist tries to force the other's hidden form of libidinal excess to manifest itself, and the sadist believes that this will produce enjoyment for herself or himself. That is to say, the sadist wants to see evidence of her or his victim's subjectivity through fear, anxiety, and pain.

In order to produce the expression of subjectivity in the victim, the sadist must turn herself or himself into the object that elicits this subjectivity. In this sense, sadism involves not, as we often think, turning the victim into an object through the sadist becoming an absolute subject.[11] Instead, the sadist becomes an object to arouse the subjectivity of the victim. When the sadist causes expressions of these emotions they feel they have elicited something foundational about the victim's subjectivity. The logic of sadism reveals that the sadist doesn't seek her or his own enjoyment directly, but rather through the libidinal excess of the other. And the logic of sadism is the logic of torture. The torturer aims at obtaining a glimpse of the subject itself—a glimpse of their unconscious.[12]

In the introduction, I give a precise example of this from *Hostel: Part I* in which a failed doctor explains his reason for torturing his victim. He explains that he wants to touch the essence of the victim's life, to be part of it through its destruction. Clearly this has more to do with just biology. This essence he refers to relates to the subject and the ineffability of subjectivity, the unconscious, and its relation to the body. And later on in this chapter I explore the representation of the torturer/serial killer in the *Saw* films who explains that he is torturing the victims in order to make them realize they want to be alive. That is, he wants to be the one that provokes them into expressing and valuing their subjectivity.

Among the many contemporary representations of torture, it is only in the extreme genre of torture porn that the centrality of the enjoying torturer comes to the fore. The sadistic practices of the torturer bespeak a quest to discover how to provoke anguished expressions of subjectivity itself. In these films, the tortured body is not just a body but a subject. During the act of torture, the suffering of the body reveals a subject that relates to this body and its pain. Every act of torture envisions the appearance of this subject. Some of the similarities between these images and the images from Abu Ghraib visually link the military torturers with these outrageous monstrous killers and torture addicts.

HOSTEL AND THE NAIVE AMERICAN

Hostel: Part I and *Hostel: Part II* more concretely address enjoyment than any of the other torture porn films.[13] The notable difference between these two films is their gender focus: the first film features three male friends and the second three female friends. This difference in gender leads to the revelation of cultural assumptions about gender and violence, but the link between torture and enjoyment remains the same in spite of gender difference. Where the two films remain completely parallel is the basic setup of the plot: young American tourists are lured into a remote Slovakian town on some pretense, and then they are systematically kidnapped and brought to a torture factory.[14] The torture factory is located in a dilapidated building on the outskirts of the town. In this old factory, an organization, Elite Hunting, provides victims to its clients, who pay for the pleasure of torturing and killing them.

Both films start with the scenario of young American tourists on vacation seeking pure pleasure with no concern or interest in the countries they are traversing. The films depict them as foolish and gullible. The men interest themselves only in sleeping with women and getting high, while the women interest themselves only in attracting men and shopping for spa services. The films mock these characters by suggesting that the reason they become trapped in the torture scheme is that they lack any broad knowledge of the world and focus solely on their own pleasures. The victims are victims not because of what they know but how they enjoy (their wild vacation, lack of caution, and so on), which contrasts them with the victims of state-sponsored torture depicted in documentaries like *Taxi to the Dark Side* (Alex Gibney, 2007). By associating the victims with their innocence rather than their presupposed guilt, the *Hostel* films make a clear intervention into the political question of torture. This intervention happens through the structure of the horror film, which often condemns characters that express their sexual desire.

A common trope in the horror film is to punish the most sexually active characters with death. The fact that the torture victims in these films are young sexually active men and women means that the plots follow one of the common horror genre tropes. Importantly, this conservative gesture on the part of the horror genre, most often aimed at young women, ends up clashing with the contemporary fantasy that torture works as an information procurement tool. The end result is a torturer driven by desire rather than one looking for information. Torture porn then features characters who torture for pleasure and depicts their victims as people so focused on their own pleasure seeking that they are vulnerable to torture. In this way, the victims have no practical knowledge that their torturers are going after, which takes them completely out of the logic of biopower.

The enjoyment also manifests itself in the image that lures the tourists. The location that attracts the victims is a beautiful spa situated in a town with natural hot springs. The films follow the main characters from their European travels to a quaint Slovakian youth hostel. But they end up in the huge and barren factory where the torture takes place. Using the decayed industrial setting as the backdrop for the actual torture serves two purposes. It makes the torture chamber a zone of exception that is radically different than the settings in the rest of the film. And secondly, the dungeonlike qualities of the torture chambers links it thematically both to medieval torture and the look of a contemporary prison as seen in the Abu Ghraib photos.

When Todd (Richard Burgi) and Stuart (Roger Bart), for example, approach the torture factory in *Hostel: Part II*, the first shot is of an old industrial building with a steel fence around it. Guards in black with dark sunglasses, machine guns, and attack dogs are posted at the entrance. The guards could just as well be military, considering the look of their clothes. The next sets of shots emphasize the guards' inspection and the menacing nature of the dogs. As they are led inside, they pass through a cavernous empty room (possibly the old factory floor) with rubble and broken windows. The mise-en-scène of this long shot encourages the viewer to assume this torture factory is built on something already dead and buried. Once they are in the torture factory they are provided costumes that resemble those of a meat factory worker with a hint of sadomasochistic ritual. The outfit is all dark brown and black with a huge rubber butcher's overall bib. These costumes transition them from the militarylike mise-en-scène of the opening of this scene to some of the dungeonlike qualities in the next scenes. When Stuart enters his torture chamber, the walls are industrial and dark with one whole panel of the wall made of rock and a grate, which appears to be older and more sinister than the rest of the room. In the center of the room sits his torture victim: a young woman chained to a chair with a black bag over her head. Thus the mise-en-scène of the room combines the look of the Abu Ghraib prison with a fantasy of the medieval torture chamber.

Exactly what lures the young victims to this torture factory is the main focus of the first part of both films. Sex in general as a lure for the characters is much more pronounced in the first *Hostel*, which features young male characters. The men in the film treat women as objects to consume. Even at the beginning of the film, they talk about the success or failure of their trip in terms of how many women they will sleep with. In addition, the character that lures them off their path and to Slovakia does so by suggesting that the women in Slovakia are plentiful and easy. Both films lure the spectator into the mood of the film with bawdy sexual discussions in order to suggest the wild and sexual nature of its main characters. *Hostel: Part II* opens with the three female characters serenely painting a male nude model during an art class in Italy. Thus their visual introduction seems much more tasteful than that of their male counterparts in the first film. Their dialogue, however, reveals the same emphasis on sexuality. For instance, one woman mocks another to a third by saying, "Do you think she's ever seen a cock before?" The film thus immediately suggests that the main characters are thinking mostly of sex and are not prudish or naive. This itself becomes a crude marker for the unconscious as a form of desire and pleasure.

The films are ambiguous in terms of their judgments of these characters. The characters are in some sense punished for their consumerist, sexist, and xenophobic attitudes because they are tortured and killed. And yet the viewer remains at least somewhat sympathetic to the characters, since the tension of the plot revolves around whether they escape or not. It is through the male characters in both films that the connection between prostitution and torture is drawn. In *Hostel: Part I*, the friends of one victim, Paxton (Jay Hernandez), pay so that he can have sex in a brothel. *Hostel: Part II* depicts a friend paying for another's ticket to torture and kill his victim. In both cases, the friends make a big deal that having this kind of pleasure is their right as men and will establish them as real men. *Hostel* also makes a clear visual parallel between the brothel and the torture factory. An analysis of this visual parallel reveals the connection that is made in the *Hostel* series between torture and enjoyment.

By establishing the parallel between the brothel and the torture factory, torture porn links sexual enjoyment to the act of torture. In *Hostel*, though Paxton's friends fund a visit to a prostitute, he goes into the room with her only grudgingly. Ultimately, he can't go through with it. But as he leaves, he enjoys looking into the doors of the other rooms in the corridor of the brothel. This tracking shot is very specific. Each door is made of translucent glass, and Paxton sees the silhouettes of the specific sex act happening in each room. These tableaux vary from the missionary position to the woman on top to scenes of sadomasochism. He sees one scene that looks like torture, and he hears a woman scream. He opens the door to help her, but what he finds is not a woman in distress but a sadomasochistic act in progress. Rather than appreciating his intervention, the woman informs Paxton that he must pay to watch.

In this scene, Paxton begins with the refusal of the prostitute. But as he confronts the various sexual scenarios while walking out of the brothel, he experiences a different kind of enjoyment of the brothel, a visual enjoyment of the sexual spectacle. When he intrudes on the sadomasochistic act, he does so in order to prevent the violence that he imagines taking place in the room. Though he discovers a sexual act instead of a violent one, this particular encounter sets the stage for what follows in the film because it links the idea of torture with the idea of sexual pleasure.

Later, the film employs the same type of tracking shot in the torture chamber that it uses in the brothel. This formal parallel leaves no doubt concerning the role that enjoyment plays in torture. After escaping from a torture scenario, Paxton hides on a cart full of body parts that is being rolled down a hallway of the torture factory. As he moves down the corridor, Paxton again looks into each of the different rooms that he passes. In each room, rather than seeing different sexual acts, he sees different scenes of torture, which for the first time make clear where he is and what is going on. Some of the scenes look very similar to the earlier sexual scenes of the original tracking shot, and some look like classic scenes of torture. In the scene at the brothel, Paxton's voyeurism is certainly acceptable. No one questions a young male's desire to look at scenes of sex. Though it is socially unacceptable to look at and enjoy acts of torture, the parallel between the two scenes renders this enjoyment comprehensible, if not justified.

In this formal way, the films suggest the violence of prostitution while at the same time suggesting the sexual component of torture. In the brothel, Paxton is the paying customer, but in the torture factory he is the "product," the body to be bought for the pleasure of another. The second tracking shot is from the view of the victim looking in horror at the fate he is escaping. The character himself does not have any epiphanies about these structural changes he's gone through—from perpetrator to victim. In *Men, Women, and Chainsaws*, Carol Clover argues that shifting the identification of the viewer from perpetrator to victim is an important trope in the horror genre. Clover discusses horror films from the 1970s, in which the viewer literally switches character identification.[15]

In *Hostel*, Paxton himself moves between these two positions.[16] He does not overtly realize this switch, but the film's form makes the relation very clear. On the level of mise-en-scène (the similar tableaux in each room) and the type of camera work (the tracking shot down the hallway), the film itself draws together the prostitution industry with this fantasized torture industry. Though it is a fantasy constructed in the film's narrative structure, the idea of a torture industry that caters to customers who seek pleasure through torture responds to the real question of why people torture. The answer in *Hostel* is that torture occupies the same position as prostitution. Both prostitution and torture depend on the amalgamation of sex and violence. Other scholars have also noted that this reversal is a trope in the horror genre. Jason Middleton says, "Director Eli Roth includes a number of references to famous and influential horror films in his *Hostel* movies, and *The Texas Chainsaw Massacre* is one of the most prominent subjects of homage here: not only is there a significant scene involving a chainsaw in both *Hostel* and *Hostel: Part II*, but, at a broader level, both films' narrative structures are premised upon a reversal of positions between exploiter and exploited."[17] This reversal in *Hostel* allows the viewer to focus on the shifting terrains of enjoyment even within the torture chamber.

One of the key insights of psychoanalysis is its theorization of the inextricable link between sex and violence. Though we typically stereotype Freud as a pansexualist, violence plays an equally crucial role in his thought. Even prior to his discovery of the death drive, Freud discusses how violence constantly intrudes on sex and vice versa. In the 1905 *Three Essays on the Theory of Sexuality*, he writes, "there is an intimate connection between cruelty and the sexual instinct."[18] Freud understands that one cannot purify sex or violence from the other. Sex and violence consistently intrude on each other and are very complicated intersubjective relations between people defined by the intersection of culture, the psyche, and the body. Both are also expressions of the subject and the way the body is an experience of and expression of this subjectivity.

There is no tortured body, only a tortured subject, and torture porn foregrounds the latter. The image of torture that predominates has its basis in the biopolitical body. The practice of torture, however, cannot continue within the current fantasy structure if we grasp the victim as a subject rather than just a body instinctually organized to survive. The aim of torture is not knowledge, no matter how loudly authorities announce this justification.

Many television shows and films depicting torture concentrate on the issue of whether torture actually produces information or not, whether the fantasy underlying torture practice holds up. In the *Hostel* films, this is not an issue. There is no knowledge at the end of torture; the end point of torture in the *Hostel* films is death. Death is the only end possible because the torture relationship in these films is presented as one that can never be resolved. Once a client tortures, he or she is forever addicted to that experience because he or she believes in the promise of finding something essential about the subject in their response to torture, yet this essence is always just out of reach.

But the question lingers: why does the torturer think violence, control, and taking someone near death will provoke expressions of subjectivity? What is this fantasy? In a sense, even this torturer is wrong because, though the torture victim will certainly express emotions of fear and anxiety and cry out in pain, there is no reason that the torturer would be able to recognize subjectivity in this expression more than in any other. Once the torturer comes face to face with the fact that they will never be able to access a person's subjectivity, then they often react by trying to destroy it. This is why in *Hostel* and *Saw*, though very different films about torture, the torturers most often end up killing their victims (unless they escape, which is rare). And this is also why torture porn often depicts the torturer as immediately addicted to torture. Customers return to the torture chamber like addicts return to cigarettes or casinos. In fact, the films suggest that other forms of enjoyment, like extreme sexual perversions, pale in comparison with the enjoyment that torture offers. The *Hostel* films are especially focused on the enjoyment of the torturer.

In one torture scene in *Hostel: Part II*, for example, the door opens to reveal that in the middle of the room is a huge bathtub surrounded by lit candles. Despite its location in the dank industrial-like torture factory, the mise-en-scène of the scene mirrors the general theme of the spa that Beth (Lauren German), Whitney (Bijou Phillips), and Lorna (Heather Matarazzo) had come to enjoy in Slovakia. The difference here is that above the luxurious bathtub surrounded with candles Lorna hangs naked and upside down over the bathtub with her mouth muzzled, while her hands and feet are bound. A woman, whom we've never seen before, walks into the scene. She is dressed in an elegant bathrobe and takes it off to reveal her naked body. She then licks her lips while running a scythe up and down Lorna's body. The torturer begins by taking off her victim's muzzle, and Lorna takes advantage of this liberty to plea for her life. The woman cuts off the back of Lorna's head with one swift violent swipe and lies down beneath Lorna as the latter's blood drips all over her until she is bathed in blood. This prompts her to have an orgasm while rubbing the blood all over herself. Then she cuts Lorna's neck, and the blood rushes out. As a result, the torturer bathes completely in the blood. More than any other scene, this gruesome scene of torture links together violence and sex. The scene not only shows the torturer experiencing an orgasm covered with the victim's blood, but it also depicts the room as a site of female sexual enjoyment, with bathtub, candlelight, and elegant robe. This scene explicitly represents the intersection of the woman's sexual enjoyment with the most extreme violence. Similar to the surgeon's statement that he tortures to reach the essence of a subject, this female torturer attempts to use the violence to create a sexual intimacy. Blending excessive and aberrant sexuality and violence so completely, the scene lays bare the subject as the obscene underside of the contemporary torture fantasy.

Elsewhere in *Hostel: Part II*, we can see this same dynamic at work. *Hostel: Part II* introduces us to best friends Todd and Stuart, upper-class white American businessmen who have won the bid on torturing two of the main heroines. This trip together to the torture factory marks their yearly male-bonding vacation. Todd and Stuart had previously gone to Thailand on a pleasure trip to take in the prostitution there. In some ways, this alludes to the young men in the first film who bond over and assert their masculinity with their sexual conquests.[19] To make these characters seem more depraved than the heroes of the first film, however, *Hostel: Part II* takes the prostitution further. Rather than the upscale Amsterdam brothel that the young American men visit, these middle-aged businessmen have taken a vacation in Thailand to visit brothels that traffic in very young girls . Thus they have already bought pleasure that involves domination and degradation of their victims.

Seeking pleasure in prostitution with women most often forced into the situation signals an enjoyment necessarily constituted through the other's suffering. The best friends in *Hostel: Part II* emphasize this in an exchange they have when Stuart is feeling nervous about going forward with the torturing. He says,

> STUART: Do you think we're sick?
> TODD: Fuck no. Dude you look anywhere in the world where there's no law, whether it's fucking Chad or New Orleans. And this is the shit that people are doing, bro. We're the normal ones.
> STUART: Any idea what you are going to do in there?
> TODD: You don't even want to know.

This conversation, like many similar ones in the films, paints the torture chamber as a zone of exception, a space where law ceases to operate. Todd compares the torture chamber to Chad or New Orleans, but he might just as easily have invoked Abu Ghraib. The photographs from the prison reveal a zone of exception where the protections of law do not save the prisoners.

But the zone of exception in *Hostel* is not the site for what Giorgio Agamben would call bare life. Agamben's idea of biopolitics is nowhere to be found in these films, despite their insistence on the state of exception. There are no beings reduced to bare life in torture porn. Instead, the zone of exception is a thoroughly sexualized zone replete with enjoyment. The exception from the law carves out a space where one can enjoy without restraint, and this is a form of exceptionality that Agamben never considers. When Agamben focuses on the state of exception, his examples (such as Nazi Germany or Guantanamo Bay) do not emphasize the sexualized status of this site. The violence of the state of exception, as Agamben theorizes it, is necessarily asexual. It deprives subjects of their sexuality when it deprives them of their political being. This contrasts Agamben's state of exception with both Abu Ghraib and with the form found in torture porn.[20]

But even though the torture chamber is a zone of exception, this zone of exception exposes the unconscious of regular society. It functions as a kind of return of the repressed. This is emphasized when Stuart is finally in the torture chamber and turns out to have more of a taste for the torture than his more enthusiastic friend. Stuart has been assigned Beth as his victim. The viewer initially feels some relief at this, figuring that Stuart will not go through with the torture. It turns out, however, that Stuart's repressed hatred toward his wife as a result of his emasculation at her hands over the years comes bubbling out in the zone of exception of the torture chamber. At one point, Beth tries to appeal to someone she believes is a relatively kindhearted family man. Stuart has chained her up, and Beth says, "Don't you have a wife?" She hopes that this question will trigger his sympathies. Instead, he shows her a photograph of the wife and says, "I can't kill my wife." He says this with his voice dripping with hatred and pain, as if what he is about to do is the logical conclusion to the way he's been treated in his home life. Thus the film suggests that Stuart's desire to mutilate Beth and his ability to go through with it are just the obscene underside of his normal bourgeois family life.[21] And it is this obscene underside that you find in the zone of exception, not bare life.

Throughout its plot and mise-en-scène, but especially through the characters of Stuart and Todd, *Hostel: Part II* posits that there is a relationship between torture and enjoyment. This is what the smile on the torturer's face from the Abu Ghraib photos point to, which so many films, television shows, and commentators have failed to illuminate. By placing torture within a series of fantasy scenarios, the films can point out an aspect of torture that no one else acknowledges so directly. In *Hostel*, there are no pure biopolitical bodies. In *Hostel*, one can't help but be a subject.

SAW AND ENDLESS UNENLIGHTENMENT

But the torture porn genre is not homogeneous. In fact, the *Saw* series is vastly different than the two *Hostel* films. The differences further highlight some of the underlying revelations about torture in America. If *Hostel* is torture porn exploring the role of sexual enjoyment within torture, then the *Saw* films posit torture as the path to enlightenment, one that depends upon the comprehension of the primacy of one's bare life. In this sense, the *Saw* films seem to defy the link that the *Hostel* films establish between torture and enjoyment. They appear to have more in common with *24* than with other torture porn films. The films' premise bespeaks many of the tenets of biopolitics and the torture fantasy, but it ultimately exposes the limits of both. A show like *24* relies on the importance of bare life over all else and postulates that torture leads to information that provides the solution to a threat. In the case of the *Saw* films, the torture aims at instilling knowledge about the value of life through confrontation with death, but no knowledge actually results from the torture. The *Saw* films show that knowledge is an alibi for torture, but not the cause of it. They are torture porn because they emphasize that one tortures in order to enjoy.

The main character in the *Saw* films tortures so that the victims can come to a realization about the quality of their lives and thereby improve them. He embarks on a project of giving knowledge about life and even, to put it in Foucault's idiom, "making live," just like a regime of biopower. But the films give the lie to the premise behind the torture that they depict, which is what distances them from *24* and allows them to be categorized with *Hostel*. On the one hand, the tortured bodies don't survive the torture and thus cannot reach the promised enlightenment. On the other hand, the bodies cannot fulfill the directive to live more fully because they are not just bodies. They are lacking subjects. They lack information about who they are and why they do what they do, and the films make evident this lack, this failure of the body to be nothing but a body.

Within the filmic reality of the *Saw* films, death appears as the ultimate reality that compels people to embrace life.[22] According to the logic of the torture they depict, the victims have to confront their imminent death, and, even more, they must understand the violent acts they are willing to commit in order to stay alive. Only facing their own death in this way allows the victims to appreciate the life they have. This is a very different portrait of torture than that of the *Hostel* films, where torture doesn't aim at bringing any of the characters to this kind of enlightenment. Torture in *Hostel* is simply a form of deranged entertainment perpetrated by weak men, sexually perverted women, and serial killers. In *Saw*, torture is a violent puzzle constructed with a definite purpose. This is the basic premise of the serial killer who sets up all the torture scenarios, but the impossibility of this enlightenment is what shakes its very structure.

In contrast to *Hostel*, the films start only after victims have been caught. They wake up to find themselves trapped, and they must figure out why they are where they are. This is the beginning of the torture scenario. The victims find themselves in hundreds of scenarios over the seven films made. Though they differ widely in structure and milieu, the one common feature in all these torture scenarios is the pain that the victim must endure. Often locked into machines that pierce their bodies or even attach to their organs, the victims wake up in pain and must desperately figure out what is happening.[23] Many times a tape recorder is left for them to turn on or a television illuminates just after they wake up. The device gives instructions as to how they might extricate themselves from the torture machines.

The way to escape the machine is usually more painful than the torture machine itself. For example, in *Saw III* a woman wakes up to find herself strapped into and hanging from an elaborate machine that is fastened to the inside of her chest. In order to retrieve the key that will unlock the device, she has to stick her hand into a container of acid that burns away flesh. This theme recurs throughout: the victims have to put their hands into fire or acid or a vat of needles in order to reach the key in time to release them from their torture chamber. In other scenarios, the victims have to harm or kill other people in order to save themselves.

The designer of the torture, John Kramer (Tobin Bell), is revealed in the first film.[24] The police officers investigating the killings have labeled him a serial killer and nicknamed him Jigsaw for killing his victims only after putting them through a complicated and violent puzzle (or "game," as Kramer calls it). As the film unfolds, it reveals that when he found out that he had cancer and was going to die, Kramer tried to kill himself. It is during this botched suicide that he discovers a new appreciation of life and decides that others need to have this experience as well. He justifies his actions by repeating throughout the film that he gives people an opportunity to appreciate life, and he often mutters, "Most people are so ungrateful to be alive." He sees the sadistic torture that he inflicts on his victims as freeing them and giving them insight. He believes that torturing the body itself is what will produce the new self-awareness and need to live. Forcing the victim to experience the potential death of their body through the pain of torture will lead them to understanding the value of their body. Death becomes the vehicle for authentic life.

DEATH AND BIOPOWER

The explicit justification for torture in *Saw* closely approximates the biopolitical logic that undergirds contemporary state-sponsored torture.[25] Though the goal for detainees at Guantanamo Bay or other prisons is not a proper appreciation for life, the torture similarly envisions a sort of enlightenment. The contemporary fantasy of torture (as represented by the Bush administration's approach) aims at the production of knowledge about terrorist plots. This fantasmatic justification rests on the idea that the torture victim's body represents the ground of the person's being and thus that the body is the road to truth. Authorities who torture believe, like Kramer in *Saw*, that the threat of the body's imminent death produces the most important form of knowledge.

Kramer (as Jigsaw, the serial killer) is someone we get to know in different ways over the first four films: more of his motivation and backstory is revealed in each film. In *Saw IV*, for example, we learn that, added to his own brush with death, his wife loses her baby while pregnant because a junkie in her drug clinic violently pushes her down. This incident furthers Kramer's devotion to torture. He believes that if the man who pushed his wife had valued his own life then he wouldn't have been on drugs, wouldn't have tried to rob the drug clinic, wouldn't have pushed his wife, and thus wouldn't have killed his unborn child. Torture, in *Saw*, functions as a corrective, as a means for making life better for those who are tortured and for the world in which they live.

Kramer's focus on life leads to a focus on death. This is one of the ironies of the biopolitical outlook that biopolitical theorists struggle to explain. If the point of biopower is to make bodies live, one must explain why regimes of biopower, like that in Nazi Germany, expend so much energy on taking life. Michel Foucault's explanation, which comes near the conclusion of his lecture series, consists in identifying the presence of racism within the world of biopower as the culprit for instances of making death. In his lecture series "Society Must Be Defended," Foucault claims, "Once the state functions in the biopower mode, racism alone can justify the murderous function of the state."[26] Racism enables biopolitical regimes to distinguish between those it wants to keep alive and those it must put to death.

The problem with this explanation—other than the fact that it arrives in the form of a deus ex machina at the conclusion of Foucault's analysis of biopower—is that it fails to account for the zeal with which regimes of biopower put subjects to death. The Nazis did not simply kill Jews but went to extreme and even self-destructive lengths in the pursuit of Jewish annihilation. In other words, the racism (or in this case anti-Semitism) can't simply be explained as a throwback that allows for the state to murder. Approaching racism in this way relegates it to some previous mode of behavior that surfaces only for a specific use by the state and thus obfuscates the contemporary modes of racism. This in turn eliminates any complex reading of exactly how and why racism functions today. Furthermore, it ignores the role that enjoyment plays in racism. Because Foucault deals with bodies rather than subjects, this is precisely the dimension of the regime of biopower that he cannot successfully theorize. The same problem exists for Roberto Esposito, though Esposito goes further in the attempt to struggle with it.

Biopolitical theorist Esposito argues that biopolitical regimes resort to imposing death because of their investment in immunizing the body.

Esposito suggests that the Nazis thought of the Jews literally as bacteria not "like bacteria." Esposito argues that ultimately, because of the way that the Nazis equated the Jew with bacteria, the disease the Nazis were fighting was death itself. Thus the Jew represented to them the direct manifestation of death. He argues,

> The disease against which the Nazis fight to the death is none other than death itself. What they want to kill in the Jew and in all human types like them isn't life, but the presence in life of death: a life that is already dead because it is marked hereditarily by an original and irremediable deformation; the contagion of the German people by a part of life inhabited and oppressed by death. The only way to do so seemed to be to accelerate the 'work of the negative,' namely, to take upon oneself the natural or divine task of leading to death the life of those who had already been promised to it.[27]

Esposito regards immunization as the ultimate biopolitical project. In this way, Esposito suggests that certain racisms today are heavily ensconced in the terms of biopower. If the structure of society positions individuals as simply bodies, nothing could be worse than death, and immunization would become requisite in order to keep death at bay. But what escapes both biopower as a social structure and the biopolitical theorist's critique of biopower is that there are not just bodies in the world; there are also subjects who desire and enjoy in ways that are not completely predictable. That is to say, subjects enjoy in ways that often sabotage what society wants of them or what they think they want for themselves. *Saw* depicts Kramer making a similar mistake as Foucault and Esposito—viewing the encounter with death as a tool for facilitating life. The film, however, reveals that Kramer's rationale does not hold up, that he tortures for the sake of enjoyment rather than enlightenment.

In *Saw*, Kramer sees his victims as the walking dead, and he feels that the only way to cure them is to bring them to the brink of death. Focusing on death above all else becomes a way to avoid all questions of desire or enjoyment. For Kramer, his victims' apathy and lack of accomplishment turn them into the embodiment of death. For example, he accuses one young man of being consumed by apathy even though he had a privileged childhood, another of dealing drugs and being sent to jail multiple times, another of sinking into apathy and anger after the death of his son, another of prostitution and lack of love. What's remarkable about Kramer's victims is that they are so unremarkable. For the most part, they haven't committed any serious crimes or transgressed any moral imperative. For Kramer, their apathy and lack of affect indicate a failure to live.

There are many ways that Kramer might have interpreted their apathy and lack of will. Their apathy could, for example, bespeak a lack of desire, and his project could have been to make them desire, to awaken their desire. Or he could see them as enjoying too much. He could conclude that their apathy is a kind of enjoyment that threatens his own enjoyment and makes him hate them. But Kramer doesn't see them in this way. As a true believer in the biopolitical conception of the individual, he sees them as dying, and he wants to give them the gift of life through the portal of death. He wants them to appreciate the aliveness of their own bodies, the raw life that exists in their bodies. Life is the fundamental value for Kramer, and he tortures in the name of this value.

The *Saw* films expose the limit of the torture fantasy because they can't imagine what the victim's life would be past their enlightenment. The majority of the victims in *Saw* never reach enlightenment and instead die horrific deaths. We have only two counterexamples: the serial killer himself and the first woman in the first *Saw* film, Amanda (Shawnee Smith). During her torture puzzle, Amanda is fitted with a strange helmet and must get the key to unlock the helmet within a certain amount of time. Failing that, her head will explode. The key is hidden in someone's stomach, and this person is lying in the room. Kramer tells her that the man is dead, but in fact he is just drugged. Amanda kills him when she hacks into his stomach, and she makes it out of the room alive because she completes the task on time. After escaping the torture chamber, Amanda goes on to become Kramer's protégé. Rather than returning to a normal life with a renewed sense of the importance of life, Amanda's new appreciation of bare life leads her to devoting herself to helping the dying Kramer with his torture scenarios. Life leads Amanda straight to death. Ultimately, Kramer stages an elaborate new puzzle for her in *Saw III* that she fails, and she dies at the end of the film. Both Amanda and Kramer, despite their supposedly enlightening encounters with death, turn to horrifically killing and torturing people.

As *Saw* presents it, the game of torture has no end point, no possible resolution other than the incitement to additional acts of torture. The impossible kernel that constantly prevents the winning of the game is the very subjectivity of the torturer and of the victim. One can't win the game because there is enjoyment only in playing it, not in winning it. When Amanda takes over for Kramer (because he is too sick with cancer to continue), she allows her thirst for revenge to cloud her ability to create torture scenarios from which the victim really can escape.[28] Kramer chastises her for this, telling her that she's failing his original intention to bring these people to enlightenment. Her actions, however, end up highlighting the fact that Kramer's victims don't escape either. No one can win in the game of torture that Kramer sets up, and yet his biopolitical theory of torture depends on the possibility of winning. The many sequels that audiences supported further highlight the endless nature of this cycle.

The metaphor of torture as a puzzle or game that drives *Saw* identifies a core element of torture, and it constitutes the key insight of the films. The contemporary torture fantasy espouses that the game at the heart of torture is winnable both for the torturer and the victim. The torturer wins by getting the information, and the tortured win by retaining their life or by avoiding excessive suffering. But the film undercuts the logic of the game by showing the absence of winners on either side. Kramer himself doesn't win: he never accomplishes his stated goal of forcing the apathetic to embrace life. The tortured victims don't win because they all end up dead. Despite clear differences from the *Hostel* films, the *Saw* films take a related stand against the prevailing torture fantasy that imagines torture as an information procurement tool that does not necessarily permanently harm the torturer or the victim.

All torture porn films take torture out of the realm of immediate national need and place it in a more individual and personal level. These films ask, if torture can produce military secrets, why can't it produce personal secrets, or why can't it demand personal change? The *Saw* films also pose the question of torture's overall usefulness: if the torture fantasy is correct and the body is the road to truth, then why not use torture to discover other truths? But the films show that the body is in fact not the road to truth, that we cannot discover truth through the body.

The *Saw* films demonstrate this in the endlessness of Kramer's attempts to violently push his victims into an awareness of their own truth. As the films progress, the torture devices penetrate the body further and further. Kramer implants his torture devices deeper into the body with each film in an attempt to provoke the enlightenment that he seeks. Though these devices ultimately eviscerate the body, they do not produce any enlightenment. Each failure reveals that the body is not equivalent to the subject and that the subject exceeds the body.

The body in *Saw* is a battered, tortured, bleeding body that fails nearly every test. No matter how long Kramer searches for the bare life body that he professes to believe in, he never finds that body that is controllable and knowable. Trapped in his labyrinths are the dead bodies of his victims, but there are no answers in those bodies except the impossible frustration that the body—even its possible death—is not the whole answer. The body is penetrated, twisted, peeled apart, smashed, and blown up over and over in the *Saw* films. Yet Kramer and his disciples who continue the work after he dies are no closer to the truth after this morass of destruction—and neither are the victims. This may also mirror the fate of the torture porn film itself. Its inability to challenge its own reliance on the disavowed enjoyment of the torture spectacle ends up blunting the critique that they make concerning the torture fantasy.

What torture porn films have in common is that they push torture into the realms the world saw exhibited in the Abu Ghraib photographs both on the level of mise-en-scène and narrative content. The official justification for torture is biopolitical, but in the end the body that this contemporary torture fantasy envisions doesn't exist. Torture porn counters this official justification by exposing the subjectivity and the enjoyment that subverts every act of torture. There are several ways that torture porn's critique is lessened.[29] Most viewers don't think of these films as critical of contemporary culture because of their genre expectations. The horror genre, in this case, both allows for the expression of this critique and also marginalizes the critique itself.[30] Viewers expect to enjoy the violent spectacle of horror and not to see how they might be partaking in the ideology that creates that spectacle. All that said, every genre has its own traditional elements that appeal to mainstream desire and yet at the same time can critique and investigate these very same desires. While torture porn may not have created the anti-torture movement that its insights should have inspired, even still, these films stand as one of the few post-9/11 filmic examples productions to consider the smile on the torturer's face in the Abu Ghraib photographs.

4

24, JACK BAUER, AND THE TORTURE FANTASY

BEATING THE CLOCK

The contemporary torture fantasy suggests that torture can retrieve information housed within the body of a terrorist. This information can then stop a terrorist's plot to kill untold numbers of people. The fantasy justifies torture as the only adequate response to an imminent threat, and it inculcates us with the impression that the body contains truths that one can access directly if one knows the proper means. This torture fantasy grows out of the ideology of biopower. Prior to the emergence of biopower, torture certainly existed, but our contemporary torture fantasy did not. The depiction of this fantasy in media representations reveals the contemporary torture fantasy's fundamental structure and the source of its widespread appeal.

The television series *24* is the perfect expression of the torture fantasy and the ideology of biopower that subtends it. All of the aspects of the series bespeak an investment in this fantasy. The series clings fervently to the idea that torture is an effective method of interrogation, and its effectiveness stems from the idea that truth resides in the body. While other aspects of the series may be complex and at times ambiguous, the torture scenes themselves are presented in a straightforwardly ideological way. Put simply: torture works on 24, especially when performed by Jack Bauer (Kiefer Sutherland), the federal agent and hero of the series. Jack's torturing methods procure information and always work to legitimate torture as the only possible response to the problem of national security and the threat that terrorism poses to this security. The believability of the effectiveness of torture, however, relies upon an extensive biopolitical ideological framework in 24 largely structured around a particular conception of time. The series reveals that biopolitics depends on producing a sense of urgency by emphasizing the finite amount of time that remains for us.

Premiering in November of 2001, 24 ran over eight seasons and ended in May 2010. (Due to its popularity, the series returned in 2014 with a twelve-episode season titled *24: Live Another Day*. The premise and approach to torture was essentially the same.) Each season represented a single day and was 24 episodes, with each episode representing one hour in that day. The form of the show occasioned a great deal of commentary when it first came out. Reviewers and producers alike lauded the show as visionary for its form. Television critic Howard Rosenberg wrote, "What lifts 24 far above the ordinary ... is that each episode covers an hour in the lives of its characters, 24 weeks of the series equaling a 24-hour period in the plot."[1] As Rosenberg's comment indicates, the concept of tying the plot to a literal interpretation of time, to a ticking clock, challenged the conventions of television. What this meant for critics was that the show was uniquely contributing to the art of television. The idea was that 24 captured something about the potential of the televisual form that hadn't previously been explored in an extended way in a narrative series.[2]

This form expressed something culturally important about contemporary society. What was innovative about the form, in fact, was that it expressed biopolitical ideology. This ideology is oriented around the body, but the body, in order to have value within the ideology, must be in danger. The chronological form of 24—the omnipresence of the ticking clock, the action taking place in real time—creates this sense of constant danger. Time is always on the verge of running out, and editing cannot elongate time, as it can in a television series with a more traditional temporal structure.

The initial support for the series centered largely on the innovativeness of the formal choice of real time and the constant presence of the ticking clock. David Nevins, executive vice president of programming at Fox said of the show, "Truthfully, I hear hundreds of pitches a year, and not often do I actually buy it in the room. But these guys came in and gave us something that moves the form of television forward. It was a bold idea. . . . They said the entire season of television is going to take place over one day. Before they got up off the sofa, I said, 'We'll buy it.'"[3] This new idea about episodes tied to real time was not, in fact, just a formal one. It was an idea that emerged from the way in which time itself has become imbued with biopolitical purpose.

The form promised a clear structure, one that followed events as they unfolded in real time, but one that also allowed for a complex plot made up of a number of different subplots. As journalist Christian Smith commented, "While the actual premise of the show is a fairly typical thriller story, it's the concept that's the kicker. . . . Although the series does bear a striking similarity to the 1995 Johnny Depp film *Nick of Time*, which used a similar assassination/real-time concept, the idea is wholly original to network television. The real-time device, along with the gimmicky split-screen editing . . . all allow the audience to follow multiple overarching subplots simultaneously."[4] Smith suggests that there is something about the real-time nature of the structure of the plot that allows for audiences to follow a more complex web of subplots. *24*, however, was not the first television show to introduce complex narrative strands. And many television shows' narratives are in fact far more complex than the narrative of *24*.[5]

What the ticking clock format did was to tie all the subplots in *24* to the clock itself, thereby suggesting a unity in these subplots and in how they should be understood. In other words, the subplots were all related to the progress of time, which was itself tied to the overarching ticking bomb plot. The ticking bomb plot varied from season to season, but always focused in some way on a crisis that threatened American citizens (sometimes thousands, sometimes hundreds of thousands) and demanded urgent work on the part of the CTU (Central Terrorist Unit) agents. Although many television shows in recent years relied on a complex web of narrative strands (some of which defined characters and environments more than they contributed to a linear plot), the narrative strands in 24 were all tied carefully to the ticking clock and thus tied carefully to a ticking bomb scenario that drove the primary narrative arc of the season.

The ticking bomb scenario is the standard justification used by all apologists for torture. It begins with the premise that a terrorist has planted a bomb in a hidden location set to explode at a specific time. Authorities capture the terrorist and want to discover the whereabouts of the bomb, but they know that they have only a limited time to obtain the information. Due to these time constraints and the many people whose lives are at risk, the authorities must resort to torture to learn about the bomb.[6] Though actual instances of the ticking bomb scenario almost never arise, they occur with incredible frequency on 24. The ticking bomb scenario, made omnipresent by the visible ticking clock, provides the narrative foundation for the series.

Ultimately, the narrative of 24 was less complex and more tied to linearity than it appeared. This suggests that the ticking clock and the use of the split screen signified complexity while in fact providing a quite narrow narrative and linear focus. This is a perfect metaphor for biopower itself. Presenting itself as a complex unavoidable contemporary power structure, it is in fact a relatively simple signifying system that buckles under the realities of the desiring subject. Journalists and viewers alike were thrilled by the new visual challenge of 24 as well as by the high concept nature of its form. By the time the series ended, however, the series became more known for its involvement in the debate on torture than for its original form. All the initial acclaim for the show's formal innovation completely transformed into criticism (or, to a lesser extent, praise) concerning the show's depiction of torture. But these are just two sides of the same coin: the twenty-four-hour clock form and the involvement of 24 in the torture debates are integrally tied to one another. When critics were praising the originality of the depiction of time on 24, they were unknowingly praising the vehicle for the justification of torture. Torture in some real sense follows directly from the chronological countdown occurring at the level of form.

The form of 24 is geared toward a sense of immediacy. This sense of immediacy begins with the twenty-four-hour clock. The clock is introduced in every episode along with the name of the series (24 depicted in numbers signifying a digital clock), the name of the episode (which is the hour it represents), and Jack's voiceover explaining that events occur in real time. The clock stands as an indication of the amount of time left in the hour and in the episode itself, and it even accounts for commercial breaks, which suggests that the clock signifies a type of realism. 24 enacts its justification for torture by relying on the ticking bomb scenario, and the torture scenes themselves are securely anchored by it. In fact, they make sense only through the importance of the ticking clock. Analyzing how this works on a detailed formal level reveals further the ideological relationship between biopolitics and the clock (or the acceptance of torture and the presence of the clock).

One exemplary scene in season 2, episode 1 ("Day 2: 8:00 am–9:00 am"), begins with a cityscape and a subtitle that tells us the events are taking place in Seoul, Korea. The next few cuts reveal an alley and an out-of-the-way building in shadows. A subsequent cut shows blue latex gloves on dials with screaming in the background, a shot of the victim's feet in plastic bags with yellow liquid in them, and then a shot of the whole victim's body, revealing he is hooked up to some large, antiquated machines. The machine in this scene is administering various drugs and electricity, and there is some smaller instrument holding the victim's eyes open. With these first few shots, we are quickly brought into a torture chamber. While not all torture scenes in 24 occur directly after the initial clock, they all are clearly linked to the urgency of the clock through the digital clock displayed at regular intervals that makes the viewer aware of how much time has passed as well as what is at stake in that time passing (i.e., the need to stop an imminent disaster).

Watching the clock constantly reminds us that CTU is literally working against the clock to save a city or the nation. Each time the clock appears, it reinforces the spectator's sense that the subplots must be resolved before the hour is up and that the larger plot must be resolved before the season ends. This is a fundamental part of what defines the ticking clock of 24: that the plot line for the season must be resolved by the end of the season. What unifies these disparate plot lines is time and urgency. Specifically, this is time as such; in other words, the ticking bomb scenario defines time itself. The emphasis on time running out indicates the role of the ideology of biopower in the structure of 24.

This is not necessarily the case with other television shows whose audiences also enjoy the complexities of their narratives. Oftentimes, larger plot lines can continue over several seasons, and this adds to the depth of their narratives. For example, in the series *Alias* (2001–2006), the mystery about strange artifacts by an ancient scientist named Rimbaldi that the CIA has been looking for and their connection to the main character and CIA agent Sydney Bristow is only revealed at the end of the whole series. Similarly, the mystery in *Battlestar Gallactica* (2004–2009) about the fate of Earth and its relationship to the actions of Starbuck, one of the ship's officers, only comes to a climax toward the end of the series. These long-term narrative structures allow for a great deal of complexity that is not always tied to the necessity of wrapping up the larger plot in one season. Thus they often expound upon other aspects of the series, such as character development, description of place, or philosophical crisis or questions.

And indeed not all ideologies are so heavily defined by their investment in time. The American dream, for example, relies on an idea of the future but not necessarily on the urgency of time. One must work hard, according to this ideology, but one need not work with the utmost urgency. Many other ideologies tend to minimize the importance of time in order to magnify a sense of timelessness to cultural behavior. Religious ideology, for example, relies on the idea of eternity, on the possibility of an escape from the ravages of time. And similarly the ideology of the coherent identity of the family (including its investment in ethnic and national identity) relies on an enduring progression of the family line in time. In many ways, biopower's reliance on the urgency of time and the ending of time ruptures the idea of time within many powerful ideological structures. Biopolitical ideology's relation to time is central to its functioning, and it is something genuinely new.

Within this biopolitical ideology, the torture fantasy relies heavily on the urgency of the ticking clock. This is why the torture fantasy requires the background of biopolitical ideology and deployment of temporal urgency. The torture fantasy links the clock to the bomb and imagines time running out and ending everything with a horrifying explosion. It is this basic idea that then becomes the reason that torture is acceptable. In other words, the constructed urgency of the clock and its link to the ticking bomb provides the reason that a suspension of political rights is acceptable, a suspension that allows for the use of and even celebration of torture.

TORTURE AND TIME

A closer investigation into the clock as a philosophical idea can shed some light onto how this ideological collusion between torture and time might have come about. The speculation on time is certainly broad and varied, but Martin Heidegger's *Being and Time* presents perhaps the most wide-ranging and substantive consideration of the impact of the clock on our lives. Of course, Heidegger wasn't a torturer (despite his association with Nazism), but his concept of temporality actually relates to that articulated in *24*. Unbeknownst to himself, Heidegger moves in the direction of a biopolitical idea of time when he criticizes our inability to take up and engage with our own finitude, a fact of our everyday life for which the clock functions as a symptom. Heidegger describes the effect of the clock in this way: "In the way time is ordinarily understood, however, the basic phenomenon of time is seen in the 'now,' and indeed in that pure 'now' which has been shorn in its full structure—that which they call the 'Present.'"[7] For Heidegger, the clock denudes the complexity of our interpretation of time by leveling off the profundity of the now.

With the acceptance of the clock and its relationship to time, the now becomes the right now, and this suggests an infinite extension of nows, an infinite that stretches both into the past and the future. Heidegger himself has two specific quarrels with the conception of time implied by the clock (rather than with the clock as such). He feels it stifles our understanding of the now, which is in fact rooted in a structure far more complex than the clock's emphasis on a succession of "right nows." On the other hand, however, Heidegger also finds fault with our understanding of time as infinite, which comes from the never-ending succession of "nows," a succession that seems implicit in the very idea of a clock. He argues that this blinds us to an authentic relationship toward death, to an adequate appreciation of our inescapable finitude. An authentic being-toward-death, in contrast, would foster a much greater sense of urgency and an acute awareness of the finite. The clock is a barrier to our authenticity insofar as it suggests that we always have more time, a time that is infinite rather than constituted through our own proper finitude.

Since Heidegger wrote *Being and Time*, however, there have been several important sociocultural shifts in relation to the clock. Most important, there has been a philosophical shift from seeing the clock as infinitely progressing forward to seeing the clock as always counting down to something (usually destructive). Some of the broad cultural changes that have affected this idea are new technological innovations—such as the nuclear bomb and the computer—that emphasize the countdown instead of infinite progression. For example, with the advent of the atom bomb and the understanding that superpowers such as the United States and the Soviet Union could destroy the earth as we know it, the countdown to total destruction became not just present in the cultural imagination, but at times—such as the nuclear scares in the 1950s or the 1980s—a national obsession in the United States.[8]

This ideological shift in thinking about time can also be seen in cultural panic over end-of-the-world scenarios that were touted as having potentially real-world material consequences, such as the Y2K scare. This scare centered around the way the computer accounted for time and its potential inability to deal with a new millennium. The shift is also visible in the more mythological end-of-the-world scenario centered on the end of the Mayan calendar in December 2012.[9] These last two scenarios privilege the way the clock or the calendar can no longer accommodate time itself. And all these obsessions with counting down to our destruction are linked to a visual countdown of the clock. The clock itself becomes a signifier of the coming destruction. Certainly it is also worth noting the difference between the analogue and the digital clock, since it is the digital clock that is most often the signifier of the countdown. I would argue that this shift to thinking of the digital clock as a countdown to destruction also shifts the meaning of the right now. The *right now* no longer signifies an infinite set of *nows* but rather signifies the potential end of all *nows*.

In this way, today, in contrast to Heidegger's conception of finitude and the clock, a sense of finitude is connected to the clock and the right now. Heidegger believes that the clock distracts us from our finitude. The clock creates a sense that there is always more time, which is why it is not conducive to thinking finitude. But with the advent of the digital clock and the countdown, the clock ceases to have a deleterious effect on our relation to finitude. We become focused on the end (or on death). This is, of course, what Heidegger had hoped for in his call for the privileging of finitude as the only ethical position, even if it hasn't come in the precise form that Heidegger anticipated.[10]

Importantly, for Heidegger, the clock is a public apparatus. He explains, "Thus when *time is measured*, it is *made public* in such a way that it is encountered on each occasion and at any time for everyone as 'now and now and now.'"[11] Heidegger refers to this public as the "they," the anonymous force of social pressure and conformity. The clock is an essential part of the presence of the "they" and its creation of an inauthentic world. In other words, one of the ways that the "they" has a public presence is through the clock itself and the way we order our lives in relation to the clock. The clock participates in creating the social order more than by just acting as a tool to gage the revolutions of the earth. Combining the "they" and the clock, Heidegger proffers a way to understand ideology, though he never uses this terminology (and even specifically criticizes it on the final page of *Being and Time*). But we can consider Heidegger's insights about the clock and its relation to the "they" as a way to understand the powerful ideological nature of the clock, especially as it is now tied to the ticking bomb scenario.

In light of other contemporary imagined and real scenarios of destruction that preceded September 11, 2001, the terrorists acts of September 11 ushered in a revitalized frenzy of the *right now* as the end of all *nows*. Following the attacks on September 11t, the constant emphasis, for example, on the national alert level (yellow, orange, red) and the immediate passage of various draconian laws (such as the Patriot Act) suggest that it was the *now* that was essential for securing our survival. This emphasis on the now trumped political rights and instead privileged the survival of our bodies. The torture fantasy encourages us to be completely immersed in the urgency of the "right now" while believing that the more we feel urgent, the more probable it is that we can save the future, or have a future at all. The urgency of the *now*, as embodied in the ticking clock, creates the sense that every moment is a state of emergency in which torturing a suspect becomes acceptable in order to avoid total annihilation. It is this clock as attached to the ticking time bomb that shaped the public discourse after September 11, 2001, and that the show 24 so adroitly hooked into.

In each season, and in many of the individual episodes, a time is given by which CTU must stop the terrorists and the clock constantly reminds the viewer that this doomsday time is approaching. Time as such feels in danger on 24. If the terrorists aren't stopped, life as we know it will end. While most narratives implicitly create a sense of time (whether whole or broken), 24 relies on a particular concept of time to explicitly shape the narrative structure.[12] The concept it relies on is tied specifically to the clock and its expression of the "they," of ideology. The specific use of the clock in 24 is meant to eradicate all potential temporal or ideological diversity in an effort to define the terms of torture and to establish it as an unquestionable tactic.[13]

There are other formal aspects to the show that work to heighten this sense of urgency. The split screen, for example, suggests urgency since we have more views of the narrative development all at once. We see not only the same action from different angles or shots but also different scenes happening at the same time in different spaces that would normally be presented to us through a crosscut. In part, the viewing experience is also based on the tension between these frames (and the tension between the split-screen and the non-split-screen scenes) as much as it is defined by the sense of mastery over the scene through multiple views. The tension between the frames heightens the urgency of the clock, which is holding them all together. This editing technique adds to the flow of the plot and to the march of time that is marked by the minute-to-minute clock, as the viewer is made aware of the multiple actors racing against the clock—competing scenarios involving either the heroes or the villains.[14]

The ticking clock produces the sense of urgency that forces the spectator to approve of Jack's use of torture, a use that has other narrative justifications (such as its effectiveness) as well. Almost any episode in which Jack tortures depicts the effectiveness and legitimacy of torture. A scene from the fourth season will stand in for the many successful torture scenes presented throughout the series. The plot of season 4, episode 1 ("Day 4: 7:00 am–8:00 am") starts by revealing Jack to be working as security and liaison for the U.S. Secretary of Defense James Heller (William Devane). Up to this point in the series, Jack's position was that of an agent for the CTU. But in this season, CTU director Erin Driscoll (Alberta Watson) has fired him. At the start of this episode, Jack has to return to CTU headquarters to discuss the secretary's stance on their budget proposal for the following year, which places him in CTU right at the time when a known terrorist is apprehended and brought into the building.

While pursuing him, the agent in charge sends the feed of his camera back to the Driscoll's office, which is where Jack is meeting with her. Though he is only an observer, Jack deftly suggests the right move that allows them to bring the terrorist in, and this signals Jack's superior skills as an agent. These are not, however, the skills that define Jack, since it is torture that constitutes his signature method. While at CTU, Jack finds out that Internet chatter suggests that there will be a terrorist attack at 8:00 (within the hour). The show then cuts to the field agent questioning the suspect, who has been brought in to CTU. The agent threatens the suspect with three years "in the hole" if he doesn't respond to the questioning, but the suspect looks completely unconcerned. The show clearly signals that mere threats have no effectiveness with hardened terrorists, and the experienced viewer of the show will laugh at this threat along with the terrorist. But then the agent leaves the room to confer with Driscoll.

After incapacitating the guard at the door, Jack bursts into the interrogation room, jams the lock, and proceeds to interrogate the suspect by torturing him. He knocks over the table to signal his capacity for violence and screams at the suspect, "I am not messing with you, you are going to tell me. WHAT IS HAPPENING AT 8:00?" Disregarding the protestations of Driscoll (who is yelling for him to holster his gun and leave the room), Jack takes out his gun and shoots the suspect in the knee. Jack screams again as he points his gun at the suspects other knee: "WHAT IS YOUR OBJECTIVE?" The man convulses in pain and is clearly frightened for his life.

As a result of his pain and fear, the suspect gives up the information. Jack learns that the secretary of defense (whom Jack works for) is the target at 8:00. Faster than imaginable, Jack procures the necessary and correct information out of this suspect, who was so clearly unmovable and unmotivated before when interrogated with nonviolent methods. Jack tortures him by causing extreme pain and threatens him with more, and the result is that Jack obtains positive results. In this particular episode, however, CTU receives the information too late, and the attack on the secretary occurs. But this failure only further justifies Jack's methods. If he had been on the job earlier, they surely would have obtained the information with enough time to save the secretary of defense. The narrative of this episode leads up to this torture scene as the climax and emphasizes the importance of torture as a method to quickly and effectively retrieve the correct information. In this way, the episode validates the method and validates Jack himself.

Jack's torture scenes throughout the series are varied: he performs many different kinds of torture, though most of it involves physical rather than emotional harm. From threatening the person's life with a knife at her or his throat to hooking someone up to a high-tech delivery system of lethal drugs to shocking her or him with the wires torn from the bottom of a lamp, Jack physically beats and scares his victims into giving him information. Generally, as in the aforementioned scene, Jack's torture is extremely efficient: it never takes very long, and it always produces information. The scenes occur in many different spaces and are shot in a variety of ways. The torture scene just discussed is shot in a stylistic way: when Jack steps into the interrogation room, the pace of the editing picks up, and when he shoots the suspect's knee, we see two low angle views of these actions. The background of the shot is black and filled with smoke from the gunshot. The show then cuts to a split screen in which Jack is screaming at the man for information as he threatens his other knee in one frame, and Driscoll is screaming at Jack to stop in the other. In this particular case, the dramatic stylistic choices showing the torture scene further emphasize Jack's status as hero. The heavily stylized scene heightens the tension and highlights the act of torture itself. Not all of Jack's torture scenes are shot with this much stylistic flare, but all of them consistently prove that torture works.

What is revelatory in 24 is that the belief in the effectiveness of torture does not stand on its own but can function because it is situated within a web of narrative and formal structures. Drawing out the central tenets of this web reveals the contours of how we have come to understand torture as effective and why the idea of effective torture, despite the empirical tenuousness of this notion, has resonated so powerfully in contemporary culture. Ultimately, what emerges is a torture fantasy that brings together a certain understanding of time as constantly working against us, combined with a belief in the utmost importance of bare life. Like the belief in the effectiveness of torture itself, both these beliefs are steeped in biopower, and the political implications of biopower become fully evident through a certain understanding of time on which the torture fantasy depends.

THE AIM OF TORTURE

Theorists analyzing biopolitics rarely consider the role of the clock and the urgency that it portends. And yet, a sense of urgency, as 24 shows, is inextricable from the ideology of biopower. In order to be effective, biopower must convince us that we are running out of time and that our survival depends on our obedience to its dictates. Giorgio Agamben comes closest to exploring time when he investigates the sovereign's use of the state of exception. When we think of a state of exception, we think of stopping a normal routine (a set relation between behavior and the clock) and entering a different set of expectations or ways of organizing our time. According to Agamben, the state of exception has become our normal state of affairs. As Agamben puts it, "in our age, the state of exception comes more and more to the foreground as the fundamental political structure and ultimately begins to become the rule."[15] This state of affairs works to secure biopower because it justifies all security measures taken to preserve life. But what Agamben doesn't see is the role that the urgency of the clock plays in the state of exception. Rather than locating us outside time, the state of exception heightens our temporality and places us under the constraints of the ticking bomb scenario. 24 leads us to think about how our concept of time participates in this state of exception or enacts a different kind of exception that has a similar biopolitical effect to the state of exception as Agamben conceives it.

Where this signifier of televisual real time is fully employed in 24 is in developing the stage upon which torture is the logical response to plot conflict.[16] On this stage, the narrative suspension of disbelief is also located in part in the ticking of the clock. It became apparent quite quickly that it seemed ludicrous that all the narrative events presented in one season of 24 could actually happen in one day. This absurdity was most clearly manifested in the experiences of Jack himself. For example, during one day he dies, is revived, and then performs heroic feats to thwart the would-be terrorists. Television critics consulted doctors to confirm the utter impossibility of this incredible recovery time. But no doctor was necessary to give the lie to Jack's ability to travel at lightning speed. He is able to traverse Los Angeles in record time with no concern for potential traffic jams. Inhabitants of the city had to suspend their disbelief at this point in order to watch the series. But locating the suspension of disbelief at the very spot where the series prompts the viewer to read authentic real time only heightens the power of the torture fantasy.

The suspension of disbelief functions as a narrative disavowal. The viewer sees the incongruities or contradictions in the plot or a formal choice yet chooses not to believe them or to ignore them. Locating the narrative disavowal at the heart of the ticking bomb scenario that is supposed to give concrete justification for torture is the quintessential ideological gesture. It both provides a kind of marker for one point at which the ideology could unravel and also solidifies it at this flawed junction. Ironically, it also displaces where the real disavowal in torture is happening: at the heart of the act of torture itself. In other words, if as spectators we are focused on our narrative suspension of disbelief functioning so obviously at the heart of the twenty-four-hour clock, then this distracts us from thinking about why torture seems like such an easy answer to complex problems of national security.

The turn to torture itself involves an act of disavowal. Torture remains an extreme and violent response to the inaccessible nature of the subject itself. Torture ritualizes violence in an attempt to destroy something that the torturer can't understand or see readily when just speaking to the other. But this performance, despite its pretensions, always already knows that it can never reach what it seeks—and this is the disavowal at the heart of torture. It purposely goes after what it cannot reach. It is in the act of pursuing the impossible that the torturer disavows this knowledge and proceeds to enact a violent abuse directed at the other who has so confounded her or him. In each act of torture, there is a repeated performance of this disavowal and an implicit confession of our inability to embrace this terrifying quality of the impossible to articulate the nature of the subject and its desire.

Torturers can no more reach any inner truth about the desire of the other through torture than they can understand their own desire. Certainly the torturer may be able to maim—physically or emotionally—the victim in a permanent way, but she or he can never erase that aspect of the victim's subjectivity that disturbs the torturer (or the agent or nation that commands the torture). That is, the torturer can't access or extract the subject's unconscious. It is forever elusive to the torturer. But on 24 there is nothing ultimately elusive, just as there is no unconscious.

24 supports the ideology of biopower by presenting torture as effective and never presenting sexual humiliation as a tactic. This is how it strips the subject out of the act of torture. In 24, unlike at Abu Ghraib and Guantanamo, there is little to no sexualized torture, and the villains, even when actually Arab, are not depicted as desiring subjects. In this way, the series perpetuates the disavowal at the heart of the torture fantasy and assists in solving the problem of the other's desire. What is revealing about the depiction of Arab characters on 24 is that they are decidedly not sexual. The show does depict stereotypical Arab villains at times, but these villains are always asexual villains.

24 depicts its Arab characters as either one-sided villains—who are marked only by their desire to destroy America—or innocent Arab characters working to save American lives. They are either on the side of good or evil, and they work diligently on whichever side they lie. This fantasy of the Arab or Arab American is a completely different portrayal then the sexual fantasies suggested by the Abu Ghraib photographs, but it is consistent with other ways that 24 betrays an investment in a biopolitical ideology. The Arab and Arab American characters on 24 are only defined by their concern for survival or destruction.[17] They are presented as defined purely by their bodies, but these bodies aren't sexual or desiring bodies because this would imply the dimension of subjectivity, which the series wants to avoid at all costs in order to sustain the torture fantasy.

The fact that the Arabs and all villains on 24 are nothing but bodies is what allows Jack Bauer to torture them effectively. The key to the perpetuation of the torture fantasy lies in the absence of desiring subjects on the series. Even Jack himself, despite his centrality in every episode, does not have the status of a desiring subject. He is a body focused on other bodies, a body completely invested in the urgency of the task confronting him. His belief in the ticking bomb scenario and the heinous acts that it authorizes defines his heroism. This heroism has nothing to do with Jack as a desiring subject. He is a calculating body who constantly engaged in utilitarian arithmetic in order to know how to act:

kill one in order to save ten, regardless of who the one is or who the ten are. Jack is heroic because he successfully uses violence and torture to procure information that solves a crisis just before it will occur. As Stephen Prince points out, "In the world of 24, his willingness to torture establishes his credentials as a hero."[18] Without Jack's willingness to torture, we would not believe in him as the heroic figure who will do whatever must be done in order to avert the crisis and save innocents.

Though the series shows that torture validates Jack's status as a hero, it also reveals the personal cost that torturing brings with it. At times it even costs him his job. He is often shown at the beginning of a season as not working at CTU anymore for various reasons, all of them stemming from his reliance on torture that doesn't quite fit with the sanctioned methods of CTU. Within the first or second episodes of the season, however, he is reinstated because he and his methods are needed for the emerging catastrophe.[19] But, more important, torture costs him his wife, who dies at the end of the first season, and it constantly puts his daughter in danger (while also leading to an estrangement from her). It costs him any romantic life he tries to pursue in the seasons after his wife dies.

Jack's recourse to torture leaves him a psychically damaged figure. Though enemies cause him physical harm, it is clear that all the years of torturing have taken a toll on him and left him unable to live a normal life. When he is on the verge of death in the penultimate season, he has no one to comfort him, and when he dreams of living a normal life as a grandfather in the final season, this image of him seems clearly untenable. At the end of his tenure as a torturer, he is unfit for the normal American existence he sought to defend.

24 AS PARADIGM

The similarity between the idea of torture on 24 and the Bush administration's ideas of torture suggests that they share the same contemporary torture fantasy. Indeed even those involved in the drafting of the Yoo torture memos at times referred to 24. Professor of International Law Philippe Sands documented the involvement of Michael Chertoff in the ideas behind the memos; Chertoff was at the Justice Department at the time and was after that the second secretary of homeland security under Bush, and coauthored the United States Patriot Act. Sands explains, "Chertoff liked a tough approach and was a fan of Jack Bauer, the lead in 24, and his fictitious counter-terrorism unit colleagues, praising them for showing the kind of character and tenacity that would help America defeat terrorism. [. . .] 'That is what we do every day,' [Chertoff] said of 24, 'that is what we do in the government, that's what we do in private life when we evaluate risks.'"[20] The links are clearly ideological, but there was some indication that the Bush administration eventually saw the connection as productive. The ideas presented on 24 became part of the fantasy material that knitted together the symbolic failures of actual torture. It seemed that when torture wasn't working in real life, even members of the military turned to 24 for inspiration. As journalist Martin Miller documents, "'Everyone wanted to be a Hollywood interrogator,' said Tony Lagouranis, a former U.S. Army interrogator at Abu Ghraib prison in Iraq who spoke to the creative teams from 24 and *Lost*. 'That's all people did in Iraq was watch DVDs of television shows and movies. What we learned in military schools didn't apply anymore.'"[21] The enhanced interrogation techniques being used at Abu Ghraib were not working, so the interrogators turned to the fictional idea of torture to augment the fantasy itself. Philippe Sands also argues that 24 contributed to making the interrogators at Guantanamo feel as though they were on the front lines of the war and thus justified why they should push their techniques further.

Jack Bauer figured prominently in this fantasy and became something of a shorthand for the torture fantasy itself. Even Justice Scalia referred to Jack Bauer to justify torture. Journalist Peter Lattman reported the now famous response by Justice Scalia. He writes, "'Jack Bauer saved Los Angeles. . . . He saved hundreds of thousands of lives,' Judge Scalia reportedly said. 'Are you going to convict Jack Bauer? . . . I don't think so.'"[22] The complexity of the cultural references and assumptions here reveals that torture requires a sidestepping of the law. It doesn't matter what crimes or atrocities Jack Bauer has committed as long as he has saved lives in the process. But this, unfortunately, is exactly what the military looking to 24 for inspiration took away from the show. The contemporary torture fantasy as a product of biopower demands a state of exception, an idea that there is a benefit to suspending the law.

The references to Jack Bauer populated political discussions as well. Tom Tancredo responded to a question during the 2007 Republican presidential primary debate by saying: "We're wondering about whether water-boarding would be a—a bad thing to do? I'm looking for Jack Bauer at that time, let me tell you."[23] From the military, to judges, to political candidates, Jack Bauer and 24 became a shorthand reference to the idea that torture works to procure information and that it is a clean and fast method. The only real downside is that the torturer may be an outsider, but he will also be a hero whose outsider status attests to his profound patriotism.

The constant emphasis on the personal damage that torture does would seem to indicate that 24, far from endorsing torture, adopts a very critical attitude toward it. But, despite the exploration of the damage that torture does to Jack, this aspect of the show cements its adherence to the torture fantasy. Jack is simply another incarnation of the Western hero, the hero who resorts to violent means to save civilization from the forces of destruction but who cannot integrate himself or his violence into that civilization. Jack is Shane (Alan Ladd) riding away on horseback at the end of George Stevens's *Shane* (1953) or Ethan Edwards (John Wayne) finding the door shut on him in the final scene of John Ford's *The Searchers* (1956). Spectators understand this repeated character type and thus can interpret Jack's loss of family, job, or freedom as only further solidifying him in the role of hero. The ticking bomb structure of the plot places this recognizable hero at the center and relies on him to continually reassert its importance. The viewer identifies with Jack's own urgency and relation to time. The damage that he experiences testifies to the authentic nature of the urgency that he confronts.

Besides the emphasis on the radical nature of the twenty-four-hour form, the series received attention for its racial diversity. 24 was in fact the first major dramatic television series to depict a black president. David Palmer (Dennis Haysbert) is a commanding, kind, and strong president on the show. In fact, the first season seems to be more about the relationship between David Palmer, as he ascends from presidential candidate to the presidency, and Jack Bauer. It also focuses on their relationships with their families and reveals how their jobs affect their families. But as the series reacts to September 11 and the threat of future acts of terrorism, the plot deemphasizes interracial relations and increasingly suggests that unity between people occurs at the level of national security. The ticking bomb scenario becomes the glue that holds together racial diversity.[24]

Ultimately, the series seems unsure about its presentation of race and gender since it teeters between conservative and progressive images throughout. The series includes defenseless women who don't know not to accept help from suspicious strangers and strong women who give their lives in defense of the country. It depicts stereotypical Arabs driven to destroy the United States as well as patriotic Arabs defying their community in order to assist in the struggle against terrorism. This farrago of character types demands interpretation, especially when we contrast it with the ideological consistency of other aspects of the series.

It is the twenty-four-clock, the ticking bomb scenario, the efficacy of torture, and Jack's heroism (which is the result of his commitment to the torture fantasy) that the show stays utterly faithful to. Arab characters can be terrorists one minute and patriots the next because this is not where the real concern of the series lies. But *24* never wavers in its adherence to the fundamental precepts of biopower. The final torture scene of the entire series, however, goes one step further and takes biopower to its end point. Jack is torturing a suspect who won't give up the information—names and numbers—that Jack needs. It seems as though, for the very first time, Jack really won't be able to obtain any information from someone by torturing him. And the man has swallowed the SIM card from his cell phone, so Jack can't get the information off his phone either.

With no possibility for effectively torturing the enemy, Jack simply kills him. After doing so, Jack hacks open the man's body and extracts the SIM card from his stomach. Jack then wipes the SIM card off on his pants, inserts it into his own cell phone, and finds the information he's looking for to defeat the terror plot. This final torture scene literalizes what Jack has been doing all along. It makes visible in a straightforward fashion the attitude that the ideology of biopower has toward the body. And, in some way, this sort of raw literal extraction of information from the body itself makes sense as a frustrated conclusion to the show. It is as if even the creators were saying that they were having trouble coming up with new and interesting methods of torture with which to extract information.

In Jane Mayer's article on *24*, she quotes U.S. Army Brigadier General Patrick Finnegan saying, "'I'd like them to stop,' he said of the show's producers. 'They should do a show where torture backfires.'"[25] There is a show in which torture backfires: *Alias*. On *Alias*, as I explore in chapter 6, torture rarely works. Instead, agent Sydney Bristow (Jennifer Gardner), the heroine of the series, relies on masquerades or aliases to discover the truth. This truth embedded in fiction rather than in the body testifies to an entirely different political structure, one that works to tear down rather than enhance the torture fantasy presented in *24*. On *24*, biopolitical ideology suggests that torture is the cause and truth is the effect. Considered in its entirety, however, the inability of *24* to evolve out of its reliance on the clock forces us to look at the rigidity of the ticking bomb scenario.

Originally an innovative form, the twenty-four-hour clock becomes a rigid restriction that the show must work harder and harder to overcome. As it does this, the narrative suspension of disbelief becomes more difficult and more obvious. The end of the series literalizes the information sought in torture by turning it into the information that can be stored on a SIM card. The idea that all the important information a person knows—or has experienced—can be stored on a SIM card represents the ultimate conclusion of the logic of biopower. The truly informative SIM card becomes the expression of the biopolitical body par excellence. Of course, this is also the impossible dream of biopower because what can never be transcribed onto the SIM card remains the desiring subject.

5

THE BIODETECTIVE VERSUS THE DETECTIVE OF THE REAL IN *ZERO DARK THIRTY* AND *HOMELAND*

BIOLOGY AS AUTHENTICITY

The appearance of Kathryn Bigelow's *Zero Dark Thirty* (2012) came a little less than a decade after the torture practices at Abu Ghraib and other sites were made public (in April 2004). The original exposure of the torture through photographs taken at Abu Ghraib sparked a very public and well-reported debate in America about the validity of torture. Much seems to have changed since 2004, with Barack Obama becoming president, many of those involved in the torture scandal tried and convicted, and countless documentaries and books arguing against torture. Nonetheless, much has also stayed the same, and the release of *Zero Dark Thirty* made evident that a contemporary torture fantasy is still active.[1] In this case, the response to the film and the director's own intervention into the debate about the film played an important role in shedding light on the interaction between representations of torture and the contemporary torture fantasy. I will consider here the role of both torture and biometrics in defining contemporary ideas about authenticity and truth in *Zero Dark Thirty*, the *Bourne* films, and *Homeland* (2011–present).[2] In these recent depictions of torture, biometrics and torture become linked, each authenticating the other or disproving each other, depending on the relationship the detective takes up to them.

The detective plays a key role in the relationship that films and television shows have to the ideology of biopower. The detective (who is usually a CIA, FBI, or some other federal agent) drives the contemporary action-oriented dramas. In order to understand how this detective functions, one must place it among the prevailing types of detectives in the modern world. Theorists have long distinguished between the classical detective (such as Edgar Allan Poe's Auguste Dupin) and the hard-boiled detective (such as Dashiell Hammett's Sam Spade).[3] The classical detective uses reason and logic to solve cases whose facts he doesn't share with the audience until the case is finally solved. This detective always remains at a distance from the case and receives financial remuneration in order to ensure that distance. The hard-boiled detective, in contrast, uses emotion to solve the case, becomes psychically invested in it, shares everything he knows with the audience (which isn't all that much), and never gets paid. He often obtains the object of his desire, but typically he must give it up to the law or destroy the object himself after obtaining it.

After the classical Hollywood era when the hard-boiled detective reigned in film noir, there has been some resurgence of both the classical and hard-boiled detectives, but they have been largely in remakes of the original genres. For example, the classical detective has reemerged in films of Agatha Christie stories and in contemporary television shows like *Sherlock* (2010–present). The hard-boiled detective has proliferated more widely. He appears in neo-noir films and television series from the 1970s to the present. But these two types of detective do not seem to exhaust the possibilities shown in contemporary film and television. Detectives today seem to be of a slightly different order.

The key to understanding contemporary detectives lies in their relationship to the facts and to their concept of how to find truth. Contemporary detectives are characterized by how they embrace or reject scientific methods of detection, surveillance, and torture. This is, I would contend, a new opposition in detection at work today. There are two prevailing orientations—the biodetective and the detective of the real. Both detectives are operative in the contemporary landscape and both act as the quilting point for how a narrative engages the contemporary torture fantasy.

The biodetective has become prominent in the film and the televisual landscape especially with the emerging importance of forensic evidence in the court system today. In television shows like *CSI* (2000–present), for example, the biodetective is successful because she or he can scientifically follow the traces of the body (in hair, fingerprints, blood, and so on) through biometric technology.[4] This biodetective invests herself or himself completely in the ideology of biopower insofar as she or he believes that the truth is embedded in the body. Evidence of the body leads this detective to the truth. For the biodetective, methods such as fingerprinting, DNA samples, surveillance, body scans, lie detector tests, and retina scans are authentic and generally infallible.

THE BIODETECTIVE

To understand this biodetective, it is important to start with the technology that is foundational to their mode of detection and their assessment of authenticity. How an ideology defines authenticity and what constitutes authenticity is the key to its structure. In general, authenticity means something that is accepted as based in fact and that has an undisputed credibility. Today the ideology of biopower has a specific form of authenticity that distinguishes it from previous ideological formations. Informed by this ideology, we associate authenticity and finding truth with biology, and the search for authenticity inevitably devolves into the search for biological causes or biological markers. The authentic has its foundation in biology. Depicting authenticity through biometrics has become an integral part of televisual and film form. Plots revolve around the discovery of forensic information or the careful integration of surveillance equipment into an investigation. And the form of the biometric technology shapes the visual form. Films and television shows spend a good amount of time presenting the screens that depict the evidence of the biometric technology (for example, tracking a suspect by satellite, looking at the DNA strands, watching as face recognition works, and so on).

Biodetectives rely on surveillance. The shot from the hidden camera in the overhead light or painting on the wall has become commonplace in films and television shows featuring the biodetective. Viewers all recognize its placement and easily identify the location and purpose of this camera angle. Similarly, the depiction of the detective, or her crew, in the van outside carefully monitoring screens that depict the images from the hidden cameras is also omnipresent. Surveillance allows for constant tracking of the whereabouts and actions of the target, and it also allows for several other biometric operations. For example, biodetectives often use face recognition technology to identify someone in the footage they are looking for, or they use heat sensors to identify the state of the body they are looking at. Surveillance suggests that tracking an individual can give you the answers to that individual. This is why surveillance embodies the ideology of biopower. While the biodetective who uses forensics will employ surveillance, it is far more present in the shows in which the biodetective employs torture. Indeed, biodetectives tend to fall into two camps: a forensic detective or a detective who relies on torture and surveillance.

Both, however, rely on the accuracy of the biological claims to tell them about the body and not about the subject. In this sense, they have the same fundamental focus despite their differences. The body is the site of their investigation. Unlike the subject, the body doesn't lack, and this absence of absence provides a sense of security, even when the biodetective is troubled by threats to national security. The individual interpellated into the ideology of biopower can know who it is and experience the sense of self-identity that stems from considering oneself a pure body. The fact that this information allows the authorities to track the body's every move doesn't offset the security of self-identity. This tracking even augments the security of the body. Biopower imprisons the subject not through its technological apparatuses but through the psychic investment that it demands.

THE BIOPOLITICAL PURSUIT OF OSAMA BIN LADEN

But despite its seeming infallibility, biopower suffers from incompleteness just like every ideology, and the necessary incompleteness of every ideology demands a collective fantasy to fill the gaps within an ideological structure. In the case of biopower, the gaps exist not in the realm of knowledge—the knowledge always appears complete—but in the emergence of the knowledge, the act by which we acquire knowledge that provides a complete explanation. As a result, it is difficult to discern these gaps, but they manifest themselves when we examine the fantasy that operates within the ideology of biopower. Two key fantasies of this ideological structure are the belief in the infallibility of biometrics and the contemporary torture fantasy. The appearance of the biodetective reveals an investment in both of these fantasies. Even though biodetectives vary in their use of biometrics and torture, both fantasies are usually operative in the figure of the biodective. These two fantasies work together to privilege the body over the subject through an idea that truth is embedded in the body.

The contemporary torture fantasy imagines the body as the source of the information that explains its own actions. Torture proponents believe that torture produces information and that this information provides the answer to how bodies behave and how they will act. This fantasy that torture is the key to truth is a fundamental fantasy of the ideology of biopower, and it predominates in many contemporary representations of torture.

The television series *24* provides the most thorough example. Structured around the ticking bomb scenario, the plot of *24* relies on surveillance and torture to provide information that will save lives, and this same dynamic occurred without fail every season. The end of the series literalized the information sought in torture by turning it into the information that can be stored on a SIM card. In a stunningly complete marriage of biometrics and torture, as I have discussed in the previous chapter, Jack finds the truth he is looking for on a SIM card he retrieved from the victim's stomach.

Like *24*, *Zero Dark Thirty* begins with the premise that biometrics and torture are ways to discover truth. The film's devotion to these two methods betrays a continuing investment in tying torture to truth. The plot of *Zero Dark Thirty* covers the decade-long hunt for Osama bin Laden after the September 11 attacks. The film culminates in a detailed depiction of the military raid of his compound in Pakistan and his resultant death. The film focuses specifically on the detective work of Maya Lambert (Jessica Chastain), a CIA analyst, whose obsessive drive to find bin Laden precipitates this military victory.[5] Maya is an archetypal biodetective who operates with a biopolitical conception of truth.

When analyzing its relation to biopower and the torture fantasy, there are several important aspects to this film: an early torture scene that seems to produce key information, the extensive use of surveillance footage, and the portrayal of the military raid that led to the killing of bin Laden. These aspects of the film are linked to the ideology of biopower that structures the film. This ideology becomes especially pronounced in the face of a threat to security and survival, which is precisely what biopower purports to privilege. The film is, of course, one of the many responses to the trauma of 9/11 and the evident threat in this attack.

Kathryn Bigelow is clear about this in the formal choice she makes at the beginning of *Zero Dark Thirty*. She starts the film with the words "September 11, 2001" on a black screen. The words then fade into the background and a black screen remains while sounds of the emergency calls made during the attacks are played. These are the actual voice recordings, and they act as a marker of documentary authenticity for the film. Thus she makes the trauma of 9/11 present through the absence of the visual and the overlaid aural documents of terror from that day.[6]

The first visual image we see is of American military personnel standing around Ammar (Reda Kateb), a Pakistani man with ties to the 9/11 hijackers, who has been tortured. They are in a makeshift torture chamber. Dan (Jason Clarke), the American CIA interrogator, walks up to Ammar and says, "I own you Ammar. You belong to me." The scene proceeds with Dan telling Ammar that if he lies or does anything Dan doesn't like he will be hurt. This juxtaposition stitches together these two scenes as if torture is the logical response to the trauma of the emergency calls that took place on September 11, 2001.

This approach of knitting together these two scenes as if one is the cause and the next is the effect sets the tone for the film. It establishes the threat to life and then posits torture as the only way to regain the security that was lost in the trauma of the 9/11 attack. In this scenario, torture provides a way of accessing the truth that will punish the perpetrators of this attack and prevent future attacks. Thus, in *Zero Dark Thirty*, torture represents the only possible path out of the trauma of 9/11, and it ultimately leads to the killing of bin Laden, which is both vengeance and prevention.

In the opening torture scene, the CIA operatives act out of the belief that the intelligence that will lead to bin Laden is lodged in the bodies of their detainees. A little later in the film, Dan tells his boss that Ammar must know about the Saudi group. He says, "He's got them in his head, he needs to disclose them." This seemingly innocuous statement is actually incredibly revelatory. Here Dan further underscores the idea that the body, or in this case the head, is a container that just needs to be opened in the correct way, and that torture is the method to do this.

During the next scene with Ammar, torture determines the pacing of the scene, as the violence increases with the passing of time. Dan strips Ammar in front of Maya, puts a dog collar around his neck, makes him crawl on the ground naked, and finally confines him in a wooden box. The tension of the scene rises with each wrong answer that Ammar gives. This scene solidifies Maya as a biodectective who trusts in the answers that surveillance and torture provide. She is left alone with the naked detainee who pleads with her to help him. She calmly replies, "you can help yourself by being truthful." She thus validates the contemporary torture fantasy and her role as the biodetective by enforcing the fantasy of finding truth through torture.[7]

Later they get information out of Ammar, but the information comes from trickery. An attack has occurred, but he doesn't know that it was successful because he has been in isolation. Maya comes up with the idea of setting this trap. They give him food for supposedly already helping them, which they explain he can't remember because of the short-term memory damage of sleep deprivation. Ammar then tells them other information that later plays a role in leading them to bin Laden. This use of fiction and performance seems out of place in a film focusing on the biodetective. It is the mode of a different form of detective, one completely opposed to the biodetective. But here the fiction exists within the torture fantasy. It is subsumed to the act of torture and works only after weeks and weeks of horrible violence and sleep deprivation. The fiction is not an alternative to torture but a variation that one can employ while torturing.

Later on in the film, the effect of torture makes itself felt even when the CIA is not using it directly. Maya interrogates a key figure in the investigation, and their discussion begins with the man saying, "I have no wish to be tortured again. Ask me a question and I'll answer." There is no torture, and yet torture underlies the entire exchange. Even this easier interview is productive because of previous torture. The privileging of torture in this film does not consist simply in depicting torture as effective. It is also evident in the way the torture is situated in the form as the driving force of the action.

One important component of this structure is authenticity. Bigelow herself introduces authenticity as one of the driving forces behind plot and stylistic choices. When commenting on her approach, she says, "What we were attempting is almost a journalistic approach to film."[8] She also often told reporters that she wanted to present what it was like to hunt down and raid the complex where they found bin Laden. She described the feel of the film as "a boots-on-the-ground experience."[9] She wanted the majority of the film to follow faithfully the investigation and raid.[10] The film succeeded in this aim with the exception of one key scene: the torture scene.

Bigelow's narrative structure suggests that information gotten during the torture leads to the discovery of bin Laden's compound. But critics have attacked Bigelow for taking liberty with what actually happened in the investigation. For instance, Jane Mayer notes that Bigelow "seems to accept almost without question that the CIA's "enhanced interrogation techniques" played a key role in enabling the agency to identify the courier who unwittingly led them to bin Laden. But this claim has been debunked, repeatedly, by reliable sources with access to the facts."[11] This disingenuousness on the part of the film is not simply a concession to the exigencies of cinematic art but reflects a purely ideological choice.

Bigelow's defense of the liberty that the film takes with the facts makes clear her investment in the torture fantasy and the figure of the biodetective at the heart of this fantasy. When confronted with the historical inaccuracies concerning the role of torture in the hunt for bin Laden, Bigelow gave a response incongruous with her claim to be making a historically accurate film. She protested that she is an artist and that the film was a fictional work in which she can take liberties for the sake of creating a compelling plot. Of course, it is not insignificant that the one liberty—in the midst of a narrative replete with historical accuracy—she takes is to fictionalize the efficacy of torture. Despite the fact that this connection stands out as the one false note in an otherwise factual account, it nonetheless adheres to the biopolitical ideology of the rest of the film. The film's devotion to selective authenticity betrays a continuing investment in tying torture to truth.[12]

The first torture scene itself reveals how completely within the contemporary ideology of biopower the film is situated. In a shocking statement that almost involves the ideology itself speaking, Dan, the torturer, explains to his victim Ammar, "In the end, bro, everybody breaks. It's biology." By suggesting that it is biology that leads a torture victim to give up information, the film enacts what I have argued is the very fantasy that torture provides to shore up the validity of biopower. The information that Maya discovers through several torture sessions in the film is just one of a long line of biopolitical data that leads to bin Laden. Some of this information is discovered through torture and some through the extensive videotapes of interrogations and torture sessions. Through her reliance on this information, Maya is depicted as the ultimate contemporary biodetective.

I have proposed that ideas about torture today act as a fantasy that bridge over the gaps in biopower itself. Within *Zero Dark Thirty*, the torture scenes formally act in a similar way. The scenes are meant to explain the plot trajectory, a necessary evil that leads our biodetective to new information. Fictionalizing the efficacy of torture does not critique torture—as Bigelow has claimed she was trying to do—but rather reinforces biopower and the contemporary torture fantasy especially as it is situated in form.

In Laura Rascaroli's 1997 article on Bigelow and *Blue Steel* (1989) she makes two points that help inform a reading of *Zero Dark Thirty*. Rascaroli argues that Bigelow's cinema ruminates on vision. Bigelow's female protagonists, as in *Blue Steel*, grapple with their self-identity through their sight. Rascaroli points out that Bigelow employs the point-of-view shot attached to her female lead to emphasize the character's aggression and search for self-identity. She also suggests that in this probing look there is an attempt to find the self in the other. These formal choices in *Blue Steel* and *Strange Days* (1995) do challenge the typical dissociation of female characters and the look in the cinema, but this also helps to clarify what is largely missing in *Zero Dark Thirty*. Maya's point-of-view shot is not privileged in *Zero Dark Thirty*. She is a detective, but she doesn't have the same probing look. This obfuscates both the potential enjoyment in the look as well as any actual encounter with the other.

The biodetective never confronts the desire of the other. In fact, she or he focuses on the other's body precisely to avoid the encounter with the other's desire. The other's desire is always traumatic because it is constitutively a gap in the subject's knowledge, while the other's body appears fully knowable.[13] Biopower rests on the idea of complete knowability. Maya's encounters are all mediated through biopower and biometric technology and practices. She stares for years at video footage of interrogations with men from Pakistan, Iran, Iraq, and Afghanistan, and she is present in the room when some of these men are being tortured. All these modes of interaction prevent any kind of actual encounter with the other and the other's desire. Instead, these heavily mediated modes of detection and interaction provide many layers of social and cultural biases tied to the belief in the methods' ability to produce authenticity, to locate the truth. There is hubris in looking directly at someone else, but there is also a vulnerability as one is exposed to encountering the other's desire. It is this potential encounter that the biodetective avoids and that Bigelow formally avoids in *Zero Dark Thirty*.

The film depicts Maya staring at the figures she is researching in the surveillance videos of their interrogations, which often involve or suggest torture. The film stages Maya's unrelenting research of these interrogation videos as the key to her eventual success. The scenes of her watching the surveillance of these interrogations are filled with close-ups, pixelated grainy footage often in multiple images across the computer screen, and the contours of a small office that is almost overtaken by containers of disks and papers. Her devotion to this footage and her research defines her as a biodetective and as incredibly driven. This drivenness leads others to call her obsessed and crazy, but also leads her eventually to bin Laden.

THE DRIVE AND BEING DRIVEN

In his insightful essay on Bigelow's *Hurt Locker* (2008), David Denny argues that William James (Jeremy Renner), the main character in *Hurt Locker*, represents the subject of the drive. That is, James adheres to his drive regardless of any external incentives to abandon and heedless of any risk that this drive poses to his own survival. Because the subject's drive acts without paying attention to external constraint, it typically challenges the ideological structure the subject inhabits.[14] Thus Denny poses an essential question: if James is the subject of the drive, then why doesn't he subvert the viewer or the ideology buttressing the Iraq war in the film? Denny concludes that the film works to contain this radical possibility in the way it stages James as the object of desire. Denny explains, "James, as the embodiment of the subject of the drive, is at once the positive object that the subject looks to for the qualities of heroism and bravery *and* the object (the object *a*) that creates a gap or disturbance in the subjective point of view, one that fascinates by way of its lawless and transgressive nature."[15] Clearly, there is some similarity between James and Maya, and almost every reviewer has drawn attention to Maya's drive.[16]

But to lump James and Maya together is to proceed too quickly. While these two characters bare some similarity because they commit themselves wholly to a single activity, they are in fact quite different. Here it is important not to confuse the subject of the drive with being driven. Maya is a detective in that she has a goal that she strives for: finding bin Laden. The subject of the drive doesn't have a goal but repeats, and this repetition is not striving for any one thing in particular. The drive does not have an object. But Maya is striving after one particular target—one object of desire—the entire time.

This is quite clear in the first half of the film, but, especially once she has had friends killed during her time searching for bin Laden, she reacts to their deaths by saying, "I'm going to smoke everyone involved in this op. And then I'm going to kill bin Laden." James, on the other hand, is devoted to the activity of neutralizing bombs. This activity has a goal each time—neutralizing the bomb—but James isn't striving after only one target. There is no object that promises the realization of his desire as there is for Maya.

Both characters certainly appear alienated as a result of their devotion. *Zero Dark Thirty* shows Maya only when she is researching and interrogating targets or otherwise pursuing the case. Bigelow never even shows her at home getting ready for work or calling her family or expressing interest in anything about her surroundings. All she does is work. There is one scene depicting her socializing, but this scene exists only to show that Maya has no social concerns. In this scene, Jessica, her colleague, at dinner asks her if she is sleeping with anyone, has a boyfriend, or even has any friends. The answer to all these questions is no, and the dinner itself ends when a bomb explodes at the hotel where they are dining. Maya is even further afield from the potentially radical subject of the drive that Denny analyzes James embodying. Maya aims at a particular object, bin Laden, and she is devoted to torture as a method of finding the truth, which is altogether absent in *Hurt Locker* and the activity of James.

The biodetective in *Zero Dark Thirty* influences the structure of the film form. About Bigelow's filmic style, Laura Rascaroli argues, "Bigelow works towards a reduction of the distance between the human eye and the camera's eye, towards a more and more 'transparent' cinema, towards a transcendental vision."[17] In the age of the contemporary torture fantasy, however, this has coalesced into the final scene in which night goggles shape the viewer's experience of the raid that kills bin Laden. The night goggles create an attitude of surveillance that acts as a barrier to an encounter with the desire of the other. Even when one looks directly at the other, the night goggles provide a tint that places the other in a biometric lens just like surveillance footage does. Thus the torture scenes work in tandem with this lengthy final scene of the film in which the military raid the compound bin Laden is hiding in and kill him.

To heighten the sense of the first-person account, Bigelow provides many shots of the scene through the night goggles of the NAVY SEAL team and presents it in real time. This first-person and real-time effect attempts to reenact the experience visually, to create an authentic depiction of the raid. The role of real time in this scene harkens back to 24 and its reliance on the ticking clock, which communicates the urgency of the bomb that is ready to explode. Bigelow's film is as steeped in the ideology of biopower as 24, despite her claim to have made a film that "deconstructs" the practice of torture. Her efforts at authenticity lead her indirectly into the biopolitical trap that she tries to escape.

TRACKING BOURNE; OR, BIOLOGY AS TECHNOLOGY

The emergence of biology as the key to understanding and controlling bodies also emerges in the *Bourne* films. These films reveal the merging of torture, surveillance, and biometrics that occurs in *Zero Dark Thirty*, but their trajectory also indicates an increasing commitment to biology in recent years. In contrast to *Zero Dark Thirty*, the Bourne films take up an ambiguous relationship to the ideology of biopower. They evince an investment in it, but at times they do expose it as ideological. The hero of the *Bourne* films struggles against the forces of biopower, but these forces are very effective in tracking him. In the end, biopower is unable to control the *Bourne* hero fully, and this limitation indicates that the films are not fully invested in this ideology.

What is fascinating about the *Bourne* films is that they span the decade after the attacks on September 11, 2001. Beginning with Doug Liman's *The Bourne Identity*, which was released in 2002, and ending with Tony Gilroy's *The Bourne Legacy* (2012), these films reflect the development of the ideology of biopower in the aftermath of 9/11. The first three films revolve around Jason Bourne (Matt Damon), a CIA assassin suffering from memory loss. The final film depicts another CIA assassin, Aaron Cross (Jeremy Renner), who investigates why the CIA is trying to kill him. The first film is basically an action thriller in which Jason Bourne has to figure out who he is and then must escape the CIA. This first film is not particularly steeped in the contemporary torture fantasy. There are no depictions of torture, though the film does include violence. This absence of torture separates *The Bourne Identity* from the typical action films of the late 2000s and early 2010s. Coming out early in the decade, it still feels like an action film from the 1990s. The next two films directed by Paul Greengrass, *The Bourne Supremacy* (2004) and *The Bourne Ultimatum* (2007), are significantly more invested in the torture fantasy.[18]

Throughout both of these films, Bourne begins to have flashbacks to the behavior modification sessions that turned him into an assassin. All these sessions have the look of torture, and *The Bourne Ultimatum* reveals that torture played a central role in Bourne's recruitment. These sequels suggest that at the heart of his obedience and ability to kill so effectively are brutal torture sessions. The contrast with the first film could not be starker. It in no way hints at the role of torture in Bourne's accession to the position of CIA assassin but rather suggests that it represents an ethical failing that the amnesiac Bourne works to correct or redeem. As the decade moves on, the films become increasingly invested in the idea of torture.

The last film, however, turns completely to the biological, which makes it, despite some critical disapproval, the high point of the series.

The Bourne Legacy exposes how thoroughly the ideology of biopower dominates. In the final film, the national security apparatus controls Aaron Cross not through torture but literally through his biology. Cross comes from a generation of assassins created from viruses. The government found that a virus could function as an effective transmitter for enhancements that would boost bodily mental performance.

By controlling the virus through various pills that agents would take, the national security apparatus had control over the bodies of the agents. Indeed, these assassins seemed grateful for their new abilities and loyal to the government, which contrasts with the resistance posed to the earlier methods of torture and brainwashing. Cross rebels only when he realizes that they are phasing out, i.e., killing, all the assassins of his generation. This contrasts with the reason for Jason Bourne's rebellion in the first film. Bourne experiences moral revulsion when confronted with the prospect of killing someone in front of his young child. Control is much more effective in the case of Cross, which is why it requires an existential threat to trigger rebellion.[19]

The pursuit of Jason Bourne and of Aaron Cross also reflects the development of biodetection. The agents chasing them are all biodetectives, but those following Cross are, like Cross himself, enhanced versions. They can utilize face recognition software unavailable to the agents tracking down Jason Bourne, and they have access to a much wider range of surveillance footage. The move from *The Bourne Identity* to *The Bourne Legacy* sheds light on the changes that made *Zero Dark Thirty* possible, even though the Bourne films adopt a much less compliant relationship to the ideology of biopower that they depict.

THE DETECTIVE OF THE REAL

As the *Bourne* films show, the ideology of biopower is not the only alternative. One can challenge its dominance, and this challenge makes its presence felt in another form of detective opposed to the biodetective. This other form of detective is what I call a detective of the real. The biodetective trusts in surveillance, torture, and biometric data in order to discover the truth of the body. The detective of the real disdains these forms of knowledge and also disdains the pure body. This detective interprets the desire of the subject rather than seeking a truth lodged within the body.

In order to think more structurally about the truth of the subject, Lacan theorizes the realms of the imaginary, the symbolic, and the real. He divides the psyche into these three operations so that he can better isolate the subject's desire. In part these different registers allow Lacan to argue that any experience the subject has can never exist in only one realm or the other. For example, an experience cannot be wholly within the symbolic. When, for instance, a judge or lawyer articulates or upholds the law, she or he doesn't exist only in the symbolic order at that moment. Acting as fairly as possible, she or he still has imaginary identifications and real desires that are inevitably at play as well. Though the imaginary and symbolic categories determine the subject's social identity and how it sees itself, truth must take into account the subject's desire, which, according to Lacan, is wholly real. The real of the subject's desire is the focus of the detective of the real. As I will discuss in the following chapter, the series *Alias* (2001–2006) presents the fullest expression of the detective of the real, but she or he also appears in other less unambiguous guises.

Homeland provides an interesting case largely because of its ambivalence. The main detective, Carrie Mathison (Claire Danes), careens back and forth between the biodetective and the detective of the real, though she eventually establishes herself as the detective of the real. The detective of the real, unlike the biodetective, believes in the subject and believes that truth can only be revealed through subjectivity. The detective of the real is not entirely new, but combines aspects of the classical detective and the hard-boiled detective. On the one hand, the detective of the real certainly investigates facts, but, on the other hand, it is her or his ability to read and interact with other people's desires and anxieties that leads to success.

Biodetectives essentially read the facts as they exist in the symbolic, and sometimes in the imaginary (as in the torture fantasy), but they systematically ignore the real as meaningless, which means that they cannot see how desire distorts facts. The detective of the real, however, sees the importance of irrationality, desire, and anxiety as markers of the subject and thus of truth. For the detective of the real, fingerprinting, surveillance, and biometric technologies often are very helpful, but these technologies don't dictate their choices or assessments. Instead, the intricacy of the subject's unconscious guides the detective of the real. Instead of ignoring irrational unconscious behavior, the detective of the real relies upon their ability to read and interact with this behavior to solve a case or protect a nation. Detectives of the real are not all the same, but they do all focus on the way that truth appears at the heart of fiction and that finding truth is next to impossible if you view truth as solely embedded in the body as tracked through biometric technology or accessed through torture. With a detective of the real at the center of a story—as in shows like *Veronica Mars* (2004–2007), *Alias*, and *Homeland* (2011–present)—torture becomes deemphasized and unreliable.

Homeland depicts the CIA in the present as it tries to avert terrorist attacks. Carrie Mathison is a top CIA agent who suspects that returning war hero Nicholas Brody (Damien Lewis), whom Al Qaeda held and tortured for eight years, has become a terrorist operative working on behalf of his former captors. The first season depicts Brody evading Carrie and Carrie's attempts to convince others of her theory. She turns out to be correct and averts a major attack by having Brody's daughter call him and convince him to return home. Still, no one realizes that Carrie was correct until the next season, and the first season concludes with her undergoing electroshock treatment for her supposedly insane preoccupation with the war hero Brody. In the second season, the tables turn as Carrie becomes the only person to believe in Brody's changed nature, and this continues into the third season when she remains the only person to know of his innocence in a later attack. The backdrop of these very intense stories about Brody and Carrie is the American political scene and the CIA's current high-profile cases.

Carrie can correctly interpret Brody because she, unlike most of the other CIA agents, attempts to read his desire. Her focus on the subject's desire constitutes her as a detective of the real, but it also distinguishes her from the standard operating procedure at the CIA. Her status at the agency and even her job there seem always in jeopardy, and this risk stems directly from her concern with desire rather than facts. Even as she surveys Brody, she looks for how he desires rather than for a truth that his body might harbor.[20]

The thrust of *Homeland* is akin to *24* in that the CIA is working to stop attacks by Islamic extremists on American soil. The advertising slogan for *Homeland* was "Pledge Allegiance," which was often written above the characters whose faces were superimposed over the American flag. The series is about patriotism, but also about America's extreme anxiety over its changing role in the world and its understanding of how to approach terrorism. Even the concept of terrorism is questioned within the show. With a detective of the real at the helm who does not regularly turn to torture or find final answers in biometric technology, *Homeland* is able to pose uncomfortable questions. In an interview with Charlie Rose, aired November 13, 2013, Claire Danes reveals the show's self-awareness on this point. She explains, "it captures a new kind of anxiety and self-doubt and insecurity that we as a nation are coming to terms with." She goes on to point out that this is new on television. Danes also points out in this interview that Carrie's psychological problems are like a bomb she is sitting on. This is an important turn of phrase since it points to the logic within the narrative that the real ticking bomb is Carrie, or America itself, rather than an actual bomb planted on American soil.

The split between Carrie as biodetective and Carrie as detective of the real is interestingly mirrored in Carrie's psychic state. Even at the very beginning of the show, Carrie is presented as an excellent agent who has a small but necessarily secret problem: she is bipolar. She takes medication for this but feels it can't be on record that she is bipolar or she would lose her job. Throughout the show Carrie makes comments about being bipolar, mostly to her sister and father, who know about the disorder. At one point, Carrie comments on the medicine, explaining to her father that the most disorienting aspect of it is when you transition from the manic to the depressive side and the medicine attempts to counteract that. This works as a poignant metaphor for Carrie's swinging from her work as a biodetective to her work as a detective of the real. Similar to extremes associated with being bipolar, Carrie's work as a detective of the real is often quite extreme. In other words, she chases the real with more intensity and probably more zeal than is necessary.

The detective of the real stages a fiction to expose the other's desire. The fiction facilitates the emergence of the real of the subject's desire in a way that reality does not. But Carrie does not simply stage a fiction; she lives it. For instance, she creates a fiction that she has fallen in love with Brody in order to observe him more closely. But she really falls in love with him in the course of staging the fiction. It is her illness that prevents her from remaining distanced from the fiction that she creates, but, at the same time, this investment in the fiction, taking the fiction seriously, allows her to convince others that the fiction is real.

Her illness also enables her to interpret the real as an absence in the symbolic order. For example, during season 1, she spirals out into a massive attack of mania, which leads to her discovery of a key missing part of the timeline of the terrorist they are chasing. She has coded all the information in different colors in a manic and seemingly nonsensical way, but her coworker and friend, Saul Berenson (Mandy Patinkin), sees what she is doing. He takes what looks like a mess on the ground and posts in on the wall in a coherent form. Carrie had been repeating in apparent gibberish that it's the yellow that is the problem. When Saul arranges the colored papers on the wall, the yellow represents absence in the timeline. The CIA didn't know what the target, Abu Nazir (Navid Negahban), was doing during this time, and Carrie realizes that this is the key to understanding what the future attack might be.

This is a moment when Carrie reveals herself as a detective of the real because she sees that the lack or gap is the key and that this gap can't be filled in perfectly since it points to Abu Nazir's desire itself. Carrie often refers to the importance of lack in other ways. For example, it is common during the show for her to say, "It's not what she said, it's . . . " with the implication always being that it's the way she or he said it. In other words, Carrie reads the subject's unconscious as much as she listens to their conscious articulations.

The biometric information that she relies on becomes less and less important as the series goes on. In fact, the CIA often employs the polygraph, a classic biometric technology, but the show highlights its failings rather than its successes. The show also suggests that it's used polemically—i.e., to advance a personal agenda—rather than as a device for discovering the truth. Brody passes the polygraph even when we know he is lying, and Saul fails when he know that he's telling the truth. Later, David Estes (David Harewood), CIA assistant director, uses the polygraph to frame Saul for a crime he didn't commit. Showing the failures and shortcomings of the lie detector reveals that subjectivity remains irreducible to bodily function.

Nonetheless, torture does play a large part on *Homeland*. On the one hand, at the beginning of season 1, Carrie, acting more as a biodetective, does torture, and it works. Carrie has a suspect in an interrogation room overnight, and the programmed torture routine of freezing cold air, loud music, and lights to cause sleep deprivation runs throughout the night. She just sits there in a bored manner waiting for it to work. And it does seem to work when the suspect gives the CIA an e-mail in the morning that will help the investigation.[21] For the rest of the series, however, torture is never the preferred or successful method of investigation. The torture of Brody, at the hands of Nazir, also occupies an important role in the series. Especially during the first season, the show flashes back to his past torture, which in the end turned him into an operative for Nazir. But the meaning of this torture also shifts throughout as we learn more details. While the torture definitely damaged Brody's psyche, it is also clear that the murder of Nazir's son, whom Brody had befriended, by an American drone strike finally convinced Brody to return to the U.S. and kill the vice president who ordered the strike. Torture has multiple meanings throughout the show, but the show never privileges torture as a device for obtaining results. It does not subscribe to the torture fantasy in the end. The presence of Carrie as the detective of the real, who believes in truth lying in desire and subjectivity, far outweighs the presence of methods of biodetection.

Other important characters then echo Carrie's approach. Saul often interviews subjects and manipulates them, but he never tortures them. Near the end of season 2, he articulates this approach when he is interacting with a former colleague, Dar Adal (F. Murray Abraham), who is involved in secret operations that involve illegal killing and torture. Dar has contempt for Saul's reluctance to resort to extreme methods. He says to Saul, "Still afraid to get your hands dirty, Saul?" And Saul responds, "Still prefer to figure out a problem rather than obliterate it." This "figuring out" is the key to the detective of the real because figuring out does not refer to a belief that you can extract information from the body through biometric technology or torture. Instead, figuring it out entails investigating on the level of desire; in other words, it entails interpreting the subject rather than examining the body.

THE LIMITS OF *HOMELAND*

Here we might ask why the detective of the real on *Homeland* doesn't fully unravel the distance depicted between America and the Middle East. Despite all its self-awareness, the series does not in the first three seasons spend much time with its Muslim characters, either from abroad or from America. The show depicts, for example, Abu Nazir as a driven ideologue and not as a complex figure. What the show lacks is any character development that might allow the viewer to be sympathetic or at least ambivalent about the character. The only Muslim characters that we become acquainted with are white Americans who have joined radical Islamic groups and come back to America. Nicholas Brody and Aileen Morgan (Marin Ireland) are both given ample time to demonstrate that they have good sides and that their motives are complex and even thoughtful. The nonwhite Muslim terrorists depicted in the show, however, receive little time for complexity or exploring their point of view. In many ways, this is where the show comes up short. Both Carrie and Saul share parts of themselves during interrogations (which look more like interviews) with white middle-class Americans who look much like their interrogators. This allows them to access the real of their interlocutors' desire.

When Carrie does come face to face with Nazir and appeals to him to stop what he is doing, the gulf between them seems too wide for her to give of herself or understand his desire. She immediately thereafter has her military colleagues kill Nazir. Whereas Aileen goes to jail for life and Brody is on the run, the show sets up the expectations that the only fate for Nazir is death. The few nonwhite Muslim characters that Carrie can give of herself to in order to communicate are two women who give her information. One is Zahira Gohar (Hend Ayoub), wife of local imam Rafan Gohar (Sammy Sheik) of an American mosque that was unwittingly the site of an FBI shootout with Brody's rogue partner who is also working for Nazir. Carrie stages a meeting with Imam Gohar when she knows the Zahira will be there in order to muster her sympathies for giving up information that will help the situation. Another wife, Fatima Ali (Clara Khoury), of a Hezbollah district commander, comes forward and gives Carrie important information. Carrie had befriended her years earlier and promised her a ticket to America to help her out of an abusive marriage. The show can imagine Carrie having her femaleness in common with these women, which overcomes the cultural or racialized gulf that seems to exist with Nazir.

But the show does not allow the detective of the real to go far enough. Or possibly it posits the limits of the detective themselves as the limits of the real. *Homeland's* detectives of the real allow for a disdain of torture while still privileging the role of the CIA in protecting America. It is the detective of the real at the center of the show that enable us to see torture and biometrics in a completely different way than within the ideological constraints of biopower. The way each biometric technology gets redefined on *Homeland* exposes biopower as an ideology.

For instance, Carrie uses surveillance extensively to watch Brody when he returns, but this surveillance becomes part of her desire. She ultimately falls in love with Brody during this constant surveillance and, in a sense, she falls for not being able to understand exactly what he is doing even though she is watching him all the time. Thus surveillance becomes a tool in her investigative pursuit rather than an end unto itself. She uses surveillance not to find the answers but to find the questions, to find the points of inexplicability and lack. This suggests that when one looks right at something, even visually tracking a person's every waking moment, one still can't tell completely what the person is thinking or the nature of the person's desire.

On the other hand, surveillance in *Zero Dark Thirty* most often leads to answers and action. In fact, the higher-ups in this story often tell Maya that they need actionable intelligence. Rather than depicting a detective who works through the web of desires to find the truth, Bigelow depicts a biodetective who finds the truth through the body. Once Maya and her team find the house where they suspect bin Laden is staying, they watch the satellite image of the bodies in the house. They point out the evidence of the bodies. One of the analysts shows Maya that certain shapes are children, certain shapes are women, and certain shapes are men. Once they find a woman with no visible man, they assume they have a missing man who must be bin Laden. This biometric evidence then leads to direct action in which the Marines raid the complex and kill bin Laden. Bigelow claims that except for the torture scene she is depicting what happened. But her way of depicting what happened is thoroughly ensconced in ideologies of biopower. Bigelow's biodetective organizes the rest of the film by emphasizing the traces of the body as the key evidence that leads to action and truth.

In contrast, *Homeland* also depicts its agents finding actionable truths, but not through biometrics, surveillance, or torture. Instead, the detectives of the real in *Homeland* find the most information through methods that center on the subject and lack of knowledge. When Carrie does interact with Brody, for example, she initially finds out the most information from him by revealing her own desire and anxiety. During her interrogation of him in the second season, she reveals the truth of her desire when she tells him that she's in love with him. Carrie telegraphs her real emotions, desires, and anxieties, even if she is using them to engage her target in hopes of getting him to reveal what he knows. Similarly, Saul secures terrorist Aileen Morgan's information in season 1 by driving thirty hours with her—from the point they captured her to Langley—and getting to know her. The moment when he finally gains some of her trust is when he reveals his own failing marriage. For the detective of the real, truth is accessible through relationships, at the center of which is the subject itself.

Where the ambivalence of the series lies is in its complete devotion to the real. For *Homeland*, once an agent goes down the path of detecting the real, she or he is devoted to it completely and must give up her or his whole life in this pursuit. And even in Carrie's case, her one true love is the target she is pursuing. Thus these detectives of the real believe in pursuing the web of desire, but in this pursuit they lose themselves. They cannot separate their own desires from the fiction they create to arouse the desire of the other. This is similar to the film noir detective, and yet it seems to go further. These detectives of the real present their own desire in return for understanding the desire of the subjects they pursue. Within this format, they do turn away from torture and biometric technology, but they also completely lose any semblance of a normal life. This is evident in Carrie's struggles with being bipolar, which her job aggravates, and her lack of any other friends or lovers, and in Saul's dissolving marriage and lack of any personal life.

What *Homeland*'s detectives of the real seem unable to do is stage a fiction in order to find the truth; instead they give up all their desire to find the desire of the other. This reflects a failure to regard the fiction as a fiction, which is the final step that the detective of the real must take. It is in *Alias* where we see the example of a detective of the real who creates a fiction to reveal and ensnare the desire of the other that will lead to the truth as an alternative to the contemporary torture fantasy. In *Alias*, the detective of the real is able to treat the fiction as a fiction, which indicates her commitment to the real that this fiction reveals.

6
ALIAS AND THE FICTIONAL ALTERNATIVE TO TORTURE

SYDNEY'S PATH TO TRUTH

Unlike *24*'s consistent attempts to shore up the validity of torture, *Alias* (2001–2006), of a similar genre and moment in history, seeks truth in a way that undermines the validity of torture. *Alias* depicts a type of national security that not only doesn't rely on torture but actually posits its unreliability. The series also refuses to base the effectiveness of its operations on surveillance techniques or investigations of the body, such as one might see on a contemporary police drama that focuses on forensic evidence. Paramilitary action, surveillance, and forensics play a part in the successful missions that *Alias* depicts, but they do not have a foundational status for these missions. At the center of almost every mission shown on the series is instead the construction of a fiction, the creation of a false identity used to deceive the threat, usually an alias adopted by the heroine of the series, Sydney Bristow (Jennifer Garner).

Though critics often group *Alias* alongside *24* because it is structured as a spy thriller and it follows a small group dedicated to preserving national security, the two shows could not be more disparate. This opposition shows that *Alias* is not just different in its chosen methods but in its fundamental political bearing. In other words, it is not an accident that legislative, judicial, and military leaders invoke 24 when they defend their policies and don't think to use *Alias* as a justification. It would lack the ideological utility that 24 has because of the attitude that *Alias* takes up to the process of acquiring information.

Alias contrasts with 24 in several key ways. The central opposition between the two shows concerns the effectiveness of torture, an effectiveness that 24 (as we have seen) simply takes for granted. In the world of *Alias*, torture remains consistently less effective then all other methods the federal agents use, but especially ineffectual compared to the lead character's use of aliases to procure information. The primary task of the agents on *Alias* is to discover information or retrieve stolen high-tech items (such as bombs, satellites, or biological weapons) in order to protect national security. The agents certainly employ violence liberally throughout these tasks. What marks this series as different is its *primary* reliance on the fiction or alias as the most successful way of completing the tasks necessary for the preservation of national security. According to the conceit of the show, one particular agent, Sydney Bristow, leads the team and thus employs the most aliases. In the majority of the episodes, we see her perform a different alias (such as punk girl, nuclear physicist, prostitute, wealthy art collector, assassin, and so on) in order to acquire secret information, gain access to an otherwise restricted space, or gain the trust of an individual important to her goals. Though occasionally we see an alias fall apart after an initial success, the overall success rate of using aliases in the field for Sydney and her crew is very high.[1] The aliases succeed on the series where torture fails. The aliases further the mission and produce reliable information, whereas torture does neither.

The turn to the alias marks a direct contrast with 24. Not coincidentally, Jack Bauer on 24 almost never uses an alias. The only time he seems to take on an alias is when he wants to escape from his life as a federal agent. The alias enables Jack to retreat from the project of national security rather than to serve this project. Several seasons start by finding him living under a pseudonym with an assumed profession and life from which he is very quickly pulled to help save the country from disaster. The contrast with Sydney Bristow is stark: in her everyday life away from the agency, she never adopts an alias but confines the fiction to her national security missions. Jack's fiction is a private one, a fiction that permits him to escape public service and hide himself in private life. This occurs in between the seasons but is always swept aside once the season starts up again. Sydney's fiction, however, is always public as it is staged for work. She doesn't employ these fictions in her private life. For example, in the first few seasons of the series, Sydney was a graduate student in English when she was not working for the CIA, but this was not just a cover. She really wanted to become an English professor.[2] Key to the success of Sydney's fictional strategy at work is that she relies on her insight into subjectivity to create a successful alias and find the necessary information. This is opposed to Jack's reliance on his insight about the vulnerability of the body as a road to truth. This does not, as it may appear, create a typical divide between active male and passive female; Sydney is often as violent as Jack on a mission, but the violence is not employed in the torture chamber. Instead, Sydney's violence is employed to get her in and out of situations.

The entire structure of *Alias* revolves around Sydney and her ability to bring together intellect, brute strength, and excellent acting skills—the combination of which leads to success in the field. In one sense, this seems like the combination of talents that every good agent would have. But what makes Sydney remarkable—and what causes the series to stand out through its depiction of her—lies not in this confluence of skills but rather in Sydney herself as a desiring subject.[3] Sydney, in contrast to Jack Bauer and most other representations of secret agents, recognizes herself as a desiring subject, and, at the same time, she sees others as desiring subjects as well. To put it in the idiom of Joan Copjec, Sydney constantly reads the desire of those with whom she interacts, and time and again this is the insight that allows her to complete a mission in ways that others could not.[4]

Sydney's understanding of where the truth that she is seeking lies contrasts directly with the understanding of Jack Bauer in *24*. Sydney sees all truth as embedded in a web of desire rather than as a fact deposited in the body. In this way, truth is a much more complicated entity in *Alias*. In fact, there is no truth that is separate from the subject's desire, and following the path to desire is the only way to encounter truth. When one conceives truth in this way, one abandons the terrain of biopower and its conception of the body as the repository for truth.

Instead, each body is inscribed in a desiring subjectivity. The truth that it hides does not exist separately from the desire of the subject, and thus one cannot simply extract it as Jack Bauer does.

When beginning with desiring subjectivity rather than the raw body, fiction becomes not something to penetrate in order to access the truth but a path that one must traverse to arrive at the truth. Fiction is not an obstacle to truth; it is essential to it. At a fundamental level, *Alias* holds to Jacques Lacan's maxim that "every truth has the structure of a fiction."[5] The implicit claim of *Alias* is not that truth itself has a fictional status, that it is simply a construction, but one must use fictional constructions to find it. This conceit animates almost every episode of the show.

The preferred method that Sydney and her team of agents use on *Alias* is to stage a fiction within which they can use the target's desire and way of seeing the world to their own advantage.[6] Each subject is a subject of desire, and this desire distorts how the subject views objects in the world. On the basis of the subject's desire, certain objects do not even enter into the field of vision, while other objects, though they might be small or apparently insignificant, stand out for the subject. But in order to take advantage of the disturbance that desire introduces into the subject's perceptive field, the agents must have an idea of how their targets desire. The fictions that the agents create speak to this desire and thereby engage the subject within the fictional construction.

In *Alias*, fiction is the fantasy stage upon which the characters encounter the circuitous path of desire. The series correctly reveals that fantasy doesn't involve giving subjects what they desire but rather creating a scenario in which they can experience their desire. As Elizabeth Cowie points out, "fantasy is not the object of desire, but its setting."[7] The agents on *Alias*, especially Sydney Bristow, are adept at creating the perfect fantasmatic setting that speaks to the desire of their target subjects. This emphasis creates a very different form and structure compared to *24*.

On *Alias*, it is the path of desire that leads to the discovery of truth—whether it is where a bomb is hidden or the true nature of a relationship. Every truth remains tied to its fictional form, and the series shows that the belief that separating truth from fiction causes us to constantly miss truth altogether. The association of truth with desire leads *Alias* away from the body and toward the subject. This turn makes it impossible for the show to embrace torture in the way that 24 embraces it. By privileging the desiring subject at the center of the narrative, *Alias* is constitutively incapable of approaching torture as a productive means for uncovering truth.

In the contemporary torture fantasy, truth lies in the tortured body, and the torturer must use violence to rip away the fictions that hide it. Fiction is seen as not a path to truth but a barrier that one must eliminate to discover truth. This is the conception of truth that produces and informs the war on terror. But this is not the only problem with it. This conception of truth also inevitably fails. The miserable success rate for torture derives directly from a certain idea of truth that supports the practice. This idea sees truth as an object that can be obtained by threatening the victim's survival. The problem is that the torture victim is not just a body but also a subject attuned to the desire of the Other. While being tortured, the victim attempts to read the torturer's desire and respond to it with the appropriate fiction, not with the truth. In this way, unbeknownst to the torturer who believes in its efficacy, torture ends up being a fiction procurement device, not a privileged mode of access to truth, which is the prevailing belief about torture as espoused in films and shows like *24*.

Within psychoanalysis, the idea of truth is inextricably tied to unconscious desire and the real. One of the startling aspects of the intervention of psychoanalysis at the turn of the twentieth century was its argument that the truth of one's being lies in the unconscious rather than the conscious mind. This destabilizing idea suggests that the truth of a subject lies beyond conscious articulation and instead can only be found in indirect ways. Ways of holding one's body, gestures, slips of the tongue, and free association became important markers of the truth of one's unconscious.

Truth doesn't just concern what the subject symbolizes but also—and even more importantly—what remains absent in its symbolic identity and articulations. In Jacques Lacan's tripartite schema, the real holds a privileged position relative to the symbolic order and the imaginary. The real is a point of impossibility within the symbolic order, and yet this impossibility informs every signifying act. Desire emanates from the real, and thus the real provides the key to the subject of desire.

But Lacan does not equate truth and the real, as one might expect, and as some of his followers sometimes do. Truth is something different than the real. In fact, Lacan articulates a clear distinction in *Seminar XXIII*, where he claims, "the truth pleases, and this is what distinguishes it from the real. The real, it doesn't please, necessarily."[8] The reason the real "doesn't please, necessarily" is that encountering the real is traumatic. It indicates a desire that is always unconscious and that the subject can never satisfy in the way that it expects. One can, on the other hand, arrive at truth in a satisfying way. One can encounter it in the symbolic order and through symbolic methods, even if it involves taking the real into account. In this sense, truth can potentially be pleasing. This does not mean that truth does not have a relationship to the real. Truth becomes visible when we see the distortion that the real creates within the symbolic order. A psychoanalytic approach to the truth, then, means taking into consideration the manner in which the symbolic, the imaginary, and the real come together. This is, of course, often what good detectives do in their work. They consider facts (symbolic markers), imaginary understandings, and the subject's desire in order to lead them to what they are looking for.

The contrast between a psychoanalytic approach and a biopolitical one becomes especially pointed with regard to the status of truth. Biopolitics reduces truth to the symbolic order and thus believes it to be entirely knowable.[9] It ignores the imaginary and, more importantly, the real.[10] The trend toward wearing devices that will constantly monitor your health statistics is a good example of this. It suggests that everything that affects our health can be symbolically registered and controlled. But when searching for truth, one cannot privilege the symbolic over the imaginary and the real. To actually improve people's health, to continue this example, doctors must take into consideration the real (how their desire informs their well-being) as well as the imaginary (the impact of their conception of what health is supposed to look like). The torturer makes the same mistake as the doctor who ignores the imaginary and, most importantly, the real.[11] The contemporary torture fantasy believes only in the symbolic facts and fails to recognize how desire distorts the symbolic.

Alias engages a very different way of understanding truth and thus rejects the fantasy of torture and the preconceptions of biopolitics. While torture does work a few times in *Alias*, it is not at all the privileged mode for obtaining information, and most often the series reveals it as completely ineffectual or even misleading (and thus counterproductive). For example, in season 2, episode 11 ("A Higher Echelon"), Sydney's colleague and technological specialist Marshall Flinkman (Kevin Weisman) is kidnapped and tortured. Dr. Zhang Lee (Ric Young) tortures Marshall by pouring epoxy down his throat. Lee explains that he needs only to pour the agitating ingredient on top of this to make the epoxy harden and thus kill Marshall. Marshall resists the torture until they threaten his mother's life. Then he agrees to reengineer the software they need.

It seems torture has worked in this scene. Throughout the episode, we see Marshall working on the software, and the viewer assumes that he is simply doing the bidding of the torturer. But, at the end of the episode, it turns out he has tricked them and instead engineered a simple video game. Not only that, but while creating the video game he sent a clandestine signal alerting his colleagues to his location, which allows Sydney to come and save him. In this case, the series shows that one can respond to torture with a fiction and thereby completely undermine it. Marshall distracts his torturer with the fiction of the efficacy of torture itself. The torture doesn't work, and it also provides Marshall with the opportunity to subvert the villain's entire plan.[12]

The contrast to torture in the series is the development of elaborate fictions. These fictions always have the structure of a fantasy that has the effect of creating the reality the target comes to inhabit. Thus Sydney's approach to seeking lost government objects and information that will affect national security hews closely to Lacan's position that "everything we are allowed to approach by way of reality remains rooted in fantasy."[13] Sydney understands that fiction stages how to desire, and, as a detective, she works to follow this circuitous web of desire even when she is sometimes creating it.

In part she accomplishes this as a desiring subject herself. In her aliases, she plays characters that are pursuing their own desire, but, beneath these characters, Sydney is pursuing her desire as well. This shows that being a desiring subject activates the desire of the other. For Sydney as detective, the web of desire provides the contours within which truth can be gained. This contrasts her with the torturers and the forensic specialists that dominate the contemporary film and television landscape.

For example, in "Reckoning" (season 1, episode 6), Sydney inhabits two different aliases, and each gives her access to needed items or information. In the first scenario, the scene opens in a high-end modern art gallery. Sydney is dressed in a green modern dress with a long wig and very high-heeled shoes to match her dress. Her partner, Marcus Dixon (Carl Lumbly), is dressed for the occasion as well. They are posing as wealthy patrons interested in buying the entire collection. To distract security so Sydney can slip into the office where the item they are searching for is located, Dixon lights a cigar. The patrons around them quickly become annoyed, and the gallery manager calls security over. Once the guard is lured away from his post, Sydney slips out of the gallery and into the office to find the object. Dixon continues to occupy the gallery staff by responding to their requests to put out his cigar with an inquiry into how much the entire gallery collection costs. Upon hearing this, they let him continue to smoke his cigar while haggling over a price. More than once, he inquires whether the cigar is bothering them, and they emphatically say, "No." While Dixon is distracting everyone else, Sydney trips the alarm after obtaining the item they came for, hurries out, and enters the gallery playing her role as wealthy girlfriend. She marches up to Dixon and says, "I'd prefer the Lamborghini." To which Dixon replies with a shrug and says, "It's your birthday." He then hands his used cigar to the owner as they leave.

In this case, Sydney and Dixon stage a fantasy scene upon which the gallery staff's desire can play out. Instead of capturing the gallery owner and torturing him to give them access to his office and open the safe, Sydney and Dixon create a fantasy scenario within which the gallery owner's desire is activated so that they can lure him away from his office and gain access to his safe. They stage the scene by creating characters whose own enigmatic desire activates the desire of their target. For instance, it is crucial for the success of the mission that Dixon smokes a cigar in the gallery. He does this to hold the attention of the gallery staff, but it also indicates his own status as a desiring subject. Clearly, there are very few spaces where people smoke anymore, and especially not in art galleries. Everyone knows that smoking is prohibited inside art galleries, but it is this prohibition that creates a space for the irruption of desire. The law channels our desire not into the paths of obedience but into particular modes of disobedience, even though most of the time we do not follow our desire and instead simply obey.

Furthermore, by flaunting his enjoyment in the act of cigar smoking even though it transgresses social laws, Dixon's character is believable to the gallery staff. Because of this display of enjoyment, the gallery owner believes Dixon when he says he wants to buy the entire collection. At this point, the gallery owner's own desire to sell the art is activated, and the fictional web of desire is engaged.

After Sydney obtains the item, she and Dixon must leave undetected. To do so, they again flaunt their enjoyment. Sydney's character proclaims that she would prefer a Lamborghini to the art collection, and they abruptly leave. The gallery owner stands looking bewildered. He is bewildered at the desire of the wealthy patrons who might buy the art, but he never suspects Sydney and Dixon's fiction. Desire is enigmatic, and no one knows this more than an art gallery owner who often relies on wealthy people buying art on a whim of their desire. Sydney and Dixon stage the very unknowable nature of desire in order to make the fiction believable.[14]

THE PRODUCTION OF AUTHENTIC FEMININITY

In all of her many different kinds of aliases, Sydney (often with the aid of her coworkers) creates a fictional web of fantasy that allows her to obtain information or items that the government seeks. Later in this very episode, for example, Sydney poses as a patient who needs to be admitted to a mental institution in Bucharest in order to get close to another patient there and obtain important information. Within the structure of this series, Sydney succeeds when she turns to fiction to enchant her target and arouse the target's desire. The characters that use torture, on the other hand, rarely get what they are looking for.

The alias itself reveals an approach to truth that revolves around subjectivity rather than bare life. The way that these aliases are presented further reveals the radical nature of this idea of the priority of the fiction that animates *Alias*. Specifically, the series edits the deployment in a very unusual way, a way that violates the typical depiction of a woman in the midst of a masquerade. In this sense, editing is just as important to the political valence of *Alias* as it is to that of *24*. In chapter 3, I link *24*'s formal structure—the omnipresence of the digital clock defining the viewer's experience of the plot—to its investment in the torture fantasy. The editing in *Alias* is crucial to the alternative that it poses to this fantasy. Whereas the key to *24* and its concept of truth is the ticking clock, the key to *Alias*'s concept of truth can be found in its presentation of the alias itself.

Alias uses editing to create a short-circuit to the production of femininity that we see in the aliases that Sydney adopts. This short-circuit to the production of femininity operates formally as an instance of the real, which then highlights the role of the real in the fantasy scene that the alias is staging. An investigation into how femininity is approached in the alias reveals more about the form's opposition to biopolitics and the fantasy of torture as a tool to find truth. The performances themselves are often, but not always, contrasted to Sydney's own personality. When Sydney is at home not working, her clothes are plain and minimalist, as is her general appearance. She wears very little makeup and has straight brown hair.

Though Jennifer Garner is, of course, attractive by Hollywood standards, the show plays down any glamour that could be attached to her looks as it tries to show her as an average young working woman when she is at home in her apartment. Similarly, when she is in the office (in strategy meetings, speaking with her coworkers, etc.), she is dressed either in workout clothes or very simple office attire. This nonadorned look underscores her serious nature. Throughout the series, Sydney takes a serious approach to her work and to her home life.[15]

Her aliases, on the other hand, range from more feminine depictions (that are still quite different from her own) to truly spectacular and completely adorned feminine characters. For example, when her aliases require her to appear in dance clubs or trendy bars, she wears wigs (including red, blue, and platinum), outrageously high heels or knee-length boots, and miniskirts. She also wears a great deal of jewelry and makeup. On a theoretical level, however, the key to *Alias* is not what is shown but instead what is never shown: the preparation for these performances.

Not all preparation is hidden: the show regularly depicts Sydney and her crew preparing to go out on an assignment. We see them researching information about the item they are pursuing or listening to demonstrations from experts concerning the directions for their mission. But one aspect of the preparation is, almost without exception, missing. *Alias* never shows Sydney herself constructing her appearance for her elaborate performances of femininity. Instead, the show typically cuts from a briefing to her entrance into the scene in which she has already adopted the alias.

The radicality of this cut and this omission cannot be overstated. The depiction of women dressing and adorning themselves is a staple of film and television. In this standard depiction, femininity appears as a construction but not as a masquerade.[16] Though the focus on the woman preparing herself as feminine denaturalizes femininity, it associates femininity with the woman herself and not with the fantasy scenario to which that femininity belongs. In her account of feminine sexuality, Jacqueline Rose points out that masquerade captures the essence of femininity insofar as it does implicitly refer to this scenario. She writes, "masquerade is the very definition of 'femininity' precisely because it is constructed with reference to a male sign."[17] The traditional depiction of women putting on their femininity separates this act from the fantasy and thus disguises the masquerade that *Alias* foregrounds.

This tradition might be best embodied in a film like Garry Marshall's *Pretty Woman* (1990), whose plot revolves around the transformation of a prostitute, Vivian Ward (Julia Roberts), into an upper-class respected woman. Much of the film locates this transformation on her body itself, as multiple scenes depict changing her way of dress and her way of comporting herself from that of a lower-class call girl to the romantic partner of a millionaire. To this end, the film spends a good deal of time on Vivian shopping for new clothes, trying the clothes on, admiring how they look on her, and then finally appearing in a full makeover.

Certainly, the film reveals to us the constructed nature of femininity when it presents us these two different types (the lower-class prostitute and the upper-class romantic partner) in the same female character. It illustrates the labor that must go into changing from one to the other, but it also suggests that in this transformation Vivian Ward has finally discovered her true self. Hilary Radner argues, "These films are concerned with the theme of transformation, often represented as a magical makeover, the purpose of which is to give expression to an internal process of education, which, through the makeover trope, is linked to consumer culture."[18] Radner broadens this point to argue that *Pretty Woman* and films like it constitute a neofeminist cinema that parallels the feminist movement but links independence with consumerism, often within the structure of the romance comedy. Radner's analysis insightfully shows the way in which consumer pleasure is linked to the production of a true sense of self in the film. The pleasure that Vivian gets out of the shopping in *Pretty Woman* is not just because constructing femininity is itself a true pleasure—though it is depicted as such—but also that it is pleasurable because it is the path toward her authentic self. In this way, *Pretty Woman*—like many other film and television shows—suggests that ultimately preparing for and creating the proper femininity is both the most sanctioned and the most successful path to social acceptance as well as to authenticity.[19]

This plot trajectory, of course, is based on an even more specific tradition in the Pygmalion story. Films such as George Cukor's *My Fair Lady* (1964), Luc Besson's *La Femme Nikita* (1990), Amy Heckerling's *Clueless* (1995), and Donald Petrie's *Miss Congeniality* (2000) all have at the heart of their plots this hackneyed story of educating the woman into a more acceptable and upper-class femininity. One of the essential scenes in these films is the one in which she physically transforms. We first see her looking poor and ugly. The transformation scene involves new clothes, hairstyle, and makeup, all of which reveal, despite the fact that they further disguise the woman, her authentic inner beauty. In these films, the potential of the individual is literally located in their actual body. Their body both hides and is the secret to their fulfillment. The fact that the truth of the woman is located within her body waiting to be unleashed places these films in proximity to 24. Of course, no one tortures Vivian Ward to transform her from a prostitute into an upper-class woman, but the idea that her body contains a truth that someone might unlock parallels the prevailing conceit of 24. Though there are moments in television shows that contain moments of transformation, there are also whole reality shows based on this tradition. These reality shows dedicate themselves to making over the average woman and the supermodel alike. Shows such as *Extreme Makeover* (2002–2007), *What Not to Wear* (2003–present), *How Do I Look?* (2004–2012), and *Tim Gunn's Guide to Style* (2007–2008) spend the majority of their time filming the participants trying on the clothes and even shopping for clothes before they present the women as a final product.[20] The outcome of this emphasis is that the woman is finally produced as her true best self (usually upper-class, trendy, etc.), which is meant to make her a happier person.

THE HARD CUT TO THE FICTION OF FEMININITY

Alias works entirely against this grain. The hard cut to the performance of the alias that the series utilizes every time emphasizes the performance at the expense of the preparation. Here I will turn to one alias in the series that perfectly exemplifies the role of the hard cut and the absence of any preparation. "Phase One" (season 2, episode 13) begins with an alias performance. The episode opens with a shot of an empty hallway with a door at end of hallway. All of a sudden, the door opens dramatically to reveal Sydney clad in lingerie. The camera tracks back down the hallway as she walks forward until she stops to pose with a riding crop in her hand. The entire scene has the look of a music video (and AC/DC's "Back in Black" is blaring as background music). It presents a typical sexist fantasy of the woman as an object of male sexual desire. In this way, the camera work formally presents Sydney's fiction. The form of the editing itself shifts from its typically straightforward way of depicting Sydney to a more traditionally gendered way of portraying the woman as object of the male's look. The form is also gesturing to the music video, with her hair blowing and her walk down the hallway slightly in slow motion. Thus the form itself signals that we are in a fantasy realm, specifically a male fantasy of the perfectly objectified woman.

The implications here are twofold: the alias is presented to the viewers as much as to the characters in the scene, and the form of the scene is from Sydney's subjective position. In this case, the subjective position is the fiction that she is working to project and that the look of the scene helps to project. The man for whom she is performing evaluates her by looking her up and down and then says, "No, the red one" (in French). The scene then cuts to the same door as before, which again opens to reveal Sydney, now in the red lingerie outfit. The viewer never sees her dressing for either of these performances.

Sometimes, the show reveals why she needs to create a certain alias. For example, she must act like someone who is missing or disguise herself as a scientist who could get into the facility the agency must access. But other times, as in this episode, the show does not explain the alias, and this adds an element of detection for the viewer to try to figure out why she is performing this particular alias. After approving the red lingerie outfit, it becomes clear that the man thinks Sydney is a prostitute that he has hired. Once she is on the bed with him, she uses her bracelet to pull out a wire that she could use to strangle him and pins him down. She says, "What was wrong with the black one? Do you think it's comfortable wearing clothes like this?" In response, he tries to push his emergency button, and she says, "This isn't my first day on the job; I disconnected your call button." Both these statements, while falling into the tradition of the pithy lines that action heroes utter during their physical struggles, also emphasize the working aspect of her aliases. Her comment about her annoyance that he wasn't happy with her first outfit suggests that wearing the lingerie is an uncomfortable but necessary aspect of the job and holds none of the romance that advertising suggests. And her second statement emphasizes that her experience allows her to be completely unflustered even when finding herself in this seemingly demeaning situation.

In fact, she is in complete control, as is evident both in her physical prowess over a man much larger than she and her disconnecting his call button. After finding out where her target (the computer server) is, she delivers a swift blow to his head.[21] She proceeds to get dressed, access the server, and transmit the data to the CIA. It is clear that the reason she was able to find her target information is because of the fantasy scene that she created, not the violence she uses at the end, which simply incapacitates the man after she finds out what she needs to know.

The episode then cuts to a brief flashback in which we are presented with the events that led up to this moment. We might expect a flashback scene to show us Sydney putting on the lingerie, but instead we see a repetition of the seduction scene itself, which is repeated from the perspective of a camera in Sydney's earrings. The repetition of this scene allows for some important reinvestigations of the issues the first scene raises. Giving us Sydney's literal point of view (from the earring camera) allows us to step outside the fantasy space she created. It shows the viewer Sydney's perspective while weaving the pattern of this fantasy. The perspective allows for a critique of the "woman as object" fantasy. What is important to note is that the show gives us both the fantasy that Sydney is presenting and an approximation of her actual point of view. In this sense, the viewer doubly experiences Sydney's alias, though this is the only time that the series does this.

Still, this double inscription of Sydney's performance of the alias emphasizes her role as desiring subject within the fiction she creates. In other words, the earring camera perspective signifies Sydney's desire to perform the mission. Unlike the first presentation, this scene crosscuts between Sydney's experience and that of her colleague and boyfriend Michael Vaughn (Michael Vartan), who is following the events by monitoring the earring camera with fellow agent Eric Weiss (Greg Grunberg) from another plane. Vaughn is clearly upset at her peril and then deeply satisfied when she beats her opponent (a bodyguard who comes upon her after she has found the computer server). After this fight, the scene dramatically ends when Sydney shoots out the plane window to rid herself of the rest of the bodyguards (who are sucked out the hole in the plane that Sydney's gunshot has created), puts on a jump suit, curls herself into a ball, and lets go so that she is also sucked out the gaping hole of the plane to rendezvous with the other agents. During this scene, Vaughn and Weiss are left to just watch in shock. At the end of the scene, Weiss and Vaughn appear agitated, and Weiss says, "She's all yours."

Crosscutting between her activity and that of her male colleagues' inactivity reinterprets the male look. Instead of a look of mastery with the woman as object, the male look here is one of helplessness with the woman as the subject of desire. Seeing the scene from her point of view, they automatically come face-to-face with the leering man who has hired her as a prostitute. The disgust on their faces in reaction to this man creates an implicit critique of that leering male position. At the same time, they are banking on her alias working in order to succeed in their mission. The filming of the scene separates the success of the alias from any investment in it or in the image of femininity that it conveys. Femininity in the series is a fiction that functions as a fantasmatic trap for desire.

Sydney is able to perform femininity in precisely the appropriate way because she can read the deadlocks in the symbolic order and create a fantasy space to assuage these deadlocks. This has the effect of putting people at ease and making her performance invisible as a performance. The key to the analysis of *Alias* lies in the complex relationship between the paths of desire as it is staged within the fantasy in these moments. This particular episode's multitiered representation of the point-of-view shot in depicting experience stems from the complexity that is present (whether implicitly or explicitly) in every one of Sydney's aliases. She is able to make herself into a figure of the real, and this figure always engages her target.

There have been several excellent forays into how one might analyze the real in the visual field. Joan Copjec's work on photographer Cindy Sherman's *Untitled Film Stills* (produced between 1977–1980), however, is particularly relevant for analyzing Sydney's aliases because it theorizes the relationship of the real to fantasy in the realm of the feminine. Sherman's photographs are staged film stills that depict many different types of femininity that Sherman herself adopts. Copjec suggests that the key to reading Sherman's photographs is not the different narratives or characters that her *Untitled Film Stills* create but rather that they show the same woman (the photographer) in each of the photographs. Sherman's face itself, Copjec suggests, acts as the gaze—that stain embodying the real—because of is constant ambiguity. This is contrasted with the fantasy space of the film still setup, and it is the tension between the two that creates meaning and sets viewers on their own voyage of desire and confrontation with the fantasy scene.

Importantly, Copjec argues, the photographs force us to see that there is no authentic identity that the feminine fantasy hides. Rather, Sherman confronts us with our own fantasies and desires by equating the woman with the masquerade. Copjec argues, "It is as if these photographs were endorsing the thesis of film theorists regarding the closeness of the woman to the screen image. . . . But where film theorists condemned this theoretical and cinematic conflation of the woman with the image, the *Untitled Film Stills* does not. It accepts that there is 'no exit' for woman from the level of appearance, that 'womanliness' *is* always but masquerade."[22] Copjec's analysis points out that truth exists within the structure of the fantasy itself; it is not something hidden within some more authentic space. Sherman understands this and engages the viewer's desire through this provocative embrace of the fantasy structure of femininity itself.

Alias operates under a similar assumption. Sydney searches for truth within the fantasy space she creates. She engages the desire of those around her during an alias through her belief in appearance as such. Purposely staging the fantasy scene allows for a confrontation with the truth of the desire that this scene arouses. Sherman's stills reveal the way the fantasy scene harnesses desire and provokes the viewer through the partial object (Sherman's face) rather than an object that connotes wholeness. Sydney takes up this same position of the partial object.

The hard cut to the alias in *Alias* allows for Sydney to be the partial object because it does not present her as a whole authentic woman. The absence of any depiction of the preparation of the alias shows, at the same time, that the alias has no outside, just like the film stills of Cindy Sherman. The implication of this is not that deconstructing the ideology will simply tear it down, but instead that one must recognize the limit inherent in the language of authenticity itself.

The aliases neither serve to make her happier nor reveal her authentic self. And, yet, there is still something in this performance qua performance that represents Sydney as subject. Sydney seems sure of her abilities in espionage but never sure of her identity. She clearly embraces these performances as fiction, and it is her facility with this fiction—and her belief that it is only within the fiction that truth is discovered—that structures her identity and the show's discourse. Even when Sydney's own father can't remember something essential to national security, Sydney relies on creating a fantasy space to probe his mind for the truth. She and the agency recreate a scene of his past. She poses as her mother in a scene on a set the agency constructed to look exactly like his old house in 1981. In staging this scene, they discover that Jack revealed secrets to his wife, who was in fact a Russian undercover agent. They also recover the important location they were seeking for their mission.

THE MOTHER DOESN'T EXIST

The show posits that one reason Sydney has this unique skill as a detective—she understands that one must arouse the real of desire in order to arrive at truth—comes from the traumatic knowledge she has about her mother, specifically about the noncomplementary relationship between mother and child. The counterpoint to Sydney's aliases within the show itself is the way countries like the USSR demand far more difficult aliases from their women agents. The KGB demanded that Irina (Lena Olin), Sydney's mother, take on an alias full-time for decades. In order to infiltrate the CIA, she had to adopt a long-term fiction and even have a child with a CIA agent.

The line between the truth and the alias, in Irina's case, is constantly in question, especially for Sydney, who wonders if her mother ever loved her or if that motherly love was also a performance since she was conceived as part of Irina's alias (which was as wife of Jack Bristow, Sydney's father and a CIA agent). One of the recurrent motifs of the series is the ambiguity of Irina's desire. Trying to point to the complexity and the severity of Sydney's questions and questioning looks, Irina, several times throughout the series, replies with this phrase: "the truth takes time."[23] During their first encounter, Irina has Sydney tortured for information—but does not find any this way—and then Irina herself shoots Sydney in the arm. During the next encounter, Irina shows up again, and just when a viewer thinks she's going to kill Sydney, she instead kills someone trying to kill Sydney and tells her, mysteriously, "the truth takes time."

Later on in the series, in an episode titled "The Truth Takes Time" (season 2, episode 18), Irina leaves behind this same riddle for Sydney after she has escaped her captivity with the CIA (which she in part elected to endure to prove her love to Sydney). The message was left through Morse code that emanates out of her mother's earrings, which supposedly belonged to Sydney's grandmother. A seemingly contradictory artifact, the earrings fit perfectly within the form of the show. Passed down through three generations, the earrings are both high-tech and an ancestral heirloom. Common symbols of femininity, these diamond earrings have been refashioned in such a way that only a well-trained agent could decipher their message. As the reader of the message sent through Morse code, Sydney relies on her skills as an agent. Thus the earrings are employed in an unfeminine way, but ultimately the message they send is one sent by a mother to her daughter about their relationship.

The truth it points to, however, remains just as confused by the end of the series.[24] The truth, it turns out, is unattainable no matter how long you wait. It holds the place marker of the impossible in the mother-daughter relationship, which stems from the original deadlock of identity. In reaction to this emotional situation, Dixon tells her, "No one can be blamed for trusting her own mother." Implicit in this statement is the idea that no one can be blamed for her own mother's desire. Or that no one can be blamed for the fact that even her own mother has an unconscious.

Irina's professed love for Sydney seems evident in the way she looks at her and the sacrifices she makes for her at certain times. The relationship between Sydney and Irina reveals how fiction inserts itself even into what we believe are the most authentic relationships—between mother and daughter. The constant questioning of the maternal relationship points to the status of the real within the maternal. At the heart of the maternal relationship is not just a pure motherly love but rather a different version of Lacan's "there is no sexual relation": something like "there is no mother-child relation." Ideology relies on this relationship being seen as one that provides wholeness for both parties. The mother receives all she needs when she provides love, education, and protection for her child. What ideology does not allow room for is the woman's desire, which continues to exist even after she becomes a mother. *Alias*, however, suggests otherwise. It takes up Jacques-Alain Miller's statement that "woman takes precedence over the mother."[25] Behind every loving mother is a woman who is a desiring subject.

The angst-ridden investigation into the mother-daughter relationship that occurs over five years of this series provides an unusual opportunity to illuminate the noncomplementariness of that mother-child relationship. Within the structure of this series—set up by the fictional performances of Sydney's aliases and the privileging of Sydney as a desiring subject—the mother-daughter relationship necessarily had to be thrown into question. In turn, understanding this noncomplementariness helps Sydney come to a psychoanalytic conception of truth as the truth of the subject's desire. She is confronted with a mother (and an Other) whose desire she must investigate rather than trust, and this frees her from the biopolitical conception of truth, a conception based on the idea of a secure Other as the background against which one can uncover truth. *Alias* suggests that our relationship to truth depends on our recognition that the Other doesn't exist, that the secure bond informing our relations to others is not wholly symbolic and thus doesn't exist in the way ideology would like us to believe. Sydney's ability as a detective derives ultimately from her recognition that desire is as important as the facts.

DETECTING THE REAL

Sydney's mode of detection fundamentally sets her apart from Jack Bauer. She is a creator of fictions that capture desire rather than a torturer of bodies that contain a hidden truth. Her status as a detective also sets her apart from all the different kinds of biodetectives that appear in shows like *CSI* and films like *Zero Dark Thirty*. Sydney is instead a detective of the real. She excels at navigating or creating the web of fantasy within which she can often procure the real of the subject's desire. Recognizing the way the truth relates to the real, however, destroys many of her relationships (especially with her mother). But, at the same time, it allows for an ethics that acknowledges subjectivity and thus provides a real alternative to the biopolitical way of seeing the world.

Sydney does not look for what's hiding in plain sight like the classical detective, nor does she fully involve herself with the criminal like the hard-boiled detective. While she may at times display elements of both these forms of investigation, Sydney represents a new form that corresponds to the exigencies of the contemporary world. She is the foremost exemplar in contemporary film and television of the detective of the real. Though *Homeland* develops this form of detective as well, *Alias* presents it in the most unqualified way. As a detective of the real, Sydney sees lacking subjects rather than fully present bodies, and this enables her to interpret their desires rather than torturing their bodies.

Sydney approaches each case through the construction of a fiction that will provide access to the real of desire, and it is the commitment to fictionality that separates most clearly the detective of the real from other forms of the detective. Though other detectives employ fictions during their investigations—Auguste Dupin deploys a ruse in order to steal the stolen letter in "The Purloined Letter," for instance—they do not make fiction the foundation of their work in the way that Sydney does. The fiction is incidental for the classical and hard-boiled detectives, as it is for the biodetective. The biodetective places much more trust in information gained through torture or biometric surveillance than that which is obtained through a fiction. For the detective of the real, the situation is entirely different. The privileged position of the fiction enables the detective of the real to create a frame in which the subject's desire will emerge—and this desire holds the key to understanding why the subject acts as it does.

Within the world of *Alias*, a world built around this detective of the real, there is no psychic space for the development of the torture fantasy. The torture fantasy cannot take root. Its conception of the truth as embedded in the body, the image of the ticking clock, and the idea that truth is governed by power neither acknowledges subjectivity as such nor the subject's desire. *Alias* shows that we will only overcome our desperate willingness to resort to torture at the point when we accede to a conception of truth centered on the desiring subject rather than an object housed within the body.

The fundamental opposition today is that which exists between 24 and *Alias*. The great success of the former within the popular imagination and within political discourse signals the ascendance of biopolitical ideology. If we invest ourselves in this ideology, we invest in a logic that ultimately leads to the torture chamber. But the existence of *Alias* indicates that there is a viable, if less popular, alternative. The first step in struggling against biopower and the torture it produces consists in recognizing it as an ideology. Biopower functions not by controlling bodies but instead, like other ideologies, by harnessing the enjoyment and directing the desire of the subjects that it addresses. As an expression of biopower, the contemporary torture fantasy functions in a similar way. Disavowing this enjoyment, as I have argued throughout this book, is central to how the contemporary torture fantasy operates. The myriad representations of torture in film and on television, however, bring this enjoyment into view and suggest that it is possible to see the subject where a body appears. Seeing a subject instead of a body is the only true barrier to torture.

NOTES

INTRODUCTION: CONFRONTING THE ABU GHRAIB PHOTOGRAPHS

1. Many of these images can be viewed in the gallery that the *Guardian* put up as an attempt to make them available to the public: www.theguardian.com/gall/0,8542,1211872,00.html (accessed January 11, 2014).

2. George Bush, *Decision Points* (New York: Crown, 2010), 169.

3. Giorgio Agamben, *State of Exception*, trans. Kevin Attell (Chicago: University of Chicago Press, 2005), 3.

4. Agamben argues that there is a connection between American actions in the war on terror and those of the Nazis during World War II. This connection is evident in both official declarations—such as the designation *enemy combatant*—and in unofficial activities like the torture at Abu Ghraib.

5. See Barton Gellman and Dana Priest, "U.S. Decries Abuse but Defends Interrogations," *Washington Post*, December 26, 2002, www.washingtonpost.com/wp-dyn/content/article/2006/06/09/AR2006060901356.html (accessed February 11, 2014); and Eyal Press, "In Torture We Trust?" *Nation*, March 31, 2003, www.thenation.com/article/torture-we-trust (accessed February 11, 2014).

6. See Marc Lacey, "Iraqi Detainees Claim Abuse By British and U.S. Troops," *New York Times*, May 17, 2003, A11; and David Lamb, "When MPs' Push Becomes a Charge," *Los Angeles Times*, August 18, 2003, http://articles.latimes.com/2003/aug/18/nation/na-soldiers18 (accessed July 16, 2014).

7. See Jonathan Alter, "Time to Think About Torture," *Daily Beast*, November 3, 2004, www.thedailybeast.com/newsweek/2001/11/04/time-to-think-about-torture.html; and Alan Dershowitz, "The Case for Torture Warrants" (2002), www.alandershowitz.com/publications/docs/torturewarrants.html (accessed February 12, 2014).

8. Scholars such as Alessia Ricciardi have investigated the direct aesthetic connections between the Abu Ghraib images and past films. Ricciardi specifically looks at Pier Paolo Pasolini's *Salò or the 120 Days of Sodom* (1975) to unpack the relationship between violence and sexuality. She argues, "Watching *Salò* thirty years later, one finds that the film's provocative aesthetic appeal has not notably changed. However, with regard to its ideologically scandalous position, its use of sexuality as a metaphor for power, the story is different. *Salò*, it turns out, shares the most troubling elements of its iconography with the photographic record of torture at Abu Ghraib." Alessia Ricciardi, "Rethinking *Salò* After Abu Ghraib," *Postmodern Culture* 21, no. 3 (2011), http://muse.jhu.edu/ (accessed February 19, 2014).

9. President Obama signed an executive order in 2009 prohibiting any interrogation methods not authorized by and listed in the Army Field Manual. But human rights groups point out that this does little good when it is the Army Field Manual itself that needs to be rewritten. For example, it separates out "war on terror" prisoners as not subject to the same rights as prisoners of war. Additionally, this Appendix M, as it is labeled, allows for many enhanced interrogation techniques such as sleep deprivation, solitary confinement, and others. For further explanation see Jeffrey Kaye, "Contrary to Obama's Promises, the US Military Still Permits Torture," *Guardian*, January 25, 2014, http://www.theguardian.com/commentisfree/2014/jan/25/obama-administration-military-torture-army-field-manual (accessed February 19, 2014); and Scott Horton, "Obama's Black Sites," *Harper's Magazine*, May 12, 2010, http://harpers.org/blog/2010/05/obamas-black-sites/ (accessed February 19, 2014).

10. Wisnewski provides a comprehensive look at the many legal definitions of torture. J. Jeremy Wisnewski. *Understanding Torture* (Edinbugh: Edinburgh University Press, 2010), 5.

11. See Marquis de Sade, *Justine, or the Misfortunes of Virtue* (Cambridge: Oxford University Press, 2013), originally published in 1785; and *The 120 Days of Sodom, or the School of Licentiousness* (New York: Grove, 1994), originally published in 1787.

12. For other discussions of this history of torture, see Lisa Hajjar, *Torture: A Sociology of Violence and Human Rights* (New York: Routledge, 2013).

13. For an excellent discussion of the implications of this juridical approach, see Justin Clemens, *Psychoanalysis Is an Antiphilosophy* (Edinburgh: Edinburgh University Press, 2013).

14. Michel Foucault, *Discipline and Punish: The Birth of the Prison*, trans. Alan Sheridan (New York: Random House, 1978), 3.

15. The following is the exact wording of the Eight Amendment: "Excessive bail shall not be required, nor excessive fines imposed, nor cruel or unusual punishment inflicted." Many of the cases that have referred to the Eight Amendment have parsed

out whether a punishment was disproportionate to the offense in cases involving capital punishment or life imprisonment.

16. Generally evaluating what "cruel and unusual" means relies on what legal analysts often refer to as evolving standards of decency. Even as recently as 1972, the courts continued to work on defining these standards. In *Furman v. Georgia*, 408 U.S. 238, Justice Brennan elaborated that there are four principles that determine whether a punishment is cruel and unusual. First in this list was that a punishment must not degrade human dignity, and it specifically refers to torture as a prime example of such an offense.

17. The U.S.'s history is rife with examples of corrupt legal systems in which no one was prosecuted for these acts. It also has, however, many cases in which people have been prosecuted and convicted for these infractions.

18. The language of the Geneva Conventions reads: "No physical or mental torture, nor any other form of coercion, may be inflicted on prisoners of war to secure from them information of any kind whatever. Prisoners of war who refuse to answer may not be threatened, insulted, or exposed to unpleasant or disadvantageous treatment of any kind." Part 3, section 1, article 17.

19. Convention Against Torture and Other Cruel Inhuman or Degrading Treatment or Punishment was adopted by the General Assembly of the United Nations on December 10, 1984, and ratified by twenty nations on June 26, 1987. The work on this convention started in 1975 when a declaration was made to protect people from torture and a Commission of Human Rights studying the questions of torture was formed. As of September 2013, the Convention Against Torture has 154 signatories.

20. George W. Bush, "Statement in Support of Victims of Torture," White House Press Release (June 23, 2003).

21. *Memorandum for Alberto R. Gonzales*, counsel to the president, Re: Standards of Conduct for Interrogation Under 18 U.S.C (2340–2340A), U.S. Department of Justice, Office of Legal Counsel, filed August 1, 2002.

22. This was reported in the news. See, for example, "U.N.: U.S. Tortures Guantanamo Detainees. U.S. Takes Issue with Preliminary Report," *NBC News*, February 13, 2006, www.nbcnews.com/id/11333496/#.UvzatfYdRog (accessed February 1, 2014).

23. It is, of course, Louis Althusser who contends that the primary function of ideology involves interpellating individuals as subjects. Althusser's formulation seems especially out of date when we examine contemporary representations of torture. Even though this is an almost wholly ideological terrain, one finds bodies but not subjects.

24. This separation of mind and body forces Descartes and subsequent thinkers to try to resolve their interdependence. Descartes argues for their absolute distinction, but he nonetheless must accept that a reciprocal influence exists. This leads him to the most fantasmatic development within his thought—the pineal gland, a mysterious organ that functions as the site where mind and body interact.

25. Colette Soler, *Lacan, l'inconscient réinventé* (Paris: Presses Universitaires de France, 2009), 200.

26. Instead of theorizing mind and body as two possible sides of an opposition, psychoanalysis conceives of both sides as impossible to grasp. If we try to situate ourselves on the side of the mind, we don't just lose the body, but the mind as well. This is what Jacques Lacan is getting at in his account of the subject's fundamental division in *Seminar XI*. He states, "If we choose being, the subject disappears, it eludes us, it falls into non-meaning. If we choose meaning, the meaning survives only deprived of that part of non-meaning that is, strictly speaking, that which constitutes in the realization of the subject, the unconscious. In other words, it is of the nature of this meaning, as it emerges in the field of the Other, to be in a large part of its field, eclipsed by the disappearance of being, induced by the very function of the signifier." Jacques Lacan, *The Four Fundamental Concepts of Psychoanalysis*, trans. Alan Sheridan (New York: Norton, 1978), 211.

27. A. Kiarina Kordela attempts to synthesize the project of biopolitics and that of psychoanalysis, and she does so by viewing the body itself as an interruption in discourse. She claims, "A psychoanalytic theory of biopolitics . . . requires that Foucault's account of biopolitics be revised through a reconceptualization of the body and bios as the excess to, or lack in, discursive construction." A. Kiarina Kordela, *Being, Time, Bios: Capitalism and Ontology* (Albany: SUNY Press, 2013), xvi.

28. William Schultz, *The Phenomenon of Torture* (Philadelphia: University of Pennsylvania Press, 2007), 261.

29. We should nonetheless commend Schulz for arguing that torture doesn't work rather than just engaging in a moral diatribe against it. Calling into question the effectiveness of torture is one way of challenging the biopolitical ideology that grounds the practice of torture. But it fails in the end to undermine the torture fantasy because it doesn't emphasize the role that enjoyment plays in torture. This critique recognizes that torture doesn't produce truth, but it doesn't recognize what torture does effectively produce—that is, enjoyment.

30. Julia Lesage, "Torture Documentaries," *Jump Cut: A Review of Contemporary Media* 51 (2009).

31. See Jean Lartéguy, *Les Centurions* (Paris: Presses de la Cité, 1960).

32. In an interview with Mike Wallace on *60 Minutes*, Alan Dershowitz supported torture in the case of the ticking bomb scenario and said, "If anybody had the ability to prevent the events of Sept. 11 . . . they would have gone to whatever length." The justification is always tied to a retroactive explanation. David Kohn, "Legal Torture?: Civil Libertarian Believes Torture Will Be Used in War on Terrorism," *60 Minutes*, January 17, 2002, www.cbsnews.com/news/legal-torture/ (accessed February 11, 2013).

33. Political scientist Darius Rejali notes, "But too often fantasy sells better than reality. *Les Centurions* won the Prix Eve Delocroix in 1960 and sold half a million copies, a privilege no book on the real Algerian war can claim. It won praise for its military realism, and French Paras embraced the novel." Darius Regali, *Torture and Democracy* (Princeton: Princeton University Press, 2007), 547.

1. TORTURE, BIOPOWER, AND THE DESIRING SUBJECT   165

34. Ibid., 487–488.

35. Rejali explains, "A survey of the famous cases suggests as well that interrogators who did not torture were more successful in harvesting accurate, timely information. . . . Contrast these cases with the four important prisoners who were tortured, Ben M'hidi (the head of the FLN in Algiers), George Hadhadj (editor of the underground newspaper), Ali Boumandjel (the FLN foreign minister), and Henri Alleg (editor of the *Alger Républicain*). These prisoners gave up nothing other than their identity as opposition members, and two were killed to avoid bad publicity." Regali, *Torture and Democracy*, 490.

36. The effectiveness of the ticking bomb scenario also has its basis in fundamental anxieties that accompany modern democracy. Journalist Jane Mayer explains, "Lartéguy's scenario exploited an insecurity shared by many liberal societies—that their enlightened legal systems had made them vulnerable to security threats." Jane Mayer, "Whatever It Takes: The Politics of the Man Behind 24," *New Yorker*, February 19, 2007, www.newyorker.com/reporting/2007/02/19/070219fa_fact_mayer?currentPage=all (accessed Februrary 12, 2014).

37. See www.parentstv.org.

38. Stephen Prince, *Firestorm: American Film in the Age of Terrorism* (New York: Columbia University Press, 2009), 240.

39. In *The Phenomenology of Spirit*, Hegel claims, "truth is not a minted coin that can be given and pocketed ready-made. Nor *is* there such a thing as the false, any more than there *is* something evil." G. W. F. Hegel, *The Phenomenology of Spirit*, trans. A. V. Miller (Oxford: Oxford University Press, 1977), 22.

40. *Alias* provides an implicit critique of the political philosophy of Carl Schmitt, which views politics as dependent on the distinction between friend and enemy. During every season of the series, it becomes impossible to distinguish clearly between a friend and an enemy, and the two positions often switch multiples times.

1. TORTURE, BIOPOWER, AND THE DESIRING SUBJECT

1. For some of the main evolutionary thinkers today, see Richard Dawkins, *The Selfish Gene* (Oxford: Oxford University Press, 2006); Daniel Dennett, *Darwin's Dangerous Idea: Evolution and the Meanings of Life* (New York: Simon and Schuster, 1996); Steven Pinker, *The Blank Slate: The Modern Denial of Human Nature* (New York: Penguin, 2003); Edward O. Wilson, *Social Conquest of Earth* (New York: Liveright, 2012); and Robert Wright, *Moral Animal: Why We Are, the Way We Are: The New Science of Evolutionary Psychology* (New York: Vintage, 1995).

2. Many contemporary psychoanalytic cultural theorists write about this desiring subject as a subject at the heart of politics and philosophy, and in doing so they are interrogating how desire and politics work together. See Richard Boothby, *Freud as Philosopher* (New Brunswick, NJ: Routledge, 2001); Jennifer Friedlander, *Feminine Look: Sexuation, Spectatorship, Subversion* (New York, SUNY Press, 2009); Paul Eisenstein and Todd McGowan, *Rupture: On the Emergence of the Political* (Chicago:

Northwestern University Press, 2012); Yannis Stavrakakis, *The Lacanian Left* (New York: SUNY Press, 2007); Slavoj Žižek, *The Ticklish Subject: The Absent Center of Political Ontology* (New York: Verso, 2009); and Alenka Zupenčič, *Ethics of the Real: Kant and Lacan* (New York: Verso, 2012).

3. René Descartes, *Meditations on First Philosophy*, trans. John Cottingham (Cambridge: Cambridge University Press, 1986), 59.

4. This is not an unchallenged view. There have been several attempts to marry biopolitics and psychoanalysis. See, for instance, A. Kiarina Kordela, *Being, Time, Bios: Capitalism and Ontology* (Albany: SUNY Press, 2013).

5. I often equate biopower and biopolitics because, as I argue in what follows, both operate according to the same fundamental assumption concerning the philosophical priority of the body and the absence of a subject complicating this body's self-identity.

6. The term *biopower* first became popular as a result of Michel Foucault's mention of it in the first volume of the *History of Sexuality*. Describing this new form of power, he writes, "there was an explosion of numerous and diverse techniques for achieving the subjugation of bodies and the control of populations, marking the beginning of an era of 'biopower.'" Michael Foucault, *The History of Sexuality*, vol. 1: *An Introduction*, trans. Robert Hurley (New York: Random House, 1978), 140.

7. Gilles Deleuze and Félix Guattari, *A Thousand Plateaus: Capitalism and Schizophrenia*, trans. Brian Massumi (Minneapolis: University of Minnesota Press, 1987), 90.

8. Though there are vast differences between the thought of Foucault and that of Deleuze, this is their fundamental point of intersection and what constitutes the basis for their philosophical comradeship. Both are champions of the body and critics of the signifier for the violence that it does to the body.

9. Michel Foucault, *Security, Nation, Population: Lectures at the Collège de France, 1977—1978* (New York: Picador, 2009), 1.

10. Michel Foucault, *Society Must Be Defended: Lectures at the College de France, 1975–1976* (New York: Picador, 1997), 247.

11. Michel Foucault, *History of Sexuality*, 1:142–143.

12. See Foucault, *Security, Nation, Population*.

13. Foucault offers a famous celebration of the body at the end of the first volume of *The History of Sexuality*. He says, "It is the agency of sex that we must break away from, if we aim—through a tactical reversal of the various mechanisms of sexuality—to counter the grips of power with the claims of bodies, pleasures, and knowledges, in their multiplicity and their possibilities of resistance. The rallying point for the counterattack against the deployment of sexuality ought not to be sex-desire, but bodies and pleasures." Foucault, *The History of Sexuality*, 1:157.

14. It should not be at all surprising that Foucault wrote a panegyric to *Anti-Oedipus* when prefacing that work. His position on the body as the site of resistance is exactly congruous with that of Deleuze and Guattari.

15. Michael Hardt and Antonio Negri, *Multitude: War and Democracy in the Age of Empire* (New York: Penguin, 2004), 158.

16. Roberto Esposito also calls for a positive biopolitics as a potential antidote. See Roberto Esposito, *Bios: Biopolitics and Philosophy* (Minneapolis: University of Minnesota Press, 2008).

17. For Agamben, bare life appears exactly where political freedom should be. He says, "Modern democracy's specific aporia: it wants to put the freedom and happiness of men into play in the very place—'bare life'—that marked their subjection." Giorgio Agamben, *Homo Sacer: Sovereign Power and Bare Life* (Palo Alto: Stanford University Press, 1998), 9–10.

18. Ibid., 127.

19. See Hannah Arendt, *The Origins of Totalitarianism* (New York: Harcourt Brace, 1951); Walter Benjamin, *Illuminations,* trans. Harry Zohn (New York: Schocken, 1989); Carl Schmidt, *Political Theology: Four Chapters on the Concept of Sovereignty* (Chicago: University of Chicago Press, 2006).

20. Giorgio Agamben, *Means Without End: Notes on Politics* (Minneapolis: University of Minnesota Press, 2000), 7.

21. Ibid., 59.

22. Ibid., 56.

23. Louis Althusser, "Ideology and Ideological State Apparatuses," in *Lenin and Philosophy and Other Essays,* trans. Ben Brewster (New York: Monthly Review Press, 1971), 171.

24. Slavoj Žižek, *The Sublime Object of Ideology* (New York: Verso, 1989), 45.

25. W. J. T. Mitchell, *Cloning Terror: The War of Images, 9/11 to the Present* (Chicago: University of Chicago Press, 2011), 71.

26. Even though Freud never discusses the signifier in the way that Lacan does, he nonetheless chronicles how subjection to the signifier disturbs the individual and constitutes the subject. The attention that psychoanalysis pays to language as decisive is not a pure addition that Lacan makes but is present at least implicitly from the beginning.

27. No matter how diligently they work to engage psychoanalytic theory, constructivists will always run up against the role that the body plays in it and will view it as too naturalist. On the other side, naturalists will always dismiss psychoanalytic theory as too committed to constructivism. The point is not that psychoanalysis is a compromise position between the two but that it excludes completely the two alternatives.

28. Sigmund Freud, *Dora: An Analysis of a Case of Hysteria,* trans. James Strachey (New York: Collier, 1963), 105.

29. Jacques Lacan, *The Four Fundamental Concepts of Psychoanalysis,* trans. Alan Sheridan (New York: Norton, 1978), 39.

30. Jacques Lacan, *Le Séminaire, livre XVI: D'un Autre à l'autre, 1968–1969,* ed. Jacques-Alain Miller (Paris: Seuil, 2006), 321. A few years later, he makes an even more direct statement about the relationship between enjoyment and the real. He claims, "enjoyment is from the real." Jacques Lacan, *Le Séminaire, livre XXIII: Le sinthome, 1975–1976,* ed. Jacques-Alain Miller (Paris: Seuil, 2005), 78.

1. TORTURE, BIOPOWER, AND THE DESIRING SUBJECT

31. Sigmund Freud, *Notes Upon a Case of Obsessional Neurosis*, trans. Alix Strachey and James Strachey, in *The Standard Edition of the Complete Psychological Works of Sigmund Freud*, ed. James Strachey (London: Hogarth, 1955), 10:166.

32. Ibid, 167.

33. Torture is in no way residue from the past. J. Jeremy Wisnewski points out that we should not assume we are beyond torture, that this is partly what creates problems in thinking about it and making astute political and juridical prohibitions on torture. See J. Jeremy Wisnewski, *Understanding Torture* (Edinburgh: Edinburgh University Press, 2010).

34. Slavoj Žižek, *Violence* (New York: Picador, 2008), 45.

2. THE NONSENSICAL SMILE OF THE TORTURER IN POST-9/11 DOCUMENTARY FILMS

1. Even though we tend to think of fantasy as illogical and unstructured, every fantasy obeys a precise logic, which is what enables it to be effective in obscuring the gaps in ideology. Jacques Lacan traces this logic in his "Seminar XIV," entitled "The Logic of Fantasy." See Jacques Lacan, "Séminaire XIV: La logique du fantasme," unpublished manuscript.

2. Jacques Lacan, *The Four Fundamental Concepts of Psychoanalysis*, trans. Alan Sheridan (New York: Norton, 1978), 104.

3. For more work on gaze as stain, see Joan Copjec, *Read My Desire* (Cambridge: MIT Press, 1994); Slavoj Žižek, *Looking Awry: An Introduction to Jacques Lacan Through Popular Culture* (Cambridge: MIT Press, 1992); Jennifer Friedlander, *The Feminine Look: Sexuation, Spectatorship, Subversion* (Albany: State University of New York Press, 2008); Todd McGowan, *The Real Gaze: Film Theory After Lacan* (Albany: State University of New York Press, 2007); and Hilary Neroni, "Documenting the Gaze: Psychoanalysis and Judith Helfand's *Blue Vinyl* and Agnes Varda's *The Gleaners and I*," *Quarterly Review of Film and Video* 27, no. 2 (2010).

4. Mulvey's conception of the gaze became so dominant in film studies that it completely obscured Lacan's understanding of the gaze as the point that disrupts the image. *Screen* theory thus had the effect of eliminating disruption, which is the key to any psychoanalytic interpretation.

5. Slavoj Žižek, *Living in the End Times* (London: Verso, 2010), 400.

6. Žižek is at once more pessimistic than *Screen* theory and more optimistic about ideology. He theorizes the subject's investment in ideology as much more thorough than *Screen* theory, but at the same time, he sees the necessity of gaps within ideology from which one can mount a challenge to it.

7. Slavoj Žižek, "'I Hear You with My Eyes'; Or, The Invisible Master," in *Gaze and Voice as Love Objects*, ed. Renata Salecl and Slavoj Žižek (Durham: Duke University Press, 90–128), 115.

8. Ibid.

2. THE NONSENSICAL SMILE OF THE TORTURER   169

9. Yannis Stavrakakis, *The Lacanian Left: Psychoanalysis, Theory, Politics* (Albany: SUNY Press, 2007), 243.

10. Susan Sontag, "Regarding the Torture of Others," www.nytimes.com/2004/05/23/magazine/23PRISONS.html (accessed June 15, 2009).

11. See www.salon.com/news/abu_ghraib/2006/03/14/introduction/ (accessed January 23, 2014).

12. Brian Whitaker says, "In contrast, opinions of Patai's book among Middle East experts at US universities are almost universally scathing. 'The best use for this volume, if any, is as a doorstop,' one commented. 'The book is old, and a thoroughly discredited form of scholarship,' said another. None of the academics I contacted thought the book suitable for serious study, although Georgetown University once invited students to analyse it as 'an example of bad, biased social science.'" Brian Whitaker, "'Its Best Use Is as a Doorstop,'" *Guardian*, May 24, 2004, www.theguardian.com/world/2004/may/24/worlddispatch.usa (accessed February 28, 2014).

13. Ibid.

14. Raphael Patai, *The Arab Mind*, rev. ed. (New York: Haterleigh, 2002), 130.

15. Whitaker, "'Its Best Use Is as a Doorstop.'"

16. In discussing the historical situatedness of documentaries, Paula Rabinowitz says, "The cinematic choices these visionary directors made have an eerie parallel in the diminished political possibilities available in the Reagan era. As such the films serve as guides to the place of women in the nation, the place of language in identity, the place of documentary in politics." Paula Rabinowitz, *They Must Be Represented: The Politics of Documentary* (New York: Verso, 1994), 204. Though she is discussing a different group of films, her point still resonates for these current documentaries about Abu Ghraib. As they do battle with much of the American government and media about torture, they are also evidence of the narrowed symbolic discourse surrounding these important moments.

17. For lengthy investigations on this topic, see a Mark Danner, *Torture and Truth: America, Abu Ghraib, and the War on Terror* (New York: New York Review of Books, 2004); Jane Mayer, *The Dark Side: The Inside Story of How The War on Terror Turned Into a War on American Ideals* (New York: Doubleday, 2008); and Alfred McCoy, *A Question of Torture: CIA Interrogation, from the Cold War to the War on Terror* (New York: Holt, 2006).

18. Linda Williams considers the role of the frame in the war photo. Through this line of investigation, she analyzes *Standard Operating Procedures,* about which she argues, "I hope to demonstrate that it can help show us the difference between a frame that 'conducts dehumanizing norms' and a frame that might be capable of questioning these very norms to open up our seeing and knowledge to elusive and contingent truths that lie beyond the frame's limits." Linda Williams, "Cluster Fuck: The Forcible Frame in Errol Morris's *Standard Operating Procedure*," *Camera Obscura* 73, 25, no. 1 (2010): 31.

19. Jonathan Kahana argues that *Standard Operating Procedure* does not ask enough of the soldiers in the interview. Similarly, he sees the reenactments and the narrative

170   2. THE NONSENSICAL SMILE OF THE TORTURER

structure of the film as too understated to arrive at any kind of truth. He says, "In this way, various forms of narration in the film create a self-enclosed economy of discourse about torture at Abu Ghraib, a system within which the statements of the accused have the effect not of confessions but of excuses." Jonathan Kahana, "Speech Images: *Standard Operating Procedure* and the Staging of Interrogation," *Jump Cut: A Review of Contemporary Media* 52 (2010), www.ejumpcut.org/archive/jc52.2010/sopkKahana/index.html (accessed February 27, 2014).

20. Julia Lesage, "Torture Documentaries," *Jump Cut: A Review of Contemporary Media* 51 (2009): 51, www.ejumpcut.org/archive/jc51.2009/TortureDocumentaries/text.html (accessed February 19, 2014).

21. Caetlin Benson-Allott proffers a different theory. She argues, "For if Morris is indeed suggesting that Harman possesses no better understanding of the woman in the photo than any other viewer, then he is also acknowledging the limits of his documentary." Caetlin Benson-Allott, "*Standard Operating Procedure:* Mediating Torture," *Film Quarterly* 62, no. 4 (2009): 41.

22. Kris Fallon documents Errol Morris's persistent interest in photography and its implications. He claims he looks at photography, such as the Abu Ghraib photos, in several ways. He says, "One might even be tempted to go further and credit Morris's twin alter egos, the philosopher and the detective, for each of the works, one doggedly tracking down the facts while the other tackles the more slippery issues of human consciousness." Kris Fallon, "Several Sides of Errol Morris," *Film Quarterly* 65, no. 4 (2012): 48–49.

23. Another potential interpretation of *Standard Operating Procedure* is as a reframing of those in the photographs. Just as inscrutable and ultimately mysterious, Morris's new frame provides some interpretation but insists on the confines of the frame itself to hint at the impossibility of finding an explanation.

24. Arguing that *Standard Operating Procedure* does not engage the viewers in a way that truly exposes the heart of the issues, Thomas Austin says, "I suggest that in *Standard Operating Procedure* these conventional proposals of how the viewer should respond, ethically and politically, become ambiguous, uncertain or unconvincing. As a result, the film's insertion of the events at Abu Ghraib into a discursive framework that might render them both legible and 'useful' (that is, of moral and political significance) is compromised." Thomas Austin, "*Standard Operating Procedure,* 'the Mystery of Photography' and the Politics of Pity," *Screen* 52, no. 3 (2011): 344.

25. Errol Morris was as concerned with what the photos concealed. For example, they concealed what happened in the interrogation rooms since they only depicted the interaction with the MPs. Morris explains, "One thing I'm very fond of pointing out is that photographs can both reveal and conceal. They can serve as an exposé just as well as a cover-up. And that's exactly what happened with these photographs. They concealed almost everything about Abu Ghraib." Quoted in Howard Feinstein, "Beyond the Frame," *Sight and Sound* 18, no. 7 (2008): 34 (accessed February 19, 2014) It's possible that Morris saw the smile at the heart of the photograph as concealing some sort of truth.

26. Julia Lesage makes the excellent point that Alex Gibney employs other dramatic photos to help make his point and bring in a different kind of emotional resonance. They are photos that photojournalists have taken that emphasize the power relations between the U.S. and the detainees or those being arrested. "By using the previously artfully-composed images of photojournalists, Gibney can make political points, borrow the images' emotional impact, or set up his own ironic contrasts in an astute way." Lesage, "Torture Documentaries." Lesage here points to the way that Gibney recognizes the emotional and political tie in these photos and then puts them in play alongside the Abu Ghraib photos.

27. In discussing the form of *Taxi to the Dark Side*, Julia Lesage argues that there is more aesthetic development in the presentation of other visual material. The film, she suggests, contributes to the viewer's emotional investment in the prisoners through these drawings and reenactments. She says, "The film is edited around the recurring image of a Bagram prison cell, showing shackles and chains dangling from the ceiling, from which prisoners were hung by raised hands. The recurrence of this image elicits ever-greater horror as the narrative circles back to it and as we know more of the background of torture, especially at Bagram." Lesage, "Torture Documentaries."

28. Kant's great achievement in moral philosophy is to remove duty from the domain of sentiment where it had been mired and to show that our duty lifts us above the world of feelings.

29. Paula Rabinowitz argues, "Neither the eye nor the camera can take in wholeness; wholeness, like Georg Lukács's totality, is a dream. Partiality is the province of the lens, whether in the eye or the camera." Rabinowitz, *They Must Be Represented*, 208–209. She goes on to suggest that it's the documentary directors that really push this formal nature that allows the viewer to think through the implication of our perception of the body. Clearly the depiction of bodies in the Abu Ghraib photos is not one of whole bodies. They are bodies made into partial objects, objects in the contemporary torture fantasy. And while these documentaries work to destroy that fantasy, they at times miss this fantastical element in the service of providing a whole story.

30. In *The Interpretation of Dreams*, Freud describes kettle logic. He notes, "[a man] was charged by one of his neighbours with having given him back a borrowed kettle in a damaged condition. The defendant asserted first, that he had given it back undamaged; secondly, that the kettle had a hole in it when he borrowed it; and thirdly, that he had never borrowed the kettle from his neighbour at all. So much the better: if only a single one of these three lines of defence were to be accepted as valid, the man would have to be acquitted." Sigmund Freud, *The Interpretation of Dreams*, in *The Standard Edition of the Complete Psychological Works of Sigmund Freud*, trans. and ed. James Strachey (London: Hogarth, 1953), 4:120.

31. Joan Copjec, *Imagine There's No Woman: Ethics and Sublimation* (Cambridge: MIT Press, 2002), 167.

32. Sontag, "Regarding the Torture of Others."

172   3. TORTURE PORN AND THE DESIRING SUBJECT

33. Dora Apel, "Torture Culture: Lynching Photographs and the Images of Abu Ghraib," *Art Journal*, 64, no. 2 (Summer 2005): 89.

34. Ibid.

3. TORTURE PORN AND THE DESIRING SUBJECT IN *HOSTEL* AND *SAW*

1. Jerod Hollyfield feels that the *torture porn* label has obscured the more interesting aspects of the subgenre. He says, "For Roth, the torture of the film does not act as pornography, but a glimpse into the overlooked specters that manifest when post–Cold War nationalism and the forces of the globalized market collide with American cultural perspectives." Jerod Ra'Del Hollyfield, "Torture Porn and Bodies Politic: Post–Cold War American Perspectives in Eli Roth's *Hostel* and *Hostel: Part II*," *Cineaction* 78 (2009): 28. And while I agree that these films should not be dismissed out of hand for their more conservative aspects, I do feel that the *porn* in *torture porn* is apropos if only for the nod toward the sexual nature that these horror films reveal at the heart of torture itself, which contradicts the contemporary fantasy about a cleaner, more purposeful type of torture.

2. David Edelstein, "Now Playing at Your Local Multiplex: Torture Porn," *New York Times Magazine* (2006), http://nymag.com/movies/features/15622/ (accessed July 18, 2014).

3. The imagery from media representations of torture can also be seen in other representational landscapes. As Andre Mayer observes, "Torture has even invaded our urban landscape. Last month, the Motion Picture Association of America reprimanded U.S. film company After Dark Films for a billboard promoting the upcoming thriller *Captivity*. In it, Canadian actress Elisha Cuthbert plays a supermodel who is kidnapped and tormented by a deranged fan. The offending ad, which appeared in New York and Los Angeles, featured Cuthbert in four panels, labeled 'Abduction,' 'Confinement,' 'Torture' and 'Termination.' In the final frame, she appears to be dead. While After Dark has yanked the ad, the film's current poster—in which Cuthbert looks to be buried alive—is no less vexing." Andre Mayer, "The Crying Game: Why Torture Scenes Have Gone Mainstream," *CBC Arts and Film*, April 11, 2007, http://web.archive.org/web/20070703045949/http://www.cbc.ca/arts/film/torture.html (accessed February 11, 2014).

4. The *Saw* films include James Wan's *Saw* (2004), Darren Lynn Bousman's *Saw II* (2005), *Saw III* (2006), *Saw IV* (2007), David Hackl's *Saw V* (2008), Kevin Greutert's *Saw VI* (2009), and Kevin Greutert's *Saw 3D: The Final Chapter* (2010).

5. Other examples of torture porn films include *Captivity* (Roland Joffe, 2007), *Carver* (Andrew van den Houten, 2008), *The Collector* (Arkin O'Brien, 2009), *Offspring* (Franklin Guerrero Jr., 2009), *The Human Centipede: First Sequence* (Tom Six, 2010), and *The Woman* (Lucky McKee, 2011).

6. While many have embraced the term *torture porn*, for some scholars this has been an unfortunate trend. Lowenstein argues, for example, that *torture porn* is not the best name for this group of films and instead argues for the term *spectacle horror*.

"Spectacle horror's 'loudness' as a mode of direct, visceral engagement with viewers distinguishes it from 'quieter' forms of what we might call 'ambient horror,' but this distinction should not mandate the negative value judgments that structure torture porn as a category." Adam Lowenstein, "Spectacle Horror and *Hostel*: Why 'Torture Porn' Does Not Exist," *Critical Quarterly* 53, no. 1 (2011): 42.

7. Maisha Wester claims that it has to do with the types of villains and heroes. She says, "As post–War on Terror narratives, the Splat Packs' films trouble the lines between torturer, victim, villain, and hero. In other words, at a time when the political moral efficacy of torture was centered in political debates, these directors and writers visualized the difficulty of reducing such acts to permissible or unpardonable. Notably, most of the films . . . feature average Americans both as tortured victim and torturing hero." Maisha Wester, "Torture Porn and Uneasy Feminisms: Rethinking (Wo)men in Eli Roth's Hostel Films," *Quarterly Review of Film and Video* 29, no. 5 (2012): 389. I agree here with Wester and would emphasize that this allows the films to turn away from the demands of biopower.

8. The evanescence of the musical as a dominant genre in Hollywood is very misleading. Though Hollywood rarely makes musicals today, the concern of the musical—locating and exploring how the subject enjoys itself—continues in new generic manifestations like action films, pornography, and torture porn. The set pieces in these genres interrupt the narrative with an outburst of enjoyment.

9. Evangelos Tziallas, "Torture Porn and Surveillance Culture," *Jump Cut: A Review of Contemporary Media* 52 (Summer 2010), http://www.ejumpcut.org/archive/jc52.2010/evangelosTorturePorn/ (accessed July 20, 2014).

10. Jacques Lacan, "Kant with Sade," in *Écrits: The First Complete Edition in English*, trans. Bruce Fink (New York: Norton, 2006), 656.

11. This is the central point in Lacan's analysis of sadism. See ibid., 645–668.

12. While complicated in its own right, the television show *Homeland*, though not in any way a part of the horror genre, has certain plot lines that also depict torture as damaging the victim's psychic structure, as accessing and disturbing the victim's unconscious.

13. Kevin Wetmore notes the *Hostel* films relation to American torture. He says, "The first film engages the fear of being tortured and the fear of torture in general. The second film engages the fear of becoming a torturer and the ambiguity of rendition, enhanced interrogation and the 'ticking bomb' justification for torture." Kevin J. Wetmore, *Post-9/11 Horror in American Cinema* (New York: Continuum, 2013), 105.

14. The simplistic depiction of Slovakia functions, for Jerod Hollyfield, as a critique of America. He explains, "As a result, while Roth may appear to eschew an accurate portrayal of present-day Slovakia, he presents a portrait of a nation whose history is in service to a globalized economy that absorbs national legacies into its own order." Jerod Hollyfield, "Torture Porn and Bodies Politic," 25.

15. Wetmore makes the observation that there might even be a regressive turn back in representation of women in horror films when he points out that the final girl, who was a marker of potential female power or triumph made famous by Carol

Clover, has disappeared in contemporary horror. He says, "Clover's famous 'final girl' becomes the 'final couple' in the remake of *Friday the 13th* or *Hatchet*. The 'final girls' of *Wolf Creek*, *The Devil's Rejects*, and *Martyrs* all die horrible, painful deaths, despite their resourcefulness." Wetmore, *Post-9/11 Horror in American Cinema*, 15.

16. See Carol Clover, *Men, Women, and Chain Saws: Gender in the Modern Horror Film* (Princeton: Princeton University Press, 1992).

17. Jason Middleton, "The Subject of Torture: Regarding the Pain of Americans in *Hostel*," *Cinema Journal* 49, no. 4 (Summer 2012): 9.

18. Sigmund Freud, *Three Essays on the Theory of Sexuality*, trans. James Strachey, in *The Complete Psychological Works of Sigmund Freud*, trans. and ed. James Strachey (London: Hogarth, 1953), 7:158.

19. During a scene in which the friends are out jogging, they link sexual experience with manhood when they discuss the first kid that had sex in class and how they knew it. In one scene, Todd says to Stuart, "Sometimes you meet a guy and there's just something fucking scary about him. Something that makes you think: this guy has killed somebody. He doesn't have to act tough. He never has to say it. But like an animal, you can sense it. You know that this guy's got the balls to do what few others can. And that's you after today my friend. People are going to fucking fear you. Linda is going to fucking fear you. What we do today is going to pay off everyday for the rest of our fucking lives." For these characters, though not for all the torturers depicted in this film, torture can be seen as a potent signifier of masculinity.

20. See, for example, Giorgio Agamben, *The State of Exception*, trans. Keven Atell (Chicago: University of Chicago Press, 2005).

21. About this scene, Wester points out that it reveals not that Stuart is excluded from patriarchal power but that he pursues it in other forms, notably torture. She explains, "His violence expresses not only a latent brutal desire and attitude towards his wife but a socially suppressed privilege to which his position as patriarch traditionally allows him access. Social mandate requires him to suppress such violent impulses, yet success within the market allows him renewed access in extreme ways." Wester, "Torture Porn and Uneasy Feminisms," 392.

22. Unlike the *Hostel* films, the *Saw* films do not traverse national boundaries. As McCann argues, "The Saw films situate horror in the everyday world of contemporary America but do not project that horror onto a foreign invader." Ben McCann, "Body Horror," in *See the Saw Movies: Essays on Torture Porn and Post-9/11 Horror*, ed. James Aston and John Walliss (London: McFarland, 2013), 42.

23. Dean Lockwood says that *Saw* should also be read as an expression of contemporary capitalism. He says, "My argument situates *Saw* in the context of mutations of capital and ensuing transformations of labor, specifically, the affective dimension of labor." Dean Lockwood, "Work Is Hell: Life in the Mannequin Factory," in Aston and Walliss, *See the Saw Movies*, 141.

24. Sharrett points out that the killer is also a completely mundane figure. He argues, "Jigsaw, the disgruntled, middle-class white male professional, fits in a long tradition of male characters fed up with democratic institutions, determined to set their own rules." Christopher Sharrett, "The Problem of *Saw*," *Cineast* 35 (2009).

25. Steve Jones points out that the ticking clock is also an important part of the Saw films. About the torture traps in the films, he says, "All of these traps are restricted by time as well as space (countdown timers limit the victims' options), making explicit the connection between spatial and temporal control." Steve Jones, "'Time Is Wasting': Con/sequence and S/pace in the Saw Series," *Horror Studies* 1, no. 2 (2010): 226. This provides insight into another biopolitical link to the theme of the countdown clock in 24 as linked to the justification of torture. Of course, unlike 24, in which torture always succeeds, in the *Saw* films torture always fails to be productive.

26. Michel Foucault, *"Society Must Be Defended": Lectures at the Collège de France, 1975–1976*, trans. David Macey (New York: Picador, 2003), 256.

27. Roberto Esposito, *Bíos: Biopolitics and Philosophy*, trans. Timothy Campbell (Minneapolis: University of Minnesota Press, 2008), 137.

28. The fact of Kramer's own imminent death indicates that the lesson he is trying to impart to others through torture is really a lesson for himself. Torture always reveals more about the torturer than it does the victim, despite the fact that the torture fantasy and Kramer privilege the knowledge that the victim has or will have.

29. Lockwood writes about attempts to censor torture porn, and he suggests that torture porn, in fact, could play a liberating role. But he argues that ultimately it falls short of anything radical because it is too mired in the horror genre itself. He says, "In terms of its affective strategies it is mired in the typical. The problem with torture porn cinema, as I see it, is that it fails to achieve sufficient escape velocity, so to speak, to disrupt the clichés of the aesthetic tropes to which it consistently refers." Dean Lockwood, "All Stripped Down: The Spectacle of 'Torture Porn,'" *Popular Communications* 7 (2009): 47.

30. Critics have tended to view torture porn as inherently conservative. For instance, Sharrett argues that torture porn marks a nadir in the horror genre. He argues, "It is important, I think, to place *Saw* and other such films in the context of genre history, recognizing that the issue at the center of any critique is not so much hoary arguments about the role of violence in cinema, but the regressive nature of popular cinema in the current moment, its sense of the worthlessness of human beings, and the horror film's embrace of dominant ideas about power and repression." Christopher Sharrett, "The Problem of *Saw*: 'Torture Porn' and the Conservatism of Contemporary Horror Films," *Cineaste* 35, no. 1 (Winter 2009): 37.

4. 24, JACK BAUER, AND THE TORTURE FANTASY

1. Howard Rosenberg, "Deft Timing Makes 24 Tick: Fox's new drama covers an hour of its characters' lives in each episode, building up suspense minute by minute," *Los Angeles Times* (November 6 2001): F1.

2. The use of a real-time narrative has a few antecedents in film, and they almost always use real time to create a sense of urgency, just as 24 does. In the classic example, Alfred Hitchcock's *Rope* (1948), the two murderers are on the verge of being caught for the crime during of the film's real time narrative. Hitchcock furthers the sense of urgency by eliminating obvious cuts, which differs considerably from the multilayered 24.

3. Dana Calvo, "Intrigue at Its Own Pace: With each episode covering one hour of an anti-terror agent's harrowing day, 24 bets viewers will be in the mood-for the plot device and the subject." *Los Angeles Times* (October 28, 2001): F6.

4. Christian Smith, "FOX Premieres Innovative Concept Tonight on 24," *Michigan Daily* (November 6, 2001), www.michigandaily.com.

5. The dense narrative complexity of *Veronica Mars* (2004–2007), for example, both intrigued and sometimes confused audiences but became a fundamental part of their identification with the series.

6. The powerful nature of this fantasy leads some opponents of torture to acknowledge that they would consent to torture in the ticking bomb scenario. But they insist on the exceptional status of the situation and refuse to use it as a basis for legitimizing or normalizing torture.

7. Martin Heidegger, *Being and Time*, trans. John Macquarrie and Edward Robinson (San Francisco: Harper and Row, 1962), 479.

8. This was especially true in fundamentalist Christian circles, where author Hal Lindsey popularized the notion of a coming apocalypse with *The Late, Great Planet Earth* (1970) and *The 1980s: Countdown to Armageddon* (1980). But even respected atomic scientists formed the doomsday clock in 1947, with which they measured how close the planet was to nuclear destruction on the basis of current international relations. This symbolic clock calculates time on the basis of how many minutes before midnight—or total annihilation—we have. Currently, it is 11:55 on this countdown. Hal Lindsey's *Countdown*, however, is now out of print.

9. The film *2012* (Roland Emmerich, 2009) represents the ultimate expression of the anxiety about the end of the world predicted by the Mayan calendar.

10. There are many films that struggle against the notion that we are just finite beings, often aiming directly at time itself. Here we might consider the way that recent films such as Christopher Nolan's *Inception* (2012) or Michel Gondry's *Eternal Sunshine of the Spotless Mind* (2004) use temporal disjuncture in the narrative in order to investigate the desiring subject.

11. Heidegger, *Being and Time*, 470.

12. There have been many books written on time and narrative, for example, Paul Riceour's *Time and Narrative*, which details the way time is created through a narrative configuration. See Paul Riceour, *Time and Narrative* (Chicago: University of Chicago Press, 1984).

13. In "The Art of Time, Theory to Practice," Jesse Matz points out that most narratives are defined by their relation to time. He argues, "In theory, then, human time is a product of narratives temporal dynamics." But he also argues that narrative has the potential to constitute an "art of time" and allow us to create more "temporal diversity." Jesse Matz, "The Art of Time, Theory to Practice," *Narrative* 19, no. 3 (2011): 275.

14. It does not require a great leap to see that the form also alludes to the news format. Television audiences are used to looking at several different frames on screen. Additionally, this coincides with our expectation that television, along with the Internet, is the medium that can give us life in real time.

15. Giorgio Agamben, *Homo Sacer: Sovereign Power and Bare Life*, trans. Daniel Heller-Roazen (Stanford: Stanford University Press, 1998), 20.

16. In her detailed investigation into the torture on *24*, Isabel Penido links this emphasis to a cultural shift in the military. She says, "The program, which defines inflicting torture as patriotic, is extremely popular with cadets who will go on to hold command posts in Iraq and Afghanistan. According to [U.S. Army Brigadier General Patrick] Finnegan's observations, *24*'s insistence that the law must be sacrificed to protect the security of the nation has fueled resistance to the idea that the United States military has to respect human rights, even when the terrorists do not." Isabel Penido, "Tortured Logic: Entertainment and the Spectacle of Deliberately Inflicted Pain in *24* and *Battlestar Galactica*," *Jump Cut: A Review of Contemporary Media* 52 (2010), http://ejumpcut.org/archive/jc52.2010/pinedoTorture/index.html (accessed February 15, 2014).

17. Lisa Nakamura points out that the depiction of race, torture, and surveillance are intimately related in *24*. She explains, "Both torture and information communication technologies (ICTs) are spectacular in the sense that they compel a fascinated gaze. *24*'s technologiza-tion of torture and its narrative precursor—digital identification technologies—foreground the ways in which the terrorist body is informationalized as a digital signal, a graphic file that can be decoded and recoded using the right kind of software-based tools." Lisa Nakamura, "Interfaces of Identity: Oriental Traitors and Telematic Profiling in *24*," *Camera Obscura* 70, 24, no. 1 (2009): 111.

18. Stephen Prince, *Firestorm: American Film in the Age of Terrorism* (New York: Columbia University Press, 2009), 243.

19. This is the case in season 2 (in which we learn Jack has retired but gets pulled back in to help with an impending nuclear attack); season 4 (in which we find he was fired from CTU for his torturing methods and is now working for Secretary of Defense James Heller, but is called back in to help with a ticking bomb scenario); season 5 (eighteen months after he has faked his death he is living on the outskirts of town with a woman and her son, but he reemerges at CTU to help his colleagues who are under attack); season 6 (in which Jack is still working for CTU but has been in a Chinese prison for twenty months, and the president must make a deal to get him back to help with an emergency); season 7 (in which CTU has been closed down and Jack is on trial for torture, but is pulled out of the trial by the FBI for a ticking bomb emergency); season 8 (in which Jack is still working for CTU, but is about to retire to spend time with Kim and her family and is called back in one last time).

20. Philippe Sands, *Torture Team: Rumsfeld's Memo and the Betrayal of American Values* (New York: Palgrave Macmillan, 2008), 74.

21. Martin Miller, "*24* Gets a Lesson in Torture from the Experts," *Los Angeles Times* (February 13, 2007), http://articles.latimes.com/print/2007/feb/13/entertainment/et-torture13 (accessed February 15, 2014).

22. Peter Lattman, "Justice Scalia Hearts Jack Bauer," *Wall Street Journal*, June 20, 2007, http://blogs.wsj.com/law/2007/06/20/justice-scalia-hearts-jack-bauer/tab/print/ (accessed on February 15, 2014).

23. Quoted in Shampa Biswas and Zahi Zalloua, "Introduction: Torture Democacy, and the Human Body," in *Torture: Power, Democracy, and the Human Body*, ed. Shampa Biswas and Zahi Zalloua (Seattle: University of Washington Press, 2011), 12.

24. *24* also came under attack for its depiction of torture, and it tried to respond to these attacks within the content of the show. At the beginning of the seventh season, the show's creators literally put Jack on trial. The senators of the special committee investigating CTU accuse him of torture. He admits to torturing and says he knows that it is morally wrong, but that he saved American lives doing it and so would do it again. Ironically, the FBI, to help save the nation, pulls him out of this very trial. In this second-to-last season, by including the self-reflexive critique of torture, *24* is performing the same gesture that it performs in nearly every torture scene. A character demands that Jack (or the torturer) stop, but then the torturer procures the essential information and proves the protestations wrong. Putting Jack on trial for torture at the beginning of the seventh season allowed the series, on a larger scale, to suggest that the nation needed Jack and his torturing ways.

25. Jane Mayer, "Whatever It Takes," *New Yorker* (February 10, 2007), http://www.newyorker.com/magazine/2007/02/19/whatever-it-takes?currentPage=all (accessed July 14, 2014).

5. THE BIODETECTIVE VERSUS THE DETECTIVE OF THE REAL IN *ZERO DARK THIRTY* AND *HOMELAND*

1. This film is significant in that the entire running time is dedicated to the contemporary torture fantasy as it depicts the search for and killing of bin Laden, but there are many other films coming out every year that continue to depict torture as a regular plot device. It has become a staple of the action film. Joseph McGinty Nichol's *3 Days to Kill* (February 21, 2014) and Jaume Collet-Serra's *Non-Stop* (February 28, 2014), for example, two ordinary action films, which came out in subsequent weeks, both had one or more scenes in which the hero quickly tortures his target in order to find out information in a quick and supposedly easy manner.

2. The *Bourne* films are Doug Liman's *The Bourne Identity* (2002), Paul Greengrass's *The Bourne Supremacy* (2004) and *The Bourne Ultimatum* (2007) and Tony Gilroy's *The Bourne Legacy* (2012).

3. Poe is the inventor of the classical detective, who first appears in Poe's "Murders in the Rue Morgue." The hard-boiled detective emerges in the work of a group of writers of detective fiction, including Dashiell Hammett and Raymond Chandler.

4. About shows featuring detectives relying on forensics, Yvonne Tasker says, "Even the forensic shows which came to prominence in the 2000s still work to reveal motive; despite the mantra that physical evidence doesn't lie, neither does it explain." Yvonne Tasker, "Television Crime Drama and Homeland Security: From *Law Order* to 'Terror TV,'" *Cinema Journal* 51, no. 4 (2012): 57. Tasker suggests, however, that this complexity disappears when the theme of national security enters the narrative, which she dubs Terror TV. Terror TV, for Tasker, erases the question of motive and replaces it

5. THE BIODETECTIVE VERSUS THE DETECTIVE OF THE REAL

with the urgency of the ticking bomb. Tasker distinguishes between federal agency shows such as *24*, *The Agency* (2001–20013), *Threat Matrix* (2003–2004), *Sleeper Cell* (2005–2006), *The Unit* (2006–2009), and *NCIS* (2003–present) and crime shows such as *Law & Order* (1990–2010), *NYPD Blue* (1993–2005), *Bones* (2005–present), *Without a Trace* (2002–2009), and *Lie to Me* (2009–2011). But she points out that even the crime shows become less complex when they take on the themes of Terror TV.

5. About Bigelow characters, Leo Braudy says, "This friction between an extreme version of the conventional hero and the needs of a larger group seems to me to be a constant element in the plots that attract Bigelow." Leo Braudy, "Near Dark: An Appreciation," *Film Quarterly* 64, no. 2 (2010): 29. Clearly, *Zero Dark Thirty* continues this theme with Maya's place in and struggles with the CIA itself.

6. Bigelow's use of audio from the 9/11 attack differentiates her film from other 9/11 films such as *United 93* (Paul Greengrass, 2006). Greengrass uses documentary footage—both image and sound—in order to establish authenticity in his film. By confining herself to audio, Bigelow heightens the sense of threat while lessening to some extent the sense of authenticity.

7. Many reporters remarked on the importance of the torture scene. For instance, John Anderson says, "*Zero Dark Thirty* reaches the indirect but unavoidable conclusion that torture worked, that the key piece of information that led to bin Laden was achieved through waterboarding and the variety of deprivations suffered by detainees." John Anderson, "The Hunted and the Haunted: The disturbing brilliance of *Zero Dark Thirty*," America February 11 (2013): 29.

8. Dexter Filkins, "The Pictures: Bin Laden, the Movie," New Yorker, December 17, 2012, http://www.newyorker.com/magazine/2012/12/17/bin-laden-the-movie (accessed July 14, 2014).

9. Ibid.

10. Bigelow's obsession with authenticity affected multiple levels of the film form. In discussing the sound, Bigelow says, "Paul actually hired a sound artist in Pakistan to record the noise of the marketplace in the actual town where the scene was meant to take place. I mean, who does that?" Quoted in Brooks Barnes, "As Enigmatic as Her Picture: Kathryn Bigelow on *Zero Dark Thirty*," *New York Times* (December 30, 2012), MT2.

11. Jane Mayer, "Zero Conscience in *Zero Dark Thirty*," *New Yorker*, December 14, 2012, www.newyorker.com/online/blogs/newsdesk/2012/12/torture-in-kathryn-bigelows-zero-dark-thirty.html (accessed March 13, 2014).

12. Reviewers came up with a similar interpretation at the time of the film's release. For instance, David Denby says, "[The torture scenes] damage the movie as an alleged authentic account. Bigelow and Boal—the team behind *The Hurt Locker*—want to claim the authority of fact and the freedom of fiction at the same time, and the contradiction mars an ambitious project." David Denby, "The Current Cinema: Dead Reckoning, *Zero Dark Thirty*, and *This Is Forty*," *New Yorker* (December 24, 2012), 25.

13. The desire of the other resides in the blank space in the field of knowledge. One cannot approach it through the apparatuses of knowledge, like biometric

examination, but must have recourse to interpretation. Desire is never known, but only interpreted.

14. Slavoj Žižek contends, "*The status of the drive itself is inherently ethical.*" Slavoj Žižek, *For They Know Not What They Do* (London: Verso, 1991), 272.

15. David Denny, "On the Politics of Enjoyment: A Reading of *The Hurt Locker,*" *Theory and Event* 14, no. 1 (2011), http://muse.jhu.edu.ezproxy.uvm.edu/journals/theory_and_event/v014/14.1.denny.html (accessed March 5, 2014).

16. For instance, Peter Howell claims, "The red-haired fury has to push through obstacles posed by a dismissive U.S. Embassy station chief in Pakistan (Kyle Chandler), by a hard-to-convince boss at the CIA's Virginia HQ (Mark Strong) and by the once-burned, twice-shy National Security Advisor (Stephen Dillane)." Peter Howell, "*Zero Dark Thirty* a Masterful Thriller: Review," *Toronto Star* (January 11, 2013), www.thestar.com/entertainment/movies/2013/01/11/zero_dark_thirty_a_masterful_thriller_review.html (accessed March 12, 2014).

17. Laura Rascaroli, "Steel in the Gaze: On POV and the Discourse of Vision in Kathryn Bigelow's Cinema," *Screen* 38, no. 3 (1997): 237.

18. I am indebted to Ethan Wattley for this point.

19. Nonetheless, Cross is able to rebel, and he does so by employing the very biological technology that the national security forces use to control him. By depicting this rebellion, *The Bourne Legacy* reveals its own rebellion against the ideology of biopower. Only a subject that exceeds its body could revolt in this way.

20. Carrie's insistence on the need to survey Brody in spite of laws protecting his privacy appears to establish her as a biodetective at the beginning of the series. But, as the series develops, it becomes apparent that surveillance works in service of the interpretation of desire for Carrie.

21. It is not clear, however, whether the e-mail address is ultimately helpful for the CIA or for the terrorists, which indicates that even this supposedly successful instance of torture on the show is ambiguous.

6. *ALIAS* AND THE FICTIONAL ALTERNATIVE TO TORTURE

1. Though *Alias* presents Sydney's fictions as almost always successful, they always remain fictions for her. There is never a threat that she will fall completely into the role that she's playing and lose herself in the fiction, as we often see in films or television series that depict agents working undercover. Because she is working as a double agent in the first season and a half of the series, sustaining the fiction often requires complex performances, but the series never shows the performance intruding on Sydney's own subjectivity. It is as if her lack of psychic investment in the fictions contributes to their effectiveness.

2. One of the small hints that Sydney's work, and especially her violence, bleeds into fantasy lies in her sexual preferences. Deborah Finding and Alice MacLachlon points out that *Alias* subtly links the heroine's violent abilities with her enjoyment of rough sex. They say, "Nor is the image of the female action hero who secretly (or not

so secretly) likes rough or unconventional sex uncommon.... The implication is either that violent work leads to a craving for release through equally violent sex or that the hero can only combat darkness because she possesses it, and that this darkness must manifest itself through 'dark' sexual play." Deborah Finding and Alice MacLachlan, "*Alias*, Alienation, and Agency: The Physical Integrity of Sydney Bristow," in *Investigating Alias: Secrets and Spies*, ed. Stacey Abbott and Simon Brown (New York: I. B. Tauris, 2007), 80.

3. Molly Brost argues that in the fictions of the aliases Sydney renegotiates the male gaze. She says, "As the hero of the story, she is placed in an atypical role for a female, at least as compared to the female described in "Visual Pleasure and Narrative Cinema," and though she is often sexualized, she is always shown as remaining in control of her sexuality, using it for the purpose of completing CIA missions and casting it off when necessary." Molly Brost, "Spy Games: *Alias*, Sydney Bristow, and the Ever Complicated Gaze," *Americana: The Journal of American Popular Culture* 6, no. 1 (2007), www.americanpopularculture.com/journal/articles/spring_2007/brost.htm (accessed February 14, 2014).

4. See Joan Copjec, *Read My Desire: Lacan Against the Historicists* (Cambridge: MIT Press, 1994).

5. Jacques Lacan, *The Seminar of Jacques Lacan, Book VII: The Ethics of Psychoanalysis, 1959–1960*, trans. Dennis Porter (New York: Norton, 1992), 12.

6. Manuel Garin notes that the aliases in *Alias* become part of the larger narrative in J. J. Abrams's following project *Fringe* (2008–2013). That is, the narrative itself becomes bifurcated, not just the main character. Concerning *Fringe*, Garin says, "The series' great finding is to transfer the doubling of the heroine to the narrative as a whole: it brings forward the fictional experiments that Abrams and his team had already conducted in *Alias*." Manuel Garin, "Truth Takes Time: the Interplay Between Heroines, Genres and Narratives in three J. J. Abrams' Television Series," *Communication and Society/Comunicación y Sociedad* 26, no. 2 (2013): 52. While I think this argument is incredibly insightful, I would suggest that the reason *Alias* is more successful is that Sydney's aliases remain truly fiction and thus create a stage for the truth to emerge. In *Fringe*, both universes have the status of a reality and thus neither can hold claim to truth.

7. Elizabeth Cowie, *Representing the Woman: Cinema and Psychoanalysis* (Minneapolis: University of Minnesota Press, 1997), 133. For more on fantasy as the setting for desire, see Jean Laplanche and Jean-Bertrand Pontalis, *Fantasme originaire; Fantasme des origines; Origines du fantasme* (Paris: Fayard, 2010).

8. Jacques Lacan, *Le Séminaire, livre XXIII: Le sinthome, 1975–1976*, ed. Jacques-Alain Miller (Paris: Seuil, 2005), 78.

9. Though not addressing biopolitics specifically, Stacey Abbott and Simon Brown make the insightful point that even the biological family is in question at the heart of *Alias*. They say, "*Alias* is unique in that it seems to reinstate the biological family at the heart of the narrative and as a source of support for its main character Sydney Bristow by reconfiguring the separation between chosen family and biological family.

At the same time it contests the biological family by offering a distorted representation of conventional family roles and gender dynamics." Stacey Abbott and Simon Brown, "Can't Live with 'Em, Can Shoot 'Em: *Alias* and the (Thermo) Nuclear Family," in *Investigating Alias*, 89.

10. Those invested in biopower believe that its analysis penetrates directly to the truth. For instance, the detective who privileges DNA information postulates that this information is straightforward. But DNA is a symbolic map, and one must read it just like any other map.

11. In one sense, the torturer doesn't ignore the imaginary because she or he relies on the imaginary identifications of the victim in order to procure information. But the torturer's conception of truth dismisses the imaginary altogether. The imaginary is just a tool in the hands of the torturer, not a part of what she or he hopes to find.

12. Notably, another female-centered television show about a female detective comes to the same conclusion. In *Veronica Mars*, Veronica (Kristen Bell) also uses aliases rather than force when she needs information. Indeed, her ability to imitate people and convince anyone of her assumed identity is part of what makes her a good private detective. At one point, she even says, "Despite popular opinion, you really can't beat the truth out of someone." Veronica evinces awareness of the power of the fiction and because of this does not believe in torture.

13. Jacques Lacan, *The Seminar of Jacques Lacan, Book XX: Encore, 1972–1973*, trans. Bruce Fink (New York: Norton, 1998), 95.

14. The relationship between Sydney and Dixon is essential to the form of *Alias*. This pairing of a black man and a white woman as the most important protection for American national security plays a structuring role throughout the series. While the series doesn't go so far as to have them be romantically involved, their friendship and equality play a key role in the fictions that they create in their joint search for the truth. Unlike *24*'s waning of interracial relationships and communities as the series goes on, *Alias* relies on these relationships throughout its duration.

15. Other characters in the series note Sydney's seriousness. They tell her constantly that she should relax and enjoy herself. But almost every time she attempts to do so, some traumatic event befalls her. The depictions of Sydney enjoying herself are confined for the most part to her performances of the various aliases.

16. For the classic psychoanalytic account of femininity as a masquerade, see Joan Rivière, "Womanliness as Masquerade," *International Journal of Psychoanalysis* 10 (1929): 303–313.

17. Jacqueline Rose, *Sexuality in the Field of Vision* (London: Verso, 1986), 67.

18. Hilary Radner, *Neo-Feminist Cinema: Girly Films, Chick Flicks, and Consumer Culture* (New York: Routledge, 2011), 38.

19. The path to authenticity can also go in the other direction. That is, when a woman discovers her more feminist self—she enters the workforce, becomes more of a protector for her family, becomes aware of the way her current feminine identity is oppressing her, or becomes violent—she is often depicted shedding or deconstructing her feminine appearance. For example, in Ridley Scott's *Thelma and Louise* (1991),

the two women, after their enlightenment, trade their lipstick and jewelry for cowboy hats and bandanas. At the same time, they stop worrying about their hair and change their attire from dresses to jeans. Though this film moves in the opposite direction than that of *Pretty Woman*, it remains within the same philosophical universe. It conceives of the woman as a purely symbolic construction rather than as a real subject.

20. Sarah Banet-Weiser and Laura Portwood-Stace argue that this is also the case in the cosmetic surgery reality television show. They say, "Reality makeover shows clearly and uncritically legitimate the increasing normalization of the cultural practice of cosmetic surgery in US culture, and transparently conflate personal fulfillment and individual achievement with the attainment of a physically ideal body." Sarah Banet-Weiser and Laura Portwood-Stace, "'I Just Want to Be Me Again!': Beauty Pageants, Reality Television and Post-feminism," *Feminist Theory* 7, no. 2 (2006): 255–272.

21. Elizabeth Barnes says that series like *Alias* and *Buffy the Vampire Slayer* show the contribution the women can have to the employment of violence itself. Barnes explains, "female action heroes dramatize in specific and somewhat counterintuitive ways both the potentially dehumanizing, because desensitizing, effects of violence and the redemptive potential of emotional vulnerability." Elizabeth Barnes, "The New Hero: Women, Humanism, and Violence in *Alias* and *Buffy the Vampire Slayer*," in *Investigating Alias*, 58.

22. Joan Copjec, *Imagine There's No Woman: Ethics and Sublimation* (Cambridge: MIT Press, 2002), 77.

23. David Coon argues that *Alias* walks the line of relying on sexist imagery and moving beyond this image in the depictions of Sydney. He analyzes a spate of advertisements for the series that used the tagline "Sometimes the truth hurts," and he argues that the show's position to truth positions Sydney outside the realm of objectification. According to Coon, "The image emphasizes her importance without isolating and emphasizing her sexuality or placing her in a position of objectification." David Roger Coon, "Two Steps Forward, One Step Back: The Selling of *Charlie's Angels* and *Alias*," *Journal of Popular Film and Television* 33, no. 1 (2005): 8.

24. Manuel Garin also considers this episode and investigates the relationship between truth and time not only in *Alias* but using this theme from *Alias*, also looks at other J. J. Abrams's series such as *Felicity* (1998–2002) and *Fringe* (2008–2013). He claims that through the seriality of television, Abrams—using strong female characters—slowly undermines the expected plot trajectory and with it contemporary American ideology. He argues, "Truth and lie integrate a territory in perpetual mutation, going from the romantic adventures of *Felicity* to the familiar ambiguity in *Alias* and the ontological duplication of the real in *Fringe*. Each model resonates in the precedent one and outlines a portrait of the heroine permanently split between the truths of her feminine condition (shattered and elliptical) and the lies of the universe she is doomed to save (legal, ethical)." Garin, "Truth Takes Time," 49.

25. Jacques-Alain Miller, "On Semblances in the Relation Between the Sexes," trans. Sina Najafi and Marina Harss, in *Sexuation*, ed. Renata Salecl (Durham: Duke University Press, 2000), 19.

INDEX

Abbott, Stacey, 181–82n9
Abrams, J. J., 181n6
Abu Ghraib photographs, 1–6, 10–13, 15; and documentary films 49–50, 52–54, 57–70; and torture porn, 72, 92–93
Agamben, Giorgio, 2–3, 33, 43, 47, 107, 161n4; and bare life 34–36, 84, 167n17; and cinema 36
Alias, 19–20, 72, 100, 114, 129–30, 137, 139–59, 165n40, 180n1, 181n6
Althusser, Louis, 37–38, 163n23
Amnesty International, *see* Schulz, William F.
Anderson, John, 179n7
Apel, Dora, 70, 172n33
Arab Mind, The, *see* Patai, Raphael
Arendt, Hannah, 34, 167n19
Austin, Thomas, 170n24

Banet-Weiser, Sarah, 183n20
Barnes, Elizabeth, 183n21
Battle of Algiers, The, 17
Battlestar Galactica, 100
Benjamin, Walter, 34, 167n19

Benson-Allott, Caetlin, 170n21
Bigelow, Kathryn, *see Zero Dark Thirty*
Biodetective, 116–28, 159
Biometrics, 38–39
Biopolitical body, 24–25, 27, 81, 85
Biopower, 10, 12, 18, 20, 27–33, 36, 85, 166nn5, 6; and death, 87–88; and ideology, 37–42, 95–96, 159; and the sovereign, 34–35; and time, 100–3, 107
Blue Steel, 123
Bourne films, the, 115, 126–28, 178n2
Braudy, Leo, 179n5
Brown, Simon, 181–82n9
Bush, George, 2–4, 8–9, 13, 57, 59

Centurions, Les, *see* Lartéguy, Jean
Chertoff, Michael, 110
Christie, Agatha, 116
Classical detective, 116, 158
Cloning, 39–40
Clover, Carol, 80, 173–74n15
Clueless, 150
Coon, David, 183n23

186 INDEX

Copjec, Joan, 69, 141, 154
Corsetti, Damien, 68
Cowie, Elizabeth, 142
CSI, 117, 158

Danes, Claire, 131
de Sade, Marquis, 5, 162n11
Deleuze, Gilles and Félix Guattari, 28, 166n7, 166n8, 166n14
Denby, David, 179n12
Denny, David, 124–25
Descartes, 11, 26, 163n24
Detective of the real, 116–17, 128–37, 158–59
Devil's Rejects, The, 72
Doomsday clock, 176n8
Dupin, Auguste, 116, 158

Edelstein, David, 71–72
Enjoyment: 45, 51–52, 167n30; and documentary film, 57–58, 60, 62, 65–70; and torture, 3, 72, 77
Esposito, Roberto, 88–89, 167n16
Eternal Sunshine of the Spotless Mind, 176n10
Extreme Makeover, 150

Fahrenheit 9/11, see Moore, Michael
Fallon, Kris, 170n22
Feinstein, Howard, 170n25
Felicity, 183n24
Femme Nikita, La, 150
Finding, Deborah, 181–82n2
Finnegan, Patrick, 114
Foucault, Michel, 6, 11, 29–37, 43, 85, 88–89, 162n14, 166n8, 166n13, 166n14
Freud, Sigmund, 42–44, 69, 81, 167n26, 171n30
Fringe, 181n6

Garin, Manuel, 181n6, 183n24
Geneva Conventions, 2, 7–9, 59, 163n18
Ghosts of Abu Ghraib, The, 12, 49, 58–59, 63–67
Gibney, Alex, *see Taxi to the Dark Side*
Gilroy, Tony, 127
Gleaners and I, see Varda, Agnes

Greengrass, Paul, 127
Guantanamo Bay, 4, 8, 34, 58, 84, 87, 109, 111

Hardboiled detective, 116, 158
Hardt, Michael and Antonio Negri, 33
Harmon, Sabrina, 65–67
Heidegger, Martin, 101–3
Hollyfield, Jerod, 172n1
Homeland, 115, 129–37, 158, , 173n12, 180n20
Hostel, 14–15, 72, 76–86, 174n19
How Do I Look? 150
Howell, Peter, 180n16
Hurt Locker, 124

Imaginary, 129, 143–44, 182n11
Inception, 176n10

Jones, Steve, 175n25
Jouissance, *see* Enjoyment

Kahana, Jonathan, 169–70n19
Kant, Immanuel, 68, 171n28
Kennedy, Rory, *see Ghosts of Abu Ghraib, The*
King, Rodney, 66

Lacan, Jacques, 42, 44–45, 75, 129, 142–45, 157, 164n26, 167nn26, 30, 168n1; and the gaze 51, 168n4
Lartéguy, Jean, 15–17, 164n31, 165n36
Lattman, Peter, 111
Lesage, Julia, 15, 61, 164n30, 171n26, 171n27
Lévi-Strauss, Claude, 53
Liman, Doug, 127
Lindsey, Hal, 176n8
Lockwood, Dean, 174n23, 175n29
Lowenstein, Adam, 172–73n6
Lynching photographs, 69–70

MacLachlan, Alice, 181–82n2
Marshall, Gary, 149
Masquerade, 148–49, 154, 182n16
Matz, Jesse, 176n13
Mayer, Andre, 172n3

Mayer, Jane, 114, 122, 165n36
McElwee, Ross, 57
McCann, Ben, 174n22
Middleton, Jason, 80
Milgram, Stanley, 64–65
Miller, Jacques-Alain, 157
Miller, Martin, 111
Miss Congeniality, 150
Mitchell, W. J. T., 39–40, 167n25
Moore, Michael, 57
Morris, Errol, *see Standard Operating Procedure*
Mulvey, Laura, 51, 168n4
My Fair Lady, 150

Nakamura, Lisa, 177n17
Narrative disavowal, 108, 114
Nazi Germany, 34, 84, 88–89
Nevins, David, 97
Non-Stop, 178n1

Obama, Barak, 4, 8, 115, 162n9

Passion of the Christ, The, 72
Patai, Raphael, 56
Patriot Act, 34
Penido, Isabel, 177n16
Portwood-Stace, Laura, 183n20
"Purloined Letter, The," 158
Pretty Woman, 149, 182–83n19
Prince, Stephen, 18, 110
Psychoanalytic subject, 24, 27, 36, 42–43

Quantum of Solace, 72

Rabinowitz, Paula, 169n16, 171n29
Racism; and biopower, 88–89; and depiction of Arab or Arab American characters, 109, 134–35; and torture, 55–57, 70
Radner, Hilary, 149–50
Rascaroli, Laura, 123, 126
Rat Man, 46
Real, 129–30, 143–44, 154, 158
Reality television shows, 150–51, 183n20
Rejali, Darius, 16–17, 164n33, 165n35
Riceour, Paul, 176n12

Rope, 175n2
Rose, Charlie, 131
Rose, Jacqueline, 149
Rosenberg, Howard, 96
Rumsfeld, Donald, 58

Sadism, 75–76
Sands, Philippe, 110–11
Saw, 72, 85–93, 174n22, 174n23, 175n25, 175n28
Schmidt, Carl, 34, 167n19
Schulz, William F., 13, 164n28, 164n29
Searchers, The, 112
September 11, 2001 attacks, 2–4, 9, 49, 71, 103, 119–20, 127
Shane, 112
Sharrett, Christopher, 174n24
Sherlock, 116
Sherman, Cindy, 154–55
Sherman's March, *see* McElwee, Ross
Smith, Christian, 97
Sontag, Susan, 54, 70
Spurlock, Morgan, 57
Standard Operating Procedure, 12, 49, 58, 60–64, 66, 170n23, 170n24, 170n25
State of Emergency, *see* State of Exception
State of Exception, 3, 34–35, 83–84, 107
Stavrakakis, Yannis, 53
Strange Days, 123
Super Size Me, *see* Spurlock, Morgan
Surveillance, 117–20, 124, 128
Symbolic, 129, 143–44

Tasker, Yvonne, 178–79n4
Taxi to the Dark Side, 12, 49, 58, 62–65, 68, 76, 171n27
Texas Chainsaw Massacre, 80
Thelma and Louise, 182–83n19
3 Days to Kill, 178n1
Ticking bomb scenario, 13, 15–18, 50, 98–99, 108, 113, 165n36
Tim Gunn's Guide to Style, 150
Torture fantasy, 15, 27, 41–42, 46, 50, 55, 87, 90–92, 159, 171n29, 175n28; and the contemporary detective, 115–37; and the urgency of time, 95–114

Torture porn, 13–15, 71–93
Tracking shots, 79–80
Traitor, 72
Truth in fiction, 20
24 (television series), 15, 17–20, 49, 55, 72, 85, 95–114, 119, 139–41
2012, 176n9, 178n24
Tziallas, Evangelos, 74

United 93, 179n6

Varda, Agnès, 57
Veronica Mars, 130, 176n5, 182n12

Wester, Maisha, 173n7, 174n21
Western hero, 112

What Not to Wear, 150
Williams, Linda, 73, 169n18
Wisnewski, Jeremy, 5–6, 162n10, 168n33
Wetmore, Kevin, 173n13, 173–74n15
Whitaker, Brian, 56, 169n12
Wolf Creek, 72

Yoo, John, 9, 110
Y2K scare, 102

Zapruder film, 66
Zero Dark Thirty, 20, 115–27, 135, 158, 179n5, 179n6
Žižek, Slavoj, 38, 47, 52–53, 167n24, 168n6, 180n14

GPSR Authorized Representative: Easy Access System Europe, Mustamäe tee
50, 10621 Tallinn, Estonia, gpsr.requests@easproject.com

www.ingramcontent.com/pod-product-compliance
Lightning Source LLC
Chambersburg PA
CBHW021405290426
44108CB00010B/401